Wisdom and Curriculum
Christian Schooling after Postmodernity

Wisdom and Curriculum
Christian Schooling after Postmodernity

Doug Blomberg

Dordt College Press

Cover art by Russell McKane
Cover design by Robert Haan
Layout by Carla Goslinga

Printed in the United States of America.

Dordt College Press   www.dordt.edu/dordt_press
498 Fourth Avenue NE
Sioux Center, Iowa 51250
United States of America

Library of Congress Cataloging-in-Publication Data
Blomberg, Doug.
  Wisdom and curriculum : Christian schooling after postmodernity /
  Doug Blomberg.
    p. cm.
  ISBN-13: 978-0-932914-73-6 (pbk. : alk. paper)
  1. Christian education—Curricula. 2. Wisdom—Biblical teaching.
  3. Curriculum planning. 4. Postmodernism—Religious aspects—
  Christianity. I. Title.
  BV1475.3.B56 2007
  371.071--dc22   2007010607

TABLE OF CONTENTS

FOREWORD

Following the author's lead, permit me a few autobiographical remarks. I first met Doug Blomberg in person in 1988, in the very place he so eloquently describes in the first two chapters of this book: Mount Evelyn Christian School, nestled in the hilly outskirts of Melbourne, Australia. I recall a spirited discussion in his office. The topic? Something called "distantiated knowing." As an academic, immersed in philosophical concerns but increasingly shifting attention to issues in elementary and secondary schooling, I recognized at once that Blomberg was traveling on an epistemological path marked by potholes and rocky outcroppings towards an as yet unknown destination. But I was sure already then that he would end up somewhere in a lighted clearing in the shadowy jungle called "educational theory and practice."

During the following years, the conversations continued, off and on. Doug and I met in places as diverse as Melbourne and Sydney, Sioux Center, Iowa, Grand Rapids, Michigan, Toronto, the Netherlands, the Philippines, and the United Kingdom. The encounter in the United Kingdom deserves specific mention. In the summer of 2001, it was my privilege to conduct an international symposium to explore the relation between philosophy of education and classroom practice. Comprising an intimate group from four different countries, the participants had opportunity to debate in the quiet, lovely venue generously provided by David and Ruth Hanson of the West Yorkshire School of Christian Studies (WYSOCS) in Leeds. A key point of the conversation, pressed hard by Blomberg, concerned the privileged position of theory over practice, a modernist metanarrative dating to the ancient pagan Greeks and still dominant in schooling—including Christian schooling—in the West, even today, in spite of the inroads of postmodernism in its many forms.

The modernist theory-into-practice approach, dubbed "technical rationality" by Donald Schön, asserts that the dominance of abstract reason, leads to—often behavioristic—scientific management models, and seriously crimps the possibility of students encountering and experiencing the richness and multidimensionality of God's good creation. Joined by forces of economism, modernity keeps schools chained to bureaucratic factory models driven by principles of efficiency and measurable outcomes.

No extensive surveys are needed to conclude that the structure of the Christian school curriculum does not materially differ from that in the state schools. In spite of gallant efforts to introduce thematic units and to "integrate," curriculum continues to be understood as a program of discrete, disconnected studies, to be rigorously followed and completed in the context of tests, grades, and credits. Particularly in secondary schools, the curriculum requires students to "take courses" and teachers to "cover the material," often leaving both with an indelible impression of fragmentation. Walking from one classroom to another feels like walking from one world to another.

For many years, I served college students as a philosophy professor. One main aim of my efforts was to enable our students to experience the amazing integrality, intertwinement, and coherence of all creation. I attempted to make Colossians 1:17—all things cohere in Christ—a reality. I found this task to be incredibly and discouragingly difficult. Students had been programmed to see disciplines—theoretical constructs!—indeed, the entire encyclopedia of the sciences as a conglomeration of unrelated "chunks." What previous curriculum had torn asunder, no lone philosophy professor could reassemble into an integral whole. Humpty-dumpty all over again.

The current obsession with assessment, frequently reflecting a reductionistic view of knowledge as a medley of discrete factualities, further hammers students into a fragmentation mode. When this mentality takes over a Christian school, the inner tension between the standard curriculum on the one hand and, on the other, the calling to genuine discipleship, to walk in wisdom, and to make all things new, constricts and chokes authentic Christian education—a situation that literally cries out for redemption.

The book you are about to read leads us into greener and more promising pastures. To reach them requires the author to address difficult and controversial issues. Engaging both the recent and contemporary literature, Blomberg takes pains to carefully analyze and evaluate the compatibility, or lack thereof, of our Christian commitments with those of both modernism and the varieties of postmodernism. After all, the difficult and controversial issues do not stand alone or float in space. They are determined by underlying spirits. Blomberg in this book tackles the fundamental assumptions controlling the standard curriculum and wrestles them to the ground, in an attempt to reshape them into forms patterned after the biblical theme of wisdom. The curriculum as we now have it, he argues, preaches a false gospel, a modernistic, rationalistic story that bamboozles Christian schools into believing that all is well as long as our children achieve expected scores and acquire some Christian perspective in the process.

Blomberg provides us with a fresh understanding, primed by the biblical wisdom literature, of what it means to live and learn in God's presence in a world of wonder, ambiguity, mystery, and yet trustworthiness. He rekindles a vision of schools as places where, as he puts it, "our students are passionate in the pursuit of wisdom and not just possessors of packets of knowledge."

My hope is that this book will be widely read, studied, and discussed. Clearly the last word about curriculum and wisdom has not yet been spoken. Avoiding recipes and easy answers, Blomberg opens up a vista, a realm of possibilities. What might be the implications of teaching for wisdom? What would a curriculum, freed from rationalistic and technicistic shackles, actually look like? And what would it do for our children? These questions beg for extended and sustained exploration. Ultimately, to seek wisdom is to seek the Kingdom of God above all else. And when we do seek the Kingdom first, everything else will turn out all right.

My hope is that this book will hasten the day when wisdom replaces the technical rationality of modern curriculum. That day will give the Spirit of God a good deal more elbowroom for blessing our efforts to bring up our children in the Lord.

John Van Dyk
June, 2006

ACKNOWLEDGEMENTS

In a project such as this, which draws on the experience of a working lifetime, there are more debts than it is possible to acknowledge. It will be evident that my association with the teachers, students, and families of Mount Evelyn Christian School has been most formative; though it pains me not to do so, to begin to name them would risk offending by omission. Let it suffice to mention the three principals with whom I have been privileged to serve, Jack Mechielsen, Stewart Miller, and Martin Hanscamp, both in their own right and as representatives of the staffs they have led with great vision. My thanks to all at MECS are embedded in the various fictional characters in whom they might occasionally recognize themselves, but mostly in the depiction of the school that each of them struggled joyfully to build.

Second only to the MECS community are the colleagues and teachers with whom I worked from 1979 through 2000 at the Institute (now the National Institute) for Christian Education in Australia. I have been privileged to read hundreds of essays about teachers' classrooms and curricula, and have enjoyed thousands of hours of face-to-face, telephone, and e-mail discussion. These people have also helped to shape my views of what education may be, through their dreams of what the gospel makes possible and their doubts as well as hopes concerning the extent to which these could be realized this side of Jesus' return. Meantime, they have been his hands and feet, servants seeking to usher in the new creation by erecting sanctuaries of shalom, one classroom at a time.

There are a number of teachers who have read what I have written and responded, sometimes in great detail, to it. In particular I thank Mac Nicoll, an experienced teacher and administrator in government and independent schools, for his deliberations and discussion, and Stacey Cheeseman, an erstwhile MECS teacher who, while much younger in her experience of teaching, also brought enthusiasm and insight to her reading of the draft. The project had its proximate beginning in the "Wisdom and Schooling" seminar I taught for the Institute for Christian Studies, Toronto, Canada, in 1997, and a substantial part of the manuscript was workshopped for an ICS course of the same title at Toronto District Christian High in 2000. I thank the participants in those courses, and also ICS for the opportunities it gave me to engage in research during that four-year period. Allyson Dziedzic, my Research Assistant at ICS during 2003-04, provided invaluable editorial scrutiny and advice, notably but by no means only with respect to North American sensibilities. Eva Vanderberg, my Research Assistant in 2005-06, did the lion's share of the work involved in compiling topics for the Index, and Heather Blomberg graciously assisted me in verifying the citations. The copy editor, Lisa Stracks, drew my attention to a number of important details, though could not always persuade me to sacrifice the Australian idioms that situate the text. Lorraine Voorberg, my Research Assistant in 2007-2008, undertook a final review of the proofs.

In addition to these people, there are many others who took the time to speak to or contact me after I had addressed a conference session; there are also those teachers in various schools where I was privileged to conduct workshops, most of which in recent years have danced around the theme of wisdom. Of my academic colleagues, Prof. John Van Dyk of Dordt College has been a consistent and stimulating partner in dialogue, and I thank him also for being willing to write the Foreword. Nor could I forget the career-long dialogue I have enjoyed with Rev. Dr. Stuart Fowler; I hope he and his partner Joy recognize their legacy in what I have written.

My friend, Russell McKane, has done me the honor of offering his wonderful painting, "A tree firmly planted," for the cover. Not only does it echo the book's theme, it adds another layer of richness for me in that Russell was also a colleague at MECS for many years, as well as at one time my student at the Institute for Christian Education. It goes without saying, but will be said nonetheless, that my greatest gratitude is to my wife Heather, not only an experienced teacher-librarian (yes, for many years at Mount Evelyn Christian School) with significant insight into matters educational, but most importantly a supportive, encouraging, loving—though by no means uncritical—partner. Various sections of the book have been presented at conferences and/ or published in forms that provided a basis for what appears herein. Though the manuscript was conceived with a book in view, it was originally compiled as a dissertation for the Doctor of Education degree at Monash University, in which context I owe an immense debt for detailed feedback and instructive interaction to my ultimate supervisor, Dr. Robin Small (who graciously took over the reins from Prof. David Aspin on the latter's retirement at the end of 2001).

Published sources include: "Ways of Wisdom: Multiple Modes of Meaning in Pedagogy and Andragogy," in *Ways of Knowing, in Concert*, edited by J. H. Kok, 123–146 (Sioux Center, IA: Dordt College Press, 2005); "Wisdom at Play: In the World but Not of It," in *The Crumbling Walls of Certainty: Towards a Christian Critique of Postmo-*

dernity and Education, edited by I. Lambert and S. Mitchell, 120–35 (Sydney: Centre for the Study of Australian Christianity, 1997); "A Problem-Posing Pedagogy: 'Paths of Pleasantness and Peace,'" *Journal of Education and Christian Belief* 3 no. 2 (2000), 97–113; "The Integral Curriculum," *Christian Educators Journal* 31 no. 2 (Dec 1991), 6–13; "The Practice of Wisdom: Knowing When." *Journal of Education & Christian Belief* 2, no. 1 (1998), 7–26; and *A Vision with a Task: Christian Schooling for Responsive Discipleship*, edited by Gloria Stronks and Doug Blomberg, chapter 8 (Grand Rapids, MI: Baker Books, 1993).

Doug Blomberg
Toronto
7 December 2006

Introduction

I find an Introduction to a book most helpful if it answers the "who," "what," and "why" questions. Therefore, I want to say something about who I am and who I think that you are and to give you a foretaste of what I am writing about, why I think that it is important, and why I have chosen to write in just the way that I have. Of course, the title has already given you a clue, and I presume that your interest was sufficiently piqued for you to turn to the Table of Contents and now here. So please, read on a little further.

I have been a teacher for more than half my life; for the other half, I was a student. But I doubt that it is possible to see where the one left off and the other began. When one heeds the call to teach, one accepts the gift of being a perennial learner. Thus, this book is part of a continuing personal quest. It may sound grandiose to characterize this as a search for wisdom, but I believe that this search is inseparable from what it means to be human, to be in the image of God. We are all seekers after wisdom, though all too often we find ourselves going astray. Ultimately, we order our lives in accord with what we judge to be "the good."

I have also been a Christian for more than half my life (as I write this, in fact, yesterday marks the thirty-sixth anniversary of my conversion at a Billy Graham Crusade). For me, becoming a more faithful servant of Christ constitutes "the good." My learning and teaching has, for most of that time, been a search for what it means to pursue these callings christianly. And you are probably a Christian teacher or are preparing for this vocation. (You may also be an administrator, parent, or board member in a Christian school.) In the spirit of my quest—and it is no doubt your quest as well—I wish to reflect on my life as a teacher and to include you in the conversation. After all, I agree with the observation that the most significant factor contributing to improvement in schools is "teachers talking to teachers about teaching." As teachers, we continually question the worth and effectiveness of what we are doing, at the level of goals and outcomes and at that of process. Our reflection is situated, seeking the practice of wisdom.

But as well as being a teacher, I am a philosopher of education. So I want to say something about how I understand this aspect of my vocation. Philosophers are also, by definition, "lovers of wisdom," although not, I suggest, always in ways that are most helpful. Indeed, philosophy as a way of life has too often become a search for certainty guaranteed by rational processes. As Christians, we know that our certain hope rests not in Reason, but in revelation.

I have long been convinced of the potential that a *biblical* perspective on wisdom has to function as an alternative to the dominant ideology of Reason, the "theory-into-practice paradigm." Though this has its roots in classical Greek philosophy, it came to frame the very way in which Christianity merged with the Western intellectual tradition. A wisdom perspective, with its roots not only in the East, but in revelational encounter in the history of the Hebrews, enables a different perspective on life and educational issues (Blomberg 1994, 1998b). However much the biblical story has been synthesized with (and corrupted by) the Western tradition, it remains in its heart and soul at odds with the fundamental direction of that tradition. Or so I claim.

As I hope to make clear, much of my philosophizing has emerged from my engagement in schools, specifically in Christian schools that have informed, grounded, and challenged my reflections. In this, it has had not only an historical but also an explicitly revelational context. Yet philosophy is commonly conceived as an undertaking outside time and independent of revelation. It is as though Prof. Plato or Dr. Descartes were just down the hall in their own offices, living in the same world and responding to the same conditions that I am, as "professional philosopher." The so-called essentials of their thought have been extracted and abstracted from the historical circumstances in which they wrote. These circumstances include not merely the philosophical partners with whom they were in dialogue, but the social, political, economic, and religious conditions in which they were situated.

Contrary to this ahistorical view, I think that it is not of merely incidental significance that Descartes lived in a time in which all of the certainties of the late medieval world were collapsing around him; when Europe was suffering the chaos of protracted religious-political conflict; and when the authority of the Church, which had so long determined the pervasive worldview, was in dispute. In a world falling apart, where was certainty to be found, what authority was to be trusted? Descartes' answer—that the human intellect (Reason) was able to take a firm grasp of the nature of things through clear and distinct ideas—is one that has resonated through the ages (Toulmin 1990). It is one measure of the commencement of the period designated "modern"—a period that is now in either its twilight or its heyday, depending on how one reads the signs of the times.

With some helpful prompting from others, I realized when I began this project that I wished to write in a way that would honor both the paradigm for which I am arguing and the audience I am addressing. As it happens, these two aims are not in conflict. However, realizing (in the second sense of the term) this goal was by no means straightforward. Given the nature of my training as an academic, it is difficult to find a path that allows the integration of my personal voice, the voice that I have in everyday, social relationships, with the impersonal, academic one. But if I am to counter the dominance that abstract Reason has in the conduct of schooling, I will have to allow my own voice to come through. And if schools are going to be somewhat different as a result, I have to speak to teachers and those preparing to be teachers, and not in the first place to other philosophers of education.

I referred to "helpful prompting." I have been told more than once that, although I sought an alternative to the theory-into-practice paradigm, I was employing this very paradigm to mount my case; I was in danger of "self-performative incoherence." People challenged: "Aren't you continuing the divide between theory and practice? You seek to rehabilitate experience of the everyday, but where is it in your writing?" I was urged to speak much more from my own experience (which I take by no means to exclude what I have read or reflected upon, while obviously emphasizing my lived, bodily, historical engagement with the world), which seemed to me to comport well with wisdom's bent toward learning from experience. Another significant comment was, "Your emphasis on *order* is in considerable tension with your recognition of uncertainty and the plasticity of ordinary experience, particularly when considered in the context of postmodernism. Why do you want to retain the former? Is it a question of how to maintain Christian values in the postmodern era?" The person who made this last comment (interestingly, not speaking as a Christian) later encouraged me to try to sustain the tension between order and its lack in the actual structure of the project and proposed that one way of doing this would be to include much more of the experiences of teachers and students.

Although I use a toolkit largely—though not exclusively—furnished with philosophical implements, I trust it is evident that I am not interested primarily in abstract philosophical questions. As I have said, insofar as I engage in philosophy, I am interested in it as a way of life, in particular, as a way of pursuing the good (in) life (Hadot 1995; Nehemas 1998).

3

And this is what should also characterize education and its institutional expression in schooling—who would counsel the alternative? At the same time, this requires a continual evaluation of what constitutes the good. Christian schools and teachers, in particular, are driven by the demand for ongoing reformation, so that our lives conform more daily to the image of Christ.

I have entitled this work *Wisdom and Curriculum*. I am interested in teachers' way of being with their students. Though it might strike you as strange, I believe that it is this mode of relating that constitutes the *curriculum*. For many years I have advocated an "integral curriculum" (Blomberg 1978; 1980a; 1980b; 1991; 1993; Stronks and Blomberg 1993). As well as seeking to bring further clarity to this conception, I wish to consolidate a comprehensive rationale by grounding it in a biblical view of *wisdom*.[1] I am persuaded that adopting wisdom as a goal (and also as a means) enables us to address at least two deficiencies in the current practice of schooling. These concern *what* we teach and *whom* we teach: the *subjects* of schooling, in a dual sense. But already implicit in my way of framing this dual concern is a third sense, a third set of subjects. When "we"—the teachers—are acknowledged, we have the makings of curriculum, a triadic relationship.

In this context, I recall the plea from a student classified with disabilities, who desired only a place to *be,* which the school in so many respects denied her, by treating her as an *object* to be moved from pillar to post rather than as a *subject* responsible for her own actions (Rose 1999). If the curriculum constitutes the relationship between teacher and student (and of both with subject matter), then it is first a relationship between *beings.* This is the reality underlying "whole person" rhetoric in schooling. An integral curriculum seeks to honor the being of students, to accord them respect as persons, to acknowledge their *presence.* It is thus that the curriculum will be oriented to *formation* rather than to *information,* to wisdom as a goal for students (and teachers) as well as a mode of operating for students and teachers.

Of course, the ultimate beneficiaries of schooling ought to be the students (though as I say it, I know that this, too, has been disputed, especially when schooling is oriented first and foremost to national economic productivity). Schools are spaces for learning before they are sites for teaching. I am reminded that Freire (1972) sought to overcome the dichotomy that prevails between teachers and students with his insistence on referring to "teacher-student" and "student-teacher"; admittedly, he was thinking in the first instance of adults, but I believe he would extend this same courtesy to younger people, as many advocates of a critical pedagogy have indeed since done (e.g., McLaren and Leonard 1995).

There is much that resonates with me in critical pedagogy. This is not surprising, because critique is a concomitant of wisdom. The root of *critical* is in the Greek *krinein,* to discern or to judge, and discernment and judgment are at the heart of what I have elsewhere characterized as knowing *when* (Blomberg 1998b), in an attempt to pass between the horns of the theory/practice dilemma. The meaning of wisdom is not fully encompassed by this phrase, but there is an important element of sensitivity to the moment and an orientation to action (of which both thought and speech may be considered species) that it does identify.

An integral curriculum, oriented to the promotion of wisdom, will thus be *critical,* and I propose that at its core will be the practice of problem-posing (a concept I owe initially to Freire). Problem-posing suggests a disjunction between what *is* and what *will* or *ought to be.* It is rooted in playful immersion or engagement with the world, so that disengagement cannot be a constant state, but rather a momentary possibility and potential. Its outcome, I suggest, should be "purposeful response," an informed and committed reengagement in action.

A helpful way of characterizing wisdom is as "the realization of value" (Maxwell 1984). As I hinted in an earlier paragraph, this implies both senses of the term *realization: understanding* and *implementing* what ought to be accomplished. ("Theory" is only one among a number of modes of imagining possible futures.) As such, education will be a value-laden undertaking, in which aims and goals must be regarded not as predetermined and incontestable, but as being at the center of the process. One of the benefits of the deregulation of schooling (or less politely, its marketization or privatization) is the opportunity for schools to articulate their core values and thus to distinguish themselves from one another. But there is not only a *directional* plurality of values, characterized by different visions of the good life, whether Christian, Islamic, or liberal humanist. There is also a *structural* plurality, by which I mean that there are various "ways of wisdom," a significant theme that I will explore in what follows.

Respecting not only "wisdom," but also a variety of "ways of wisdom," is a significant counter to the single voice of reason that is so often assumed to prevail. One prominent postmodern philosopher, Jacques Derrida (1976), has criticized the notion that words mean exactly what they seem to mean, and that they therefore mean exactly the same thing to the hearer as they do to the speaker, to the reader as they do to the writer. He believes it is a fundamental assumption of Western culture that words and their meanings are coterminous. *Au contraire*, Derrida insists, words are always contaminated by "traces" of previous meanings, and their very sounds suggest other words to us. To think otherwise is to be deluded by the "metaphysics of presence": that the meaning of a word is always transparently present to speaker and hearer.

On this account, there is a "slippage" between words and their meanings, and it is to me by no means a coincidence that one of the features of wisdom is its recognition and tolerance of ambiguity. Job is archetypical of this refusal to succumb to the certainty of a system. It is in part for this reason that I have chosen a variety of genres in preference to a traditional academic mode. I wish to draw attention to (or at least, not to obscure by the cold hard fact of objective academic inscription in the third person, passive voice) the very subjectivity of coming to know, the utterly perspectival nature of all knowing. In other words, I am seeking (a) style/s that embody/ies a wisdom "method"—of invitation and evocation—rather than trying to argue toward a conclusion that, by dint of its conflict with the manner in which I have approached it, will constitute a *reductio ad absurdum*.

The choice of varied genres is nothing new in this postmodern era, though it is well to be reminded at the same time of what the Teacher said long ago: "There is nothing new under the sun" (Ecclesiastes 1:9). Proverbs, Job, and Ecclesiastes, though all centrally concerned with wisdom, also demonstrate a diversity in their modes of approaching it. Just as different languages embody different worldviews, so different genres within a language invite varied orientations to the world. Each opens up its own possibilities, while at the same time excluding others. I hope that my interweaving of dialogue with more conventional sections of exposition—where the one plays on/off the other—will work to gradually build a multifaceted perspective. Given the nature of conversation, not every point is elaborated immediately upon being raised, but I trust that clarification emerges in the whole.

Blake and his colleagues have observed that whereas "the earliest complete works of philosophy are presented as dialogues . . . the genre of dialogue soon takes a back seat in the literature," so that "[t]o do philosophy was to withdraw from the overtly political world of dialogue to seek truth in the supposedly apolitical realm of monologue" (Blake, Smeyers, Smith, and Standish 1998, 22–23). Philosophizing came to be seen not as the free exchange of ideas in the *agora* (marketplace) but as an activity of pure consciousness, to be conducted as far as possible in isolation from the distractions of the world in its "blooming, buzzing confusion."

It was to be built, as Plato and Descartes each said in his own way, on the unassailable foundation of clear and distinct ideas. Diversity of opinion needed to be superseded by a single, logically clear line of thought.

Despite my aversion to the dominance of the market metaphor, philosophy does need to be in the marketplace, the public square. The "real world"—including the world of the classroom (cf. McDonald 1992)—is replete with diversity, redolent with ambiguity. Reflection on education ought to *reflect* this ambiguity, to disclose rather than to conceal it (Blomberg 1998a). In my experience, this is not only affirming of teachers: the failure to recognize—more, to honor—the messiness of the low ground is one reason at least for the antipathy of some teachers toward theory and theorists. What is needed are forms of writing that capture the complexity of the teacher's calling.

Brent Kilbourn highlights the limitations of "straight prose" for expressing depth of feeling, "because the time it takes to articulate an emotion in common language can bleed the emotion of its intensity..." (Kilbourn 1999, 29). The linearity of prose is not well suited to the multilayered activities of our lives:

> We frequently juggle a number of issues and demands at the same time. I could have simply said that in academic prose, but . . . I wanted the reader to have, in the active moment of reading, some potent reminder of that phenomenon because, while we all recognize it as a complexity of teaching, our recognition has become numbly habitual. If the manner of writing about complexity in teaching contributes to inattentive, glossed recognition, then it is not working to potently convey the message. . . .
>
> You may wonder where I stand. It is the strength of academic prose that I could be, at this very moment, quite clear about that. It is the strength of fiction that, at times, ambiguity will be stimulating in a way that shows a different view. It is the weakness of fiction that, at other times, ambiguity will be frustrating in a way that merely clouds the view. Which is it for you? (Kilbourn 1999, 29, 32)

Recognizing ambiguity helps to define a problem-space; by God's grace, this may be a space in which obedience to truth can be practiced (cf. Palmer 1983, 69). I hope my writing, in its style as well as its substance, will open up such spaces.

Joseph Dunne (1997) addresses this concern in his widely read book, capturing it in the title: *Back to the Rough Ground* (a phrase he borrows from Wittgenstein). The allusion is to the difficulty of walking on slippery ice: I well remember visiting Toronto briefly one December;

I had arrived from Australia in shoes with smooth leather soles and soon found I could venture no more than a step or two without support from friends, arm in arm on both sides. "[W]here there is no friction . . . in a certain sense the conditions are ideal, but also, just because of that, we are unable to walk. We want to walk: so we need friction. Back to the rough ground!" (Wittgenstein 1972; cit. Dunne 1997, xi). Donald Schön (1983), of "reflective practitioner" fame, evokes related imagery when he compares the messy swamps of professional practice with the high-and-dry ground from which theorists survey the terrain below.

So, a significant part of my justification for choosing "messy" forms of discourse, where many voices speak, is to be more faithful to the realities of our everyday experience of schools. As teachers, we may prefer to play on the fairway, but we end up much of the time in the rough (this is metaphor in respect to teaching, but reality in respect to my game of golf). In my experience, teachers want to know that theorists (and I do not disavow the title) understand—read, *feel*—what it is like to play alongside them, if they are to accord them credibility. The classroom is itself a place where many voices speak—and rightly so.

*****

Given this background, you will not be surprised that the first section of the book contains two chapters that draw heavily on my experience at Mount Evelyn Christian School. I describe the integral curriculum as it has been practiced there, and I report in large part by way of a fictional interview with the principal.[2]

In the second section, I focus on the nature of wisdom, particularly but not exclusively as this is understood in the biblical Wisdom Literature. The contrast with the theory-into-practice paradigm is explored in a dialogue between Solomon, Socrates, and Sophie. The roles played by the first two are no doubt evident, and it is true that they are to a large extent caricatures, speaking on behalf of traditions rather than in voices authentically their own. Sophie stands in for the classroom teacher. Of particular interest are the convergences with postmodern perspectives on knowledge and practice that emerge. Despite the widespread antipathy of Christians to postmodernism (which I have shared), I find myself looking to the lessons to be learned. Postmodernism, like the "premodern" biblical perspective, is an alternative to the modernist paradigm privileging theory. I explore the intersections in the guise of a discussion among teachers.

The third section focuses on the curriculum and seeks to break out of the conventional reification, or "thingifying," of this (as "noun") by exploring its function as verb, preposition, and adjective. This leads into another teacher dialogue in interaction with a seminal advocate of a post-modern view of curriculum, William Doll Jr.

In the final section, I am for a time more explicitly philosophical, exploring a view of wisdom as "grounded normative dispositions," in contrast to the "justified true belief" account of knowledge that has dominated Anglo-American epistemology. As I have mentioned, in defining wisdom as "realization of value," I underscore the value-laden character of schooling and that values (which I also refer to as norms) are of many kinds, enabling us to honor a broader range of human abilities than is usually the case in schools. The postmodern emphasis on *currere*, on the *process* of learning rather than on *what* it is to be learned, introduces a consideration of the growth of wisdom as a psychological phenomenon.

The concluding chapter draws the discussion together in a metaphor for learning and the curriculum: play, problem-posing, purposeful response. This is a model I have been developing over many years. Initially, I emphasized problem-posing; I supplemented this much later with "purposeful response," and completed the troika with "play" when I was at Calvin College in 1991–1992. Each of these modifications arose in response to insights and challenges from teachers and other colleagues. There is an exposition of this model in Chapter 8 of *A Vision with a Task* (Stronks and Blomberg 1993), and the final chapter here draws on that discussion but modifies and elaborates on it in several ways.

In this model, *play* points to the primal encounter with the world that is the basis of all learning. *Problem-posing* suggests that our experience of creation is deepened in a complementary manner to that which occurs through play, by addressing questions to or that arise from this primordial and ongoing encounter. Problems invite responses-in-action, the instantiation of value; *purposeful response* underscores that most important in this encounter is not detached contemplation of propositional truths but normative action, developing over time into a disposition to act normatively.

I recognize that this concise summary is overly abstract, and trust that the final chapter and the book as a whole will put the requisite flesh on these bones. The formulation itself is not sacrosanct—it is merely an attempt to point a direction by which schools may work toward fulfilling their rightful mandate for their students: "the getting of wisdom."

SECTION I

A School at Work

This first main section outlines the curricular approach of the school in which I worked in various capacities for approximately fourteen years and to which I recently returned as a replacement teacher for extended periods. This is the context in which my views on education were largely shaped, although my previous undergraduate and postgraduate study of education—not to mention the thirteen years prior to this that I had spent as a student—obviously also were a significant influence.

The first chapter has its genesis in a paper presented originally to a meeting of parents, then later developed as an introduction to the school's approach for new teachers, though it quickly moves down other avenues. The second chapter elaborates on ideas that were explored in the latter part of that same paper, in the context of a fictional interview with the school principal.

I have decided to begin this book with these pieces because it is from the experience they describe that I have gained the conviction that it is possible to do things differently in our efforts to be more faithful to what I believe God requires of us in education. And I have found when I have shared the story of Mount Evelyn Christian School with others, it has been an encouragement to them to have a concrete example of how we can "do school differently," if there is a supportive parent community. In this respect, it serves as a case study.

Many of the arguments of subsequent chapters are seen in overview here.

1

The School on the Hill

I am embarking on a personal quest. I began to be schooled at the age of four and a half, entering the Transition classroom at Coogee Public in 1956. As far as my (narrowly) vocational life is concerned, I have rarely left the confines of educational institutions. Having now passed a half-century, I want to take stock of what this journey has meant, not merely or mainly for the sake of the backward look, but to chart a course for the future. I will begin my reflection approximately halfway on my journey.

When nearing the completion of a Ph.D. in Education in 1977, I moved from my hometown of Sydney some thousand kilometers to the city of Melbourne to take up an appointment as Senior School Coordinator at Mount Evelyn Christian School. Although this was my first full-time foray into teaching, I did not arrive totally unprepared. I had been an observer in the Grade 7 classroom for three days in 1974 (many of these students were now to be my responsibility) and became a regular visitor in 1976 and 1977, as I had decided to orient the more philosophical investigations of my thesis to the question of how these would actually work out in the design of curriculum for Grades 11 and 12. By inviting me to work for extended periods in a real school environment, Mount Evelyn gave me a valuable opportunity to forge my theoretical understanding in the crucible of daily practice. For me personally, this was a significant motivation to continue these theoretical labors, which by now were becoming increasingly questionable in respect to what some of my "analytical" colleagues would have termed their "cash value."

The Integral Curriculum

Mount Evelyn Christian School—known familiarly as "MECS"— is a K–12 community (or "parent-controlled") school on the fringes of Melbourne, Victoria, Australia. Set in fourteen acres of bushland, it has about 400 students.

MECS has adopted what I have come to describe as an "integral curriculum." The term *integral Christian curriculum* had been common in the literature of the Curriculum Development Centre, Toronto, Canada. This organization had published an elementary school curriculum entitled *Joy in Learning* (de Graaff and Olthuis 1973), which had been used as a model for curriculum development at MECS as the school grew. Commencing with Prep[3] to Grade 6 in 1973, the school progressed into high school in the following year. Although there were a number of parent-controlled Christian schools that were older than MECS, it was the first to take what was indeed a bold step into secondary schooling, though most others were to follow.

What was also interesting about this move into high school was that it retained what was basically a primary school structure: a class teacher was responsible for teaching most of the "subjects," but in a relatively undifferentiated core known as "Creational Studies." Over the years that I studied the school, I began to see that it was reaching toward a model that was in principle different from that of an integrated or thematic curriculum. Where the emphasis of an "integral Christian curriculum" in *Joy in Learning* had been on the *integrality of a Christian perspective* to all that was done, an insistence on a pervasive Christian worldview, this was still perceived as being within the framework of an *integrated* curriculum. My intuition was that there was something new being developed here at MECS—not just an integrated curriculum informed by a Christian perspective, but a new shape for curriculum itself. It was in response to this developing practice, viewed through my own similarly developing theoretical framework, that I coined the phrase *integral curriculum,* a term that was soon taken up by the school as a self-descriptor and an indicator of an ideal toward which to strive.

The use of the term is at first admittedly strange to the ears, and it is helpful to think of the family of terms to which it belongs. Indeed, I have found in my own teaching that this is generally a useful strategy, because it helps students to see that the meanings—and spellings—of words are not arbitrary, just because they do not conform to a tight logical structure, nor are they "scientific." It helps students to make connections, a process that is obviously basic to what it means "to learn."

"Integral" is related to words like *integrity,* meaning "wholeness, soundness, uprightness"; to the mathematical term *integer,* which describes a whole number; to *integrate,* which means to "combine parts into a whole." (It is in respect to the latter that the distinction between "integral" and "integrated" might begin to become clear.) It means "whole or complete, necessary to the completeness of a whole." For MECS, it is a reminder that the whole world is God's world, that Christ is the sovereign Lord of all things, and that service to him is a matter for the whole of life and not just for a part of it. But it is equally an emphasis on the wholeness of creation (its integrity or *integrality*) and our experience of it.

The Judeo-Christian view of the world is that, as *creation,* it is pregnant with meaning, permeated with purposefulness. This is because it owes its existence to a personal God who made all things interdependent in their service of one another and who pronounced the finished work to be "very good." Meaning is not imposed on creation but is intrinsic to it; but neither is meaning to be construed outside the relations of one thing to another, nor of all things individually and severally to their Creator. Though it rings strange to the modern ear, things do not *have* meaning, they *are* meaning, it is their "mode of being" (cf. Dooyeweerd 1953, I, 3); much of what follows may be seen as an unpacking of this perhaps overly abstract, if not opaque, conviction.

Integral, not Integrated

Though such a concise statement might border on caricature, I think it remains legitimate to say that the school curriculum has most commonly been built around subjects and skills. Though there have been progressive protests, child-centered, project-oriented, and problem-based curricula, and, more recently, attempts to accommodate "multiple intelligences" and "learning styles" (from all of which approaches I have gained significant stimuli), these experiments have more often than not foundered on the shoals of traditional approaches. And certainly, physical, cultural, moral, and spiritual development have quite commonly been included among the aims of schools, and when these aims have been most fully realized, schools have celebrated many of the values that promote full human flourishing.

At this point, however, I wish to highlight contrasts in order to explain the import of an "integral" curriculum. And one significant contrast is with an *integrated* approach. As I have noted, to integrate is "to combine parts into a whole": so whereas the quite legitimate concern of integration has been to provide a more coherent and motivating experience for children, and perhaps even to focus on students' interests, the pieces that are brought together in themes are still derived largely from those traditional subjects and basic skills. There is indeed a commendable thematic unity that attempts to transcend subject boundaries, but which has in common with subject-based approaches an acceptance that our experience of the world is best understood through *concepts*. So deep-rooted is this belief in our culture—or, at least, our academic culture—that to suggest otherwise is to appear guilty of nonsense. At least this has been the case until recently, when we have moved into the period described as "postmodern."

The integral curriculum, however, seeks to start with life as a whole; in this respect, it may also be described as "holistic," a term that does have greater currency in educational circles (there is a "Holistic Education" Special Interest Group in the American Educational Research Association), but which is suspect amongst some Christian groups because of its New Age connotations. The notion of an integral curriculum seeks to embody a view of life as already fecund with meaning before it is divided into subject areas, which are one step removed from the integrality or wholeness of ordinary experience. The traditional subjects (in the main) are the product of theoretical-analytic investigation of this integral experience, each regarded as having a certain autonomy in respect to the others; the Hirst and Peters account of "forms of knowledge" is only one of the more recent justifications of this perspective (Hirst 1974; Hirst and Peters 1970). The contention seeking expression in the integral curriculum is that this analysis is not the *source* of meaning but a *response* to the meaning that is characteristic of creation—a quite valid response, of course, and itself crucial to human flourishing, but, nonetheless, only one *kind* of response amongst many. We see here the first indication of an attempt to break with the modernist (and classical Greek) conviction that "Reason" is the source and guarantee of the order of experience.

Ray Elliott (1974) makes a similar point about traditional subjects being "one step removed" in his critique of the Hirst and Peters account:

> But a student might say, with some justification, that he has been taught to love Criticism rather than literature or History rather than the past, if literary works and the past become for him nothing but objects to enquire into in accordance with the methods he has learned. . . .

And he continues with an observation that is particularly germane to my project in its broader outlines:

> If a student of philosophy thinks of philosophy as enquiry for its own sake, enquires into whatever the other philosophers enquire into, and is unclear about the point of the whole activity, he is at best a lover of enquiry, hardly a lover of wisdom, which is something beyond enquiry. . . . [In philosophical aesthetics] it is frequently taken for granted that when a work [of art] ceases to offer any further scope for enquiry one ceases to have any further interest in it, and turns to something else. No account is taken of the lover of art who after having come to know

a work returns to it again and again, not with the hope of discovering anything new in it but to live in it and take it to his heart. . . . (cit. Walsh 1993, 122–23)

It is important to reiterate that in advocating an integral curriculum, I am not denouncing (anymore than is Elliott) the academic disciplines as such, nor denigrating analysis and conceptualization. These are indeed significant and necessary human capabilities. But I would not give to these capacities the dominant role in establishing the content and structure of the school curriculum. Because of the polarizing presuppositions built into much educational debate, however, it is equally important to emphasize that an integral curriculum does not consider the interests of the child to be the appropriate determinant of curriculum content (though it will seek to be child-oriented, because it takes the integrality of the child's experience as a fundamental requirement for learning).

How does an *integral curriculum* differ from one that seeks to be *integrally Christian*—one that acknowledges that fullness of meaning is found in Jesus Christ and can only be approached through him? I suggest that the step from an integral Christian curriculum to an integral curriculum is a significant one. Although a Christian, Islamic, socially conservative, or liberal democratic perspective can be added to any curricular structure (one only has to include a subject entitled Religious Education, for example) or may indeed—and more effectively—*permeate* the curriculum, the notion of an integral curriculum draws attention to the fact that the curriculum structure itself embodies a value(s) framework. But the circle is joined by the suggestion that any such structure is ultimately ideological or religious in character.

A major justification for institutionalizing education in schools is that it does not leave a child's possible experiences to happenstance but seeks to chart a course of developing experience that will be more effective and efficient than serendipity (or individual parents) would allow. A curriculum creates a (school-)world within the world, because it is a selection from and sequencing of an all-but-infinite range of possible experiences. It is a conscious (re-)ordering of the world for the purposes of teaching and learning. The ends to which these processes are directed provide the criteria for the selection and organization of school experience. In its conventional sense (which I will have cause to challenge later), it sets out a course to be run, an orderly and meaningful way in which teachers and students are to proceed. This is equally true of a democratic, negotiated, or child-centered curriculum as it is of an externally prescribed curriculum, even though the sources of selection criteria are quite divergent.

One implication of the foregoing is that it is quite possible to marry a Christian perspective—what we might (following Wolters [1985] and others) call an overall choice of life-*direction*—with a curricular *structure* that embodies a quite different ultimate perspective. In particular, a school might combine a commitment to Christ as the ultimate source of meaning with a curricular framework that proclaims very clearly that it is the human capacity for rational thought that is the source: this is Van Dyk's (2002) charge. An important part of my argument is that such a conjunction will work to undermine the project of Christian schooling from the outset. It embeds a dualism that becomes part of the taken-for-granted, "it goes without saying" modus operandi of a school.

Religion

As I have said, because curriculum structure thus embodies a view of what constitutes the source of meaning, it is a value-laden—and religiously loaded—issue. But if I am to sustain the latter, much stronger claim, I need to say more about what I mean by religion.

Religion can be defined as a commitment to a source of order and meaning (Wentz 1987). Perhaps the most striking illustration of this—from a realm that is usually considered as far removed from religious concerns as possible, that of mathematics—is the following Pythagorean prayer:

> Bless us, divine number, thou who generatest gods and men! O holy, holy tetraktys, thou that containest the root and source of eternally flowing creation! For divine number begins with the profound, the pure unity until it comes to the holy four; then it begets the mother of all, the all-encompassing, the all-bounding, the first born, the never swerving, the never tiring holy ten, the keyholder of all. (Danzig 1954, 42; cit. Clouser 1991, 17)

The issue is not whether this divinization of number can be discounted by relegation to a mythological stage in human thinking, since superseded first by the theological, then by the positive-scientific (*à la* Auguste Comte). It is rather whether similar impulses, though stripped of their confessional trappings, continue to be at work in human affairs. I call in evidence contemporary physicist Paul Davies in his instructively—if provocatively—titled *The Mind of God*:

> As a professional scientist I am fully committed to the scientific method of investigating the world. . . . I have always wanted to believe that science can explain everything, at least in principle. . . . I would rather

not believe in supernatural events personally. . . . My inclination is to assume that the laws of nature are obeyed at all times. But even if one rules out supernatural events, it is still not clear that science could in principle explain everything in the physical universe. There remains that old problem about the end of the explanatory chain. However successful our scientific explanations may be, they always have certain starting assumptions built in. But one can ask where these laws come from in the first place. One could even question the origin of the logic upon which all scientific reasoning is founded. Sooner or later we all have to accept something as given, whether it is God, or logic, or a set of laws, or some other foundation for existence. Thus "ultimate" questions will always lie beyond the scope of empirical science as it is usually defined. So does this mean that the really deep questions of existence are unanswerable? . . . Probably there must always be some "mystery at the end of the universe." But it seems worth pursuing the path of rational inquiry to its limit. (Davies 1993, 15)

Davies concurs that there is a need "to accept something as given." Leaving aside for the moment the question of whether he is trapped within an unhelpful foundationalist framework, from which a coherentist or other explanation could free him, he points to the inevitability of some "ultimate" that is inexplicable within a given system. (He alludes later in the same paragraph to Gödel's Theorem, when he says that "something of that sort has already been demonstrated in mathematics" [Davies 1993, 15].)

Davies does not evidence a commitment to a particular source of meaning: he remains skeptical, opting for "mystery." But he does commit himself to "pursuing the path of rational inquiry to its limit" (Davies 1993, 15). He acknowledges with surprise the number of his scientific colleagues who practice a conventional religion, noting that whilst some are able to keep the two aspects of their lives separate, others "make strenuous and sincere efforts to bring their science and their religion into harmony." Though not adhering to a conventional religion himself, he nonetheless denies that "the universe is a purposeless accident."

> Through my scientific work I have come to believe more and more strongly that the physical universe is put together with an ingenuity so astonishing that I cannot accept it merely as a brute fact. There must, it seems to me, be a deeper level of explanation. Whether one wishes to call that deeper level "God" is a matter of taste and definition. (Davies 1993, 16)

By Davies's criteria, I am welcome to describe this "deeper level" as "religious," though I would affirm that I regard this as more than a matter of aesthetics or stipulation. Davies's own references to "conventional religion" are instructive in this respect: he seems to imply that alongside this are nonconventionally religious perspectives—such as his own. But I would not wish him to be compelled to agree.

Davies chooses for his epigraph (and the source of his title) the concluding passage from Stephen Hawking's best-selling (though purportedly little-read) *A Brief History of Time:*

> If we do discover a complete theory, it should in time be understandable in broad principle by everyone, not just a few scientists. Then we shall all, philosophers, scientists, and just ordinary people, be able to take part in the discussion of why it is that we and the universe exist. If we find the answer to that, it would be the ultimate triumph of human reason—for then we would truly know the mind of God. (Hawking 1988, 185)

It is clear from Hawking's book that he anticipates this victory of Reason one day to be attained. It should also be evident that I regard this conviction that Reason will one day penetrate to the ultimate level of existence as itself a religious commitment.

These examples, of course, prove nothing about the universality of a religious impulse; they are suggestive only. And this is all that they can be. But what is significant in the present context is that where such a commitment can be shown to exist, it provides criteria for the selection of curriculum content. A commitment to economic growth and well-being as fundamental to the meaning of the good life issues in particular kinds of educational policies, particular kinds of curriculum content—choices with which we are all too familiar today. It leads to those activities that are more economically productive (according to certain assumed criteria of productivity, usually limited to material goods) being favored over those that are regarded as less so.

Wisdom *in concreto*

I have been proposing that subject-centered and integrated curricula share the assumption that rationality is the key to human flourishing. This assumption is, of course, at the heart of the modernist project. Whereas an integrated curriculum attempts to combine dimensions derived through theoretical analysis, an integral curriculum begins with the given wholeness of experience prior to analysis. The Christian school has a premodern assumption: it begins with the confession that "all things hold together in Jesus Christ" (Colossians 1:17). This Pauline phrase unites what I have called the *structural* and *directional* dimensions of the integral curriculum: the conviction that all of reality has a coherent, intrinsically referential character and that this coherence depends upon the one through whom and for whom it was created.

Because the wholeness of experience has many sides to it besides the rational, it will have as its goal not in the first place rational understanding, but *wisdom:* concrete acting in a manner that does justice to this richness of reality (and "doing justice" is no mere metaphor, I wish to emphasize). Wisdom requires the simultaneous realization of norms (values): a *realizing*/understanding and a *making real*/actualizing of what is of significance. (Although baldly put at this point, the elaboration of this perspective and its implications for teaching and curriculum constitutes a large component of what follows.)

While the emphasis is on wholeness, children obviously cannot study the whole world at once. They will have to focus on particular parts of creation. Such focusing is a necessary requirement of any kind of learning, most evident at the level of perception, where seeing and hearing depend not only on attending to certain aspects of the perceptual field but as a corollary also on ignoring or sifting out that which is deemed irrelevant. In hearing in particular, the "message" needs to be sorted from the background "noise," but in seeing as well, how one turns one's head and then directs one's gaze delimits the focus of attention. But this selecting of a finite focus is of a different order from theoretical analysis or intellection, where one is attending *from* the concrete *entities* in interrelationship in one's field *to* the *properties* of these entities in abstraction from them.

I am suggesting that focusing on selected areas of creation is a different matter entirely from focusing on the products of academic disciplines, whether these be "pure" or integrated around themes. It is the difference between having a *slice* of chocolate cake and eating the flour or the cocoa, or more precisely, the amino acids or carbohydrates. The slice is representative of the whole cake: when I eat it, I can be confident that I know what the cake tastes like. I could not have the same confidence if I were to consume in succession each of the ingredients described in the recipe.

It could be said that this analogy is seriously flawed, because a cake is an integration of ingredients. But as *cake* it has its own identity. The taste of the cake as such cannot be derived by summing its several ingredients, any more than the meaning of the life of a person can be derived from adding together her biological, emotional, social, and spiritual functioning or by weighing and measuring the various chemical elements (which would sell on the market for $75) that make up the body. I do not know Sue by studying her digestive system, academic record, passport, and résumé. And although tasting the flour can certainly tell me about the character of flour, it barely hints at the character of the chocolate sponge cake.

This point can be expressed more philosophically as follows: God has created, either directly or mediately through human hands, a diversity of things that function in varieties of ways. Whereas the academic disciplines focus in general on the abstracted ways of functioning—Napoleon is of interest to the historian as a cultural force, but to the psychologist as a driven, perhaps megalomaniacal, bundle of emotions—our ordinary experience of creation is of the things themselves in their complex interrelations. Of course, the ways of functioning as much as the things themselves are created by God, but our primary experience of them is in the functioning of those things themselves, not in isolation from these things.

The ordinary, everyday experience of the cake may be described as "concrete," which denotes "a thing as opposed to a quality" (*Concise Oxford English Dictionary*). Concrete experience is experience of wholes (entities) rather than of functions in abstraction. Nor is concrete experience restricted to the physical, material, or sense-able world, for things function aesthetically, ethically, and confessionally (amongst other ways) just as *real*-ly as they function spatially, physically, biotically, and sensorily. A novel is not just marks on paper, with a certain weight and dimensions, but something that communicates a story, evokes an aesthetic response, raises moral dilemmas, conveys a view of life, and so on.

I hope that this will allay fears that an emphasis on concrete experience always implies doing things with one's hands or getting outside and moving about. Sitting and listening to music or reading a book are just as concrete as visiting the zoo or panning for gold: they just happen to be concrete aesthetic or linguistic experiences rather than a concrete physical experience (though they presuppose the latter). To limit the concrete to the material is to endorse a materialistic view of life.

An integral curriculum seeks to respect the creational structures as they are given. God created the land and the sea, the plants and the animals, the man and the woman. An animal in its fullness is more than the systems of assimilation, respiration, and reproduction examined in the biology laboratory; more than a component in the historical study of farming; more than an economic good for purposes of trade; more than a pet or the subject of a painting. It is all of these things, because of the rich possibilities of functioning that God has structured into creation, but it is more than these things, more even than the sum of these various parts.

The range of studies identified in the previous paragraph can give an insight into the various sides of an animal, but it is also possible thereby to lose the knowledge of the animal in its wholeness as it has been created by God. To fragment a child's experience of an animal is to fragment his or her experience of the world, promoting diffraction and loss of meaning. Treating an animal in its integrity and with integrity means meeting it not firstly as an object for theoretical manipulation, but taking it as it is *given.* Herein lies a basis for all ethical/ecological prescriptions, from treating all people as ends in themselves rather than as means to ends, to dealing sensitively with an animal or a forest.

This last statement can be defended without recourse to any *explicitly* "religious" terminology. But Christian faith takes the further step of confessing that an integral experience of the world will point to the focus and coherence of meaning in Christ, not in the first place by locating things within a theological system of doctrines, but by recognizing that all things are created to serve one another and in so doing ("Love your neighbor as yourself"), also to serve God ("Love the Lord your God with all your heart"). But intellectually as well, as we abstract and analyze, we look away from the religious root in which all things hold together; we look at separate systems of explanation rather than back toward the one who is the explanation.

Starting with the whole, we would indeed seek to open up to the child the great richness of functioning of the area under study. The integral curriculum starts at the other end of this process than the subject-centered or integrated models do. It begins with the symphony rather than the parts for each instrument, with the melody rather than the individual notes.

In Practice

The way in which MECS seeks to implement this approach can be illustrated in part by describing the roles played by the various teachers. From Kindergarten to Grade 10, the class teacher is in immediate control of curriculum implementation at each level. She is the coordinator of the learning experiences of her pupils for the year and is expected to maintain an overarching and comprehensive perspective on the unit of study. This is not to suggest that the curriculum is developed at the whim of an individual; however, taking her place within a larger team, she will lead the team at her level. At its best, a collegial or communal approach to the class program develops, with class and specialist teachers contributing their insights and expertise to the fleshing out of a coherent course of study growing out of a central direction, the particular "chunk"[4] of creation under study. The class teacher also, and no less importantly, provides a focus for pastoral care and oversight of individual students.

The Grade 8 program, for example, starts with units on agriculture and manufacturing. The English teacher oversees an investigative journalism project, in which groups of students select a product and study its growth, processing, and marketing. The science teacher assists in the analysis of products and the testing of materials. The art teachers establish a production line and over a few days a factory setting is simulated, mass producing an item that is then sold at the local shopping center and to the school community. Some "industrial relations" problems usually arise in this context, providing interesting opportunities for negotiation and conflict resolution.

Other examples include the use of novels with themes exploring issues arising from the unit; the construction of puppets involving a study of bodily proportions, the writing of a script exploring human relationships and the breeding of white mice in the Grade 7 Human Body unit; and the general introduction of library skills—such as the use of a research grid—in cooperation with the teacher and in the context of the unit.

At the senior secondary level, a more differentiated subject structure has been developed, though with a core component intended not only to deepen Christian perspective in itself but also to promote a more coherent reflection on the other areas being studied. This subject specialization is not merely a recognition of the demands of the final external examinations, but also a response to different developmental needs and potential of the students. My own role in developing this curriculum (Blomberg 1978) serves to illustrate, I trust, that I am not criticizing subject- or discipline-oriented studies in themselves but the relative importance that should be assigned to these in determining overall curriculum structure and content.

2

An Integral Curriculum: A Conversation with the Principal

Truth is an eternal conversation about things that matter, conducted with passion and discipline.
Parker J. Palmer (1998, 104)

Over the years, many principals and teachers have visited Mount Evelyn. They have a general view of the curriculum as outlined in the previous chapter, but they want more detail and justification. Sitting with the principal in his somewhat rustic office, they have conversations much like the one that follows.

"Life Is Religion"

Visitor: I noticed in the package you sent me that there are no church creeds mentioned in your Basis, though you have an Educational Creed. Don't you think that it is essential for a Christian school to make a much more explicit and detailed statement about its doctrinal foundations?

Principal: We are a parent-controlled school, not a church school. We are not affiliated with any particular denomination, but you will have noticed that our Creed is very firmly rooted in the tradition of the Protestant Reformation. We confess all of the fundamental doctrines of the faith, but there is no need in a school to insist on a particular stance on baptism or church government, for example. These things are not relevant to the daily life of the school and would only serve to divide or exclude.

Visitor: Your Creed states that "human life in its entirety is religion." I must say that this is a rather quaint way of putting it. Why don't you simply say that human beings are "religious"?

Principal: It does sound strange, I agree. But it is meant to indicate that *religious* is not just one of the things we can say about life, an adjective like *political* or *artistic,* so that you can say of a person, "Oh, he's religious," with the implication that other people are not. In our understanding, religion is not just a dimension of life, and an optional one at that. We want to say that life equals religion; it is coterminous with and saturated by religion.

Visitor: I'm not sure that I follow you. What practical difference does this make in the way that you conduct schooling?

Principal: Well, our curriculum first and foremost seeks to stress that serving God is a full-time affair. We don't want there to be a division between the so-called secular and sacred parts of the curriculum. That would give the impression that some parts of the curriculum deal with matters of everyday life, which are of only passing significance (even if they seem to be of presently pressing importance), and that other parts would deal with eternal and heavenly realities. As far as we are concerned, nothing at all can legitimately be isolated from the central issue of whom one will serve, though I admit that some things will indeed seem more remote and less crucial than others. In our view, to attempt to make a part of life stand on its own, independent of God, is the essence of idolatry.

Visitor: Idolatry! Why use an absolutist, fundamentalist word like that? Isn't that to draw the lines far too sharply?

Principal: I realize that it sounds somewhat polemical, but we do regard it as quite a serious issue. I think that one of our graduates summed it up when he came back to address a farewell assembly for senior students. He thought the essence of his school experience could be captured in the slogan, "No dualism!" We're saying that a reductionist view that seeks to explain all of life in terms of one of its aspects, such as the biotic or the historical, is not just an intellectual aberration, but is at root a religious concern.

Visitor: So, to aspire to an integral curriculum is to oppose a dualistic curriculum, and you equate dualism with idolatry, because it sets up some other principle as equal to God? But couldn't you be accused of reducing life to its religious dimension?

Principal: Yes, I guess we could be, though it seems to me that any such charge would in the end be self-refuting. A view of life that makes all other aspects *relative* to one foundational aspect gives to that latter aspect a *determining* role. It makes it the source of order and meaning. And as Wentz (1987) explains, a commitment to a source of order and meaning is an appropriate way of explaining what we mean by religion.

Visitor: Surely the response would be that this is just a matter of definition.

Principal: Well, I just don't think that there is any way of settling that question from the outside, as it were. In the end, you come back to "this is the way I see it," a confessional standpoint. This is not irrational, but it is arational. There is no such thing as a fully self-contained rational system. But I want to put this positively, because we are really more about affirming than negating. We confess that Christ is the Lord of all life and culture and that he calls his people to a ministry of reformation and transformation. This is not triumphalist. It is not that we are capable of building the Kingdom of God on earth—this won't happen until Christ returns. But because he has accomplished the mighty act of reconciliation in his death, resurrection, and ascension, we are called to erect signposts to God's peace and justice wherever we can in life.

Visitor: You say, "wherever we can." Does this mean there are areas where you can't? Are there some parts of life that are so far from God's purposes that you cannot deal with them? One of the characteristics that stands out for me in Christian schools that I have visited is their policy of exclusion: no D. H. Lawrence or fantasy novels, no detailed consideration of the theory of evolution, just its repudiation.

Principal: Because we believe in the radical and comprehensive—cosmic—character of Christ's work of redemption, we hold that no area of life can be excluded at the outset from the school curriculum. There will, of course, be many principial—concerning matters of principle—and practical influences on the selection of content and approach, but it cannot be that any facet of life is off-limits because the gospel has no relevance to it. A school is not made Christian by excluding the things you mention: it is the way in which these things are approached that will be the litmus test. It is about uncovering the religious roots of every aspect of life. Christian education is worldview education—though, in fact, I think that all schooling is education in a worldview, but it's often implicit, whereas we try very hard to be explicit about it.

Mathematics

Visitor: Well, to me, mathematics doesn't look like a religious issue at all. What's "2 + 2 = 4" got to do with Christianity? Isn't it all the same whether you're a Christian or not? How can you talk about a Christian approach to teaching mathematics? Isn't "2 + 2 = 4" simply true, whatever your religion?

Principal: Yes, I know, mathematics is a tough nut to crack. But as far as I can see, this question already assumes a secularized view of the world. By "secularized," I mean the view that life can be explained without any reference to what lies beyond "this age"—the Latin root is *saeculum*—the limits of our current experience. On this view, there are no transcendent principles impinging upon our earthly existence. The assumption is that reality can be sliced up into pieces and that the meaning of each of these pieces is self-contained, self-explanatory. It assumes that truth involves a simple statement of fact, whereas we think that it has more to do with the person of Jesus Christ than with propositions, more to do with a relationship with the one who said, "I am the truth." If you reflect on the biblical story about the Garden of Eden, the sin of Adam and Eve was to believe that they could find their own explanation without depending on God, that they could then successfully find a place to hide from him. With the eyes of faith, we confess that listening to the Word of God makes a difference—indeed, is crucial—to everything we do. The world is not self-contained, but everywhere is dependent on and open to its Creator.

Visitor: And mathematics? You haven't really addressed the question yet. Surely some things just *are:* there are facts about the world, like it is either raining or it isn't.

Principal: Fair enough. But I think that you will find that even the question about whether it is raining might get a different answer from someone who wants to spend a day at the beach than it does from farmers waiting for a drought to break. What I think is basic is this: nothing has its meaning in itself—or outside a context. The very question about two plus two and four assumes a knowledge of the English language and the way in which certain mathematical terms function within it. It also assumes most probably a number system of base ten but at least no less than base five. It takes for granted that one is talking about fairly well defined if not abstracted areas, and not about two male and two female rabbits kept together as pets for a few months or two drops plus two drops of water or two aspirin in two milliliters of water. It has made a statement that is certainly relatively true—that is, within circumscribed boundaries—into an absolute, as though it guarantees its own meaning. And I think that you would agree that belief in the Trinity certainly confounds our systems of mathematics!

Visitor: I was with you until you got to the Trinity, but I think that you are trivializing your argument rather than helping it at this point, if you don't mind me saying.

Principal: Well, you're not the first person to say that to me, I must admit, but I want to stick with it. Because what we would say is that eventually, if one traces out all of the things that are assumed by the simple mathematical statement, including, of course, beliefs about the dependability and source of the kind of order in the world that mathematics wants to talk about, one gets involved in issues of an overtly religious (and one would also say, philosophical) character. Think about the use of "zero." It originated in Hindu mathematics and was long resisted in the West because the idea of "nothing" was theologically threatening—indeed, people were persecuted for their advocacy of the concept. Similarly, the Pythagorean brotherhood, wedded to the mystical power of whole numbers and discrete ratios, could not countenance the thought of irrational numbers. Though these two examples might be taken as evidence of the impediments that religion presents to the free development of scientific understanding, they at the same time illustrate that mathematical conceptions are linked with more pervasive views of the world.

Visitor: Are you questioning the objectivity of mathematics? Surely it is reliable enough for us to be able to land someone on the moon—it could just as well have been a communist as a Christian. Indeed, many of the scientists responsible had learnt their trade as servants of the Nazis!

Principal: I think that actually helps to make my point about the dangers of separating any area of life from other areas, as though doing a job of science is a neutral undertaking, politically and religiously. But to keep focused on the issue at hand, I am certainly questioning a particular view of objectivity, the notion that something is true in and of itself, independent of human interpretation. I am not, however, questioning the importance of mathematics or of any other scientific work. I would affirm that mathematics is a valuable and powerful tool, but it is, at the same time, a limited and focused way of looking at the world. Its meaning can only be understood in relation to other dimensions of the world. To claim that mathematics is true in and of itself is not only logically false, but it is also, in my opinion, unfaithful to a biblical view of the world. That's why I am willing to call such a view idolatrous.

Visitor: Well, we started on this topic as a way of testing the claim that "human life in its entirety is religion." Does this mean that every time one does mathematics, there should be some reference to God or Jesus, to his "wonderful design," or that there should be a Bible verse tacked on to the lesson?

Meaning

Principal: I am definitely not suggesting that you can "baptize" math with a Bible verse! Nor am I suggesting that one should trace out the assumptions I have begun to identify every time one does math. What I am saying is that a curriculum structure that accepts the interconnections and interdependence in reality, rather than cutting one area off from another, will make the integral religious character of life more obvious, more often. We are then able to confront children with the fundamental religious choices that form the basis of life and thus to bring a biblical perspective to bear on even the most abstracted parts of the curriculum.

And because such a curriculum is in the deepest sense more meaningful—again, because we think of "meaning" not as something self-contained in any aspect of the universe, but as the restless referring of all things one to another—it will have more relevance and motivational power for the student. This practice of the confession that the Lordship of Christ and the response of faith makes a difference to everything must be the hallmark and the touchstone of any school that dares to call itself Christian. It gives substance to the oft-quoted "the fear of the Lord is the beginning of wisdom." I'm sorry if I'm going on a bit here, but I think that this issue is of crucial importance.

Questions

Visitor: I can see that this is something you feel quite passionate about! I'm tempted to open myself up to the charge of being trivial—did you hear that Douglas Adams died recently and that he had produced about eight pages of the novel for which he had been paid millions of dollars in advance? I started out by asking you a question about math, and, as you have been talking, I was reminded of the importance of regaining the power of asking the questions—and then of ensuring that we ask the right ones. In Adams's book, *The Hitchhiker's Guide to the Galaxy*—have you read it, it's really hilarious—

Principal: Yes, it's been quite a while, but I've read the whole "trilogy"—all five books!

Visitor: Well, you'll remember that the computer Deep Thought had worked through eons to answer the question concerning the meaning of life, the universe, and everything. When the mortals who had been bred and educated for the task were finally called to receive the answer, they were told they were not going to like it. And the machine intoned "42." It was right: they didn't like it. Deep Thought then informed them that they certainly had the right answer, but what they needed to do now was to work out the right question. Not to worry, the penultimate computer would design the ultimate computer to formulate the question, the strength of this computer being that it would incorporate organic life. Its name was to be Earth!

Principal: Isn't it ironic that the answer to the deepest questions is thought to be mathematical, yet the computer recognizes the limitations of "machine-mindedness"? But I agree about the importance of learning to ask the right questions. Socrates recognized this, but Jesus did as well. Look at the numerous times he refuses to answer the question that has been put to him and gives the answer to a more basic one instead. Or indeed, the number of times he answers a question with a question. In this respect, as well as in others, Jesus was a real teacher in the wisdom tradition. John also knew the power of a telling question; in his letter to a church being troubled by Gnostic heretics, they were to test the spirits by asking, "Did Jesus Christ come in the flesh?"

Many years ago, I took the training course for *Man: A Course of Study—MACOS*. You probably remember that it was banned in Queensland, and, because our school bought a copy of the course, we found ourselves on a banned list published by a group of concerned Christians! Thankfully, that's behind us now. But one of the handbooks states something to the effect that "Students need many opportunities to ask questions throughout the lessons. Learning to formulate questions is often as important and difficult as finding answers to other people's questions." I remember it because I think that it is a basic educational principle. In many cases, I think that it's fair to say that the answer is implicit in the question. And this is the case not only with respect to words and theories: Paulo Freire insisted that posing questions to reality is always the first step toward being able to change it. Paul's injunction to test all things, holding fast to what is good, implies the same thing: if we are not to be conformed to the world, we need to develop the power to call it into question.

We find Walsh and Middleton's (1984) four worldview questions particularly helpful in addressing the issue of religious perspective. In the development of curriculum units and in the teaching of children, these questions can be used to focus our attention on the fundamental choices. Together, of course, they imply a response to the most basic question of all: Who (or what) is God?

The "Four Questions"

1. Who am I? (What is the nature, task, and purpose of human beings?)
2. Where am I? (What is the nature of the world and universe that I live in?)
3. What is wrong? (What is the basic problem or obstacle that keeps me from attaining fulfillment? How do I understand evil?)
4. What is the remedy? (How is it possible to overcome this hindrance to my fulfillment? How do I find salvation?)

Biblical Perspective

Visitor: I've looked at some of your curriculum documents, and I noticed that they all have a section entitled "Biblical Perspective." This is obviously a practical attempt to implement the sort of thing that we've been talking about. But the notion of a biblical perspective seems to me to imply that the whole revelation of Scripture would be brought to bear on an area of study. Surely this is a big task. In my experience, most Christian teachers don't have a rigorous theological education. What practical guidelines do you use in trying to make this work?

Principal: You're right, it's a big task. It can only be possible if we are steeped in Scripture—as the Bible itself says, "our thoughts being led captive by Christ." And I should admit that I don't believe that this necessitates theological training—unless one has a very broad understanding of "theology." One helpful way of surveying the sweep of Scripture, however, is in terms of the Creation, Fall, Redemption motif. This, too, can be expressed in terms of a number of questions that may guide us in the development of biblical perspective. Let me give you this sheet (cf. Blomberg 1986).

1. What is God's intention for the particular area of creation that we are studying? What does it mean to treat these creatures with integrity, that is, in accordance with their God-given calling in life?

2. How has this purpose been distorted by the effects of sin, as reflected in human idolatry and the outworking of God's Word of judgment? Has this part of creation been severed from its interconnections with the rest so that it is thought to stand on its own as an absolute, having meaning in and of itself?

3. What are the avenues by which we may hope to bring healing and reconciliation where presently there is brokenness? In what ways does the gospel impel us to action so that the Lord's *shalom* might be at least partially restored, on the basis of Christ's mighty work of redemption?

Visitor: I can see how this reflects the Creation, Fall, Redemption motif. But don't you think that it's pretty arrogant to think that we can know God's intention for something? Do you really think that we can get inside the mind of God?

Principal: On one level, you're right. But all we really mean by that question is the same thing that we mean in any area of decision making. We can only know what God chooses to reveal to us—but then, we believe that God's creation is itself revelation, that it speaks to us, if we will only listen. This is pretty central to the biblical Wisdom Literature that we have come to see more and more as vital to our understanding of the nature of knowledge and of how we come to know. But any time a Christian makes a decision, surely he or she seeks God's will in the situation. It's in the Lord's Prayer: "Your will be done on earth, as it is in heaven." We have to carefully study the creation. But we also have to do so wearing what Calvin called "biblical spectacles." God's revelation in Scripture helps us to see more clearly—though always fallibly—how we should proceed in a situation. We don't have complete knowledge, but walking in faith is always a matter of walking without such absolute certainty. And of course, I might add, because nobody can have absolute certainty about anything, everyone has to walk in faith of some kind!

Visitor: We looked at mathematics—the most abstract, supposedly objective and neutral area of the curriculum—as a way of exploring your claims about religious perspective. Would you say that Mount Evelyn has developed a curriculum that effectively implements this goal in relation to mathematics?

Principal: Absolutely not—whether in regard to math or many other aspects of schooling! We are only too aware of our shortcomings—and I don't say that out of any sense of false modesty. But we believe that it is this concern for a biblical perspective on all that is done that must be the hallmark of a Christian school, or it isn't living up to the very large claim of being Christian, no matter how loving and caring relationships between staff and students might be.

Change

Visitor: I've been involved in schools long enough to know that change needs to be piecemeal rather than wholesale, especially in a situation in which one is so clearly accountable to the parent community. Among other things, if you try to move too quickly, you're going to have a rebellion on your hands—not only from parents, but from staff as well! What steps have you taken toward this goal in respect to math?

Principal: I always say you have to start where you are—a truism, if there ever was one! But in the first place, teachers look for whatever opportunities there are within a unit to develop mathematical skills. In the Grade 8 unit on *Using Time: Leisure,* for example, graphing, mapping, basic trigonometry, compass work, and estimation skills are employed, in preparation for the "survival camp." In the Grade 5 *B.C. to A.D.* unit, students look at some of the contributions to the development of mathematics made by the Babylonians, Egyptians, and Greeks and try to place these within their religious context. Grade 3 will make bread in their *Plants* unit and learn to use weights and measures in following recipes; they will use graphs of rainfall and sunshine in the *Weather* unit. Grade 4 students calculate trees per hectare and heights of trees in the *Forests* unit; they work with direction and distance in *Maps and Mapmaking* and practice their skills in an orienteering exercise. Statistical techniques are introduced to students in the senior high school as a means of analyzing survey results gathered for *Christian Social Perspectives.* Other statistical procedures are an integral part of the Grade 7 unit comparing various cultures.

As you have said, the steps to an integral curriculum, at any level of the school, can be gradual; in terms of accustoming people to innovations—

whether parents, teachers, or pupils—it is obviously advantageous to proceed in this manner. And it is always necessary to have an overview of the curriculum, to engage regularly in curriculum-mapping exercises so that we are not just dealing with mathematical skills and concepts in a serendipitous manner. We are just as concerned with scope and sequence as any school, and we do continue with a relatively stand-alone mathematics program alongside our other mathematical work.

Visitor: You know that one of the reasons I am here is because there are a number of parents and staff members in our school who are intrigued by what you have been doing and are interested in adopting an integral curriculum. If the board actually takes such a decision, it frightens me as to the sorts of expectations that this approach will place on teachers. Have you got any suggestions about how we might best proceed?

Principal: Well, one suggestion would be that in the primary section of the school, this change can begin by turning half—or even initially even just a quarter—of the day over to integral unit work. You can gradually begin to move out from this into the skills areas, incorporating them within the framework of the unit. You have to move at a pace with which teachers will feel comfortable, just pushing the envelope a little at a time. Of course, as a learning strategy, a further advantage of this approach is the gradual replacement of mechanical and repetitive tasks with tasks that become more meaningful. If you wish to continue with the learning of spelling lists, for example, words that have meaning within the context of the unit are not only more interesting but also more easily learned and retained. Writing, arithmetic, and artistic skills are also given more purpose within such a context. I am convinced that one of our goals, if we take seriously that people bear the image of God, is to provide children with activities in which they take responsibility for their own self-forming.

Visitor: It occurs to me from the little bit of philosophy that I've read that we have been dealing with one of the four major philosophical areas, having to do with a framework of values. I think that the fancy term for this is *axiology*—actually, I've been reading George Knight's (1980) book for my Master's study, and that's the term he uses. But you have really been saying that religious values are all-encompassing—that religion is integral to everything else, to use your own "fancy" term.

But to tell you the truth, I am pretty exhausted by our discussion, and I think that you must feel the same, although you've obviously had to field a lot of these questions before. Would it be possible for us to get together again tomorrow? I'd like to ask you about the three other kinds of questions, having to do with what you think the nature of the world is, how you see the person, and what you think it means to know something—Knight calls these *ontology, anthropology,* and *epistemology.* I think that these categories would give a pretty comprehensive coverage of the issues.

Principal: Well, looking at my diary, I had put aside the block after lunch to meet with you again if necessary, so why don't we plan on that? Now I'll take you up to the staff room to meet some of our teachers. You've already popped into some of their classrooms, so I'm sure they'll be glad to get to speak to you.

***

Creation

Principal: You said yesterday that you wanted to talk about how we see the world, the person, and knowledge. Of course, we have already touched on these issues, but I will see if I can add some more things that might be helpful. I don't expect you to agree with everything I say, of course. Some Christians think that we're way off-beam on some of these things. But it won't surprise you if I frame everything in relation to the notion of integrality.

So as far as the integrality of creation is concerned, I would say in the first place that God has created a rich and diverse world that owes its existence to him alone and has its coherence in his Son. There is one world, and the source of its meaning cannot be found within any one part of it but only in him who created it. It is an ordered, structured world, but this order comes not from any principle inherent in it but from the creative fiat—command—of God.

Visitor: So, I suppose you think that a "creation science" view is essential in a Christian school?

Principal: Actually, no, although I know that will be controversial! I think that we can sometimes underestimate the significance of the first chapter of Genesis, especially when we jump straight away to the creation-evolution debate. Being concerned about an evolutionistic view of origins, we focus on what it tells us about what happened at the beginning. With this restriction, we can then all too easily fall into an evolutionistic view of the course of human history since then—or, in more theological terms, we become "practical Deists." We regard the cultural work of humankind not as a response to the creational order under the impetus of the cultural mandate—— God's charge to humankind to till and keep the earth—but as mere accidents of chance with no abiding status. We restrict the meaning of creation to the so-called "natural world." When we are out in the bush, we extol the wonders of God's creation, rarely thinking to do so in the classroom, the kitchen, or the concert hall: unless, of course, we are even here drawn to reflect on the birds and the mountains and the trees. The "creation science" groups of various kinds do not concern themselves with economic or political science, but only with the "natural sciences." So although we have found ourselves in trouble for not endorsing creation science, I think that we actually out-creation the creationists!

Visitor: I can see how your view would be broader. All of this talk about the "integrality" of creation seems to stress that everything that exists is creaturely—

Principal: Except God, of course. We know that Paul speaks of marriage as one of those things God created to be received with thanksgiving (1 Timothy 4:3–4) and he speaks similarly of the state authorities as established and instituted by God (Romans 13:1–2). Beyond this, wherever he and the other authors of Scripture enjoin masters and slaves, parents and children, rulers and citizens to act in particular ways toward one another, they do so on the basic assumption that the manner in which human affairs are to be regulated is not merely a matter of human convention but is a response to God's purposes for such relationships. It can be a faithful or unfaithful response, but it is a response nonetheless. The creation account is foundational to this understanding, pointing as it does to the boundaries that God has established between one kind of creature and another, each with its own particular calling in the economy of creation.

Visitor: But surely you cannot take the role of slave as one intended by God at creation!

Principal: No, I certainly wouldn't, any more than I would assume that the patriarchal Roman family or the tyrannical rule of Nero represents God's purposes for the family or the state. But even when God's creational intent has been distorted as severely as it has in the roles of master and slave, the call to act in loving service remains paramount. I wouldn't even assume that the employer-employee relationship as this is structured in a capitalist society is God's creational intent. Everything we experience in the world is to a greater or lesser extent a corruption of God's purposes, because of the Fall. But as Augustine emphasized, evil is not a positive power in itself, it cannot create out of nothing. So wherever we see distortion, we should also be looking for what would bend the relationship back in the direction of love. There are "offices" here that God calls people to, and they are always a matter of relationship. But there are also issues of religious direction—is the God who is love being served?—mixed up with questions of creational structure. We can't get away from that.

Visitor: So, if that's how you see creation, how does this play out in the curriculum?

Principal: An integral curriculum seeks to open up to the child the rich diversity of the one creation. It does this in relation both to the variety of structures that God has established—not only directly but also by human hands, mediately, one might say—and to the variety of ways in which creation functions. By the latter, I mean that creation has physical, biotic, emotional, cultural, economic, aesthetic, linguistic, ethical, political, and belief dimensions—not that these exhaust the list! We don't want our curriculum to focus narrowly on one or a few of these entities or aspects or to collapse this richness into one or two categories. When that happens, it is as though we are saying that the meaning of life can be found in this area or that area of creation. Remember what I said about idolatry.

Scientism

Visitor: That reminds me of Donald McKay's (1974) description of reductionism as "nothing-buttery." Obviously, from what you're saying, an integral curriculum would reject a reductionist view of the world, one that assumes that the truth about politics can be found in the analysis of election statistics or that the meaning of war can be captured in body counts and kill ratios, that the pursuit of justice is nothing but the outworking of the class struggle, that aesthetics is nothing but the expression of personal taste, that correct use of language is nothing but the application of logical grammatical rules, that the maintenance of peace is nothing but a matter of finding the right technology.

Principal: McKay has made quite an impression on you! But I would not want to suggest that a subject-centered curriculum necessarily operates with the kind of framework that you describe. It is interesting, however, as you know, that each of your examples is drawn from actual approaches to the areas mentioned. What I would say is that a teacher who could be characterized as a rigid subject specialist, more interested in teaching the subject to the child than in teaching the child the subject, can indeed approach such an extreme. I know that putting it in terms of a polarity can be a caricature, and that teaching is always a matter of teaching *something* to *someone*. But a (Christian) science specialist did admit to me once that it had taken him a long time to be weaned of the belief that science was the most reliable and most important route to understanding the world and that he had previously been content merely to concentrate on his science and let the other areas of life take care of themselves.

Visitor: Now you've got me thinking of a book about the Manhattan Project I had to read at university. When Robert Oppenheimer was asked whether he supported the dropping of the bomb on Japan, he said that such issues of policy were beyond his responsibility, that he was there to do a job of physics, and that he would have done whatever they asked him to do, including making the bomb a different shape or painting it a different color if this were technically feasible—which hardly goes to the heart of the matter!

Principal: Yes, that's the kind of scientism we oppose. You can't compartmentalize areas of life in such a simplistic way—or rather, you shouldn't. If we recognize that creatures are called to be servants, then our curriculum will need to show how the areas of creation are intended to serve one another as they serve their God. Any area of creation that attempts to dominate rather than serve has assumed the guise of an idol. And knowledge has ultimately to be of service—"serviceable insight," they call it at Dordt College. Knowledge for the sake of knowledge is scientism. Knowledge for service is what we mean by wisdom, at least in part.

Visitor: Can you say a little more about scientism and how to avoid it? And I hope you are not saying that there is something wrong with knowledge for its own sake—don't you enjoy doing crosswords and playing Trivial Pursuit?

Principal: I do indeed—though I can't handle cryptics! Even worse, I can't stand to miss an episode of *Millionaire*. But I think that we would agree that this is not very high-level knowledge. Anyway, back to the question of scientism.

First, in general terms, we have to avoid the impression that one entity or aspect of the world is more real, more true, or more important than another. More specifically, each of the special sciences, because of its deep insight into the structure of one of the world's dimensions, can very readily fall into this trap. So, when we are selecting learning processes, we need to attend to the diversity of sides or aspects to the chunk of creation under study. It would be possible to study the heavens in purely physical terms, for example, using the methodology and results of the natural sciences as our key and perhaps supplementing this with marvel at the achievements of space technology. To do this would be to overlook that the heavens declare the glory of God, that they indeed evoke a confessional response, that they ought to remind us with Scripture's guidance that the children of Abraham are as numerous as the stars that are in the sky.

Visitor: I am sure there are many, Christians not excluded, who would be skeptical about such an approach. They would see it as a spiritualistic imposition on natural phenomena.

Principal: Yes, I know. And for me, one of the best resources on this is the only book that C. S. Lewis wrote specifically on education. It's called *The Abolition of Man* (1967)—though I am sure, traditionalist as he was in many ways, that today his title would be more gender inclusive. The famous behaviorist B. F. Skinner (1973) recognizes this as a classic defense of the freedom and dignity of humankind, which Lewis understands as having their origin in the God whom humans image. Lewis argues forcefully for the notion of normative value, and thus that certain evaluative responses—aesthetic, for example—are either, on the one hand, ordinate or, on the other, inappropriate to the reality being experienced. Against the authors of an English text, he claims that value judgments do more than merely express the emotional state of the speaker, that a (sublime) waterfall may appropriately evoke a response of humility, and that when one speaks of a shoe fitting, one is also speaking about the foot. Literary criticism ought rightly to concern itself with literary categories, he says, and not merely with the "empirical" truth or falsehood of propositions. He is obviously arguing against the old fact/value split, which thankfully seems to have less and less hold in this postmodern era.

Visitor: I have read the book, in fact, and I must say I have always found it amusing that Lewis, for all of his renown as author of the *Narnia Chronicles,* confesses that he doesn't really like children, though he says that he recognizes that he really ought to. It's the same sense of there being a normative demand that one can recognize one has fallen short of.

Principal: I used to be so keen on Lewis that I called my first cat "Clive Staples"! But if I can use Lewis as a springboard to attempt to sum up (or at least, to bring to a close!) what I have been saying about the "MECS view of the world," it is this: to confess that the whole world is God's creation is to imply something about the lingual, economic, social, aesthetic, and ethical dimensions of the world as well. It is to believe that they also owe their existence and character to the Lord God and that there are legitimate and illegitimate ways of responding here as in other areas of life. Children must be led to see the normative nature of these aspects of experience and that their responses in these areas are also to be attuned to the Spirit of God. Such ordinate responses to this multidimensional world are again what is implied by wisdom.

Visitor: Well, if you are summing up, that by no means means that you are finished! Are you ready to talk about the third area that I wanted a response to, in terms of how the integral curriculum views the person?

Principal: Thanks for the segué! I hope that doesn't mean that I am becoming tedious, though no doubt you would be too polite to tell me.

Visitor: No, in fact, as you can see, I am just struggling to get all of this down on paper.

The Person

Principal: Well, I'm not telling you anything new when I say that one of the time-honored and no doubt time-worn slogans of education is that it should be of and for "the whole person." This can mean various things, depending no doubt on one's view of the person. Nonetheless, I agree with its intent, that education will seek to nurture the development of each of the many sides of the person. Although many Christians might seem to emphasize human rationality or morality, I believe that we cannot define what it means to be human in terms of either of these, any more than we can in terms of feeling or economic productivity. We should not split the human being into parts, deciding that one is more important than the other. Our nurture addresses the whole person, physiologically, emotionally, intellectually, aesthetically, morally, socially, culturally, and—not the least—as a believer, though we shift the focus of our attention from one occasion to the next. Our curriculum thus seeks to utilize a range of ways of coming to know the world, not relying solely or heavily on a particular method or technique. At the same time, we recognize the diversity of gifts that the Lord has given to people, individually and communally, and seek to complement the nurturing of a broad and rich human functioning with attention to the development of specialized abilities.

Visitor: Can you give me an example of how this works out in practice?

Principal: Well, we've talked about arithmetic, so let's look at one of the other "3Rs"—although around here, we tend to think of four! Many reading schemes for the primary school are based on the assumption that the best way for a child to learn to read is to use a core vocabulary to construct simple sentences, which are reinforced by repetition. Certainly, such schemes are now much more interestingly and attractively presented than the earlier "Run, Dick, run" readers, but in our view, they still suffer from abstractness and artificiality. Reading reduced to a skill to be mastered overlooks the distinctive character of language in literature.

We have developed an approach that seeks to supplement one of the better reading schemes with good quality illustrated books. These have been written specifically for children so that they might experience the joy of good reading, rather than to teach them a skill. They have a creative, aesthetic, and literary integrity that captures the child's imagination and comes much closer to addressing the child as a whole person—someone who feels, fantasizes, hopes, thinks, and believes rather than merely "decodes." This is a "sharing with" program that also seeks to retain the pleasure of sharing reading with other members of the family and not to turn reading into a chore that has to be endured each evening. Activities to extend the reading experience into other dimensions are also suggested on a card included in a pocket in the book. A number of children who had previously been turned right off have now begun to rediscover the pleasures of reading in a meaningful literary context. The same is even true for some parents!

Visitor: I like the approach, but I must say that it doesn't seem to be any different from what happens in lots of schools that adopt a "whole language" approach. What makes this approach any more Christian?

Principal: Well, we don't think that being faithful to God's purposes in education means doing everything differently from the way it is done in other settings. Everyone is made in God's image and lives in God's world, so, of course, they will bump up against the normative conditions for a flourishing life. Our distinctiveness lies more in the way in which the whole package is put together than it does in the details. And, of course, there is the conscious attempt to continually acknowledge the God who is the source of human flourishing.

Aboriginal Studies

Visitor: I don't want to sidetrack you, but just in case I forget, one of the things I have heard a bit about is your trip to Central Australia and your involvement with Aboriginal people. Can you tell me something about this?

Principal: Well, it's not really a sidetrack at all, because I think that another general feature of the school that springs from an attempt to recognize the diversity of ways of knowing the creation and to engage with it as a concrete "whole" is an emphasis on out-of-school learning experiences. Excursions or field trips are a significant part of the program at all levels. Extended camps of a few days and up to three weeks are a feature from Grade 5 on, all supervised by teachers, with the active involvement of parents as well. These camps are to farms and the city, the goldfields and the beach, the desert and the bush. We also conduct work experience programs for students in Grades 8, 10, and 11.

But you're right, no doubt one of the most exciting ventures of the school has been not just the Center Trip but the development of an Aboriginal Studies program. Aboriginal culture is studied in units at Prep and Grade 5/6 levels and again in Grade 11, but the focus of this program is the Grade 10 unit, at the heart of which is the three-week trip to Central Australia. Now—just to anticipate your question—many schools make this sort of trip these days. What I think is special about the MECS trip is the quality of contact that has been established with Aboriginal people, to the extent that the group has for many years now spent a few days as the guests of the Warlpiri people at Yuendumu (which gets an honorable mention in a Midnight Oil song), and some of our friends from there have made the long trek south to visit their "southern camp." Most students in the school now have "skin names," either because they have stayed at Yuendumu or they are related to those who have. I am a Japaljarri, for instance, and my wife is a Nakamarra.

Visitor: I understand you have taken this even further—that students study Warlpiri as their second language.

Principal: Yes, it's compulsory in Grades 9 and 10. The decision to study Warlpiri rather than a number of other more usual alternatives was in large part a result of the commitment to an integral approach—though, at first, I resisted it! And it's worth noting that this decision was made after a lengthy consideration of the school's foreign language policy by a committee consisting of parents, teachers, and board members. It came after a number of years of relative failure in the foreign language program, where French and then Indonesian had been taught, with some appeal to the more academic students but with little relevance to others because of lack of connection with anything else that was happening in the school program or in their lives outside of school.

Visitor: It does seem that studying a language that children can actually use in meaningful relationships is a great plus.

Principal: Yes, and this reflects a basic pedagogical principle that has been accepted by the school, the idea that in concrete experience, one comes in contact most broadly and fully with that which is being studied in a way that evokes the broadest range of responses from students. So, when an Aboriginal Studies program was first considered, we began a search for a way of dealing with this as concretely as possible. It was when one teacher, Colin Youl, was making a careful study of the issues and realized that the original inhabitants of the Melbourne area had disappeared or been removed virtually without trace, that the search for contact with Aboriginals further afield began, leading eventually to Central Australia. The school early on purchased a coach so that a tour could be conducted without the constraints normally imposed by a commercial operator.

Visitor: This sounds like a big investment for a rather small part of the program. Were there any other motives at work besides the ones you have listed?

Principal: I suppose the basic one of loving your neighbor as yourself, expressed particularly in the need to do justice to the needy and weak. The Aboriginal people, as we have been reminded time and again over the last few years, confront us with issues of justice and reconciliation, not just on our back- or even front doorstep, but inside, where we live. And we don't think that a concern for wisdom can be separated from a commitment to justice.

Visitor: Would you say that this program has a political motivation, then?

Principal: Absolutely, because politics ought to be centrally concerned with justice. You cannot avoid addressing significant questions of justice arising from the way Aboriginals have been and are being treated.

And there is also the fact that Aboriginal culture is a rich field for the study of religion, given the relatively holistic character of Aboriginal life. Children learn to respect the integrity of Warlpiri culture and also confront the special problems facing Aboriginal Christians; this brings into focus many questions about the proper relationship between Christianity and any given culture and particularly the relationship between the gospel and European-Australian culture. These issues are studied within the broader context of other religions and worldviews, with some attention given to the distinctive features of Christianity and the various shapes it has taken in its historical development.

Visitor: You are back talking about religion again. I suppose this makes sense if human life in its entirety is religion!

Principal: Yes, this third dimension of the integral curriculum—an integral view of the person—obviously dovetails with the others we discussed earlier. The unity and coherence of human life rests in the fact that human life is religion and that all modes of functioning are religious at root. No one aspect of functioning ought to be favored over any other if one is concerned with the full development of humanness.

Visitor: Are you suggesting that the school takes on the total responsibility for the nurture of the child? That seems like a big ask! What role do other institutions, such as the family, the church, and sporting clubs, have to play?

Principal: They each have a crucial and special role to play in the child's education. Schooling is, of course, only one part of this. MECS has, in fact, taken care not to encroach on areas that we consider to be the province of the family or the church or other community groups, such as sporting clubs. There are very few extracurricular activities: if anything is thought to be worth doing, it finds its place within the curriculum rather than as an adjunct to it. But I'm afraid we're running out of time, so I should say a little about the final point, concerning the integrality of knowledge.

Knowing

Principal: We believe very strongly that the Scriptures teach that full knowledge cannot be gained by abstract contemplation, as many Greek philosophers taught in their model of theorizing. Certainly, we can use logical thought coupled with empirical investigation to describe the recurring regularities of creation. This is very important. But it is also important to recognize that we can only do so at the cost of knowledge of the individual and the particular. And the decisions and actions of daily life occur within this realm of concrete experience. Our everyday knowledge is of things, animals, plants, persons, institutions, acts, events, and their interrelations, i.e., of whole things in their many-sided functioning. Our judgment, wisdom, and skill must be applied to *this* situation in *this* personal relationship, to *this* car engine in need of repair, to *this* purchase we are contemplating.

Visitor: So what role do theoretical principles have in ordinary decision making?

Principal: A very important one, but only insofar as we have learned to integrate them into our concrete experience. And, for the most part, I don't think that schools have done a very good job of this.

Visitor: That is what I think that people are lamenting when they complain about academically talented people lacking "common sense": the gap that often exists between the two, between theory and practice.

Principal: Yes, and I know that this can imply an anti-intellectualism, which I don't want to support, but neither do I want to overlook the sting in the tail. So, we think that the locus of the curriculum must be everyday experience, rather than an abstracted academic realm in isolation from it.

Visitor: But, by the same token, it is the results of scientific thinking that most people regard as real knowledge. Are you denying this?

Principal: As I think I said yesterday, I do not want to suggest that theoretical knowledge is insignificant. Of course it's not. But we have a broader view of knowledge, as a way of describing the relationship among the person-in-community, the world, and God. To know is to be able to place things properly under the law of God, not in relation to abstract principles but in the context of the dynamic holding together of all things by the Spirit and the Word. It is to be able to see the interconnections that exist between things in the fabric of creation. It is thus a growing fabric within the mind and heart, body and soul of the person, reflecting also the many sides of humanness. It can be gained only by acting on and into the world. And it

46

is necessarily religious in character because it is rooted in the relationship of the self to God. True knowledge is wisdom.

Visitor: And you would argue that the integral curriculum embodies a holistic view of knowledge. It seems to me that the dominant tendency in schools today is still to think that the basic academic facts and skills are what are important to succeed in the workforce in particular and life in general. I think that it's interesting that one of the main reasons given for dismissing people or refusing to promote them is not that they lack competence but that "they can't get on with people." In other words, social knowing is accorded the highest priority.

Principal: Yes, and the MECS approach similarly values this social competence, or a social way of knowing—social wisdom. Although in many respects, it is part of the hidden curriculum, this emphasis springs from a commitment to Christian community rather than from the desire that children will get on in the world. Nonetheless, it involves the recognition that working cooperatively in groups is one of the normative tasks that face people in life and that schooling should foster the ability to do this. We also recognize the importance of learning to actively shape the world and seek approaches that foster initiative, independence, and self-disciplined inquiry.

I am sure that the perceived lack here is behind the emphasis in the last decade on competencies, in the Mayer and Carmichael Reports, for example—the idea that knowledge and skills need to be used, as one textbook has it, "in a combined way in work situations." Linked to this are the Karpan Report's "enterprise skills": accepting responsibility, being flexible, evaluating, initiating, deciding, negotiating, organizing and managing resources, taking risks, and thinking creatively (Meredith, Speedy, and Wood, 2001, 29–36). It strikes me that these competencies are very much in the neighborhood of wisdom and ought to be honored as *higher* rather than *lower* achievements in schooling.

And I'm afraid that I'm going to have to get back to religion again, because undergirding a person's understanding of the world is a religious heart commitment. It is important to remember that such commitment cannot be coerced. We must respect the integrity and responsible freedom of God's image-bearers as God respected that of Adam and Eve in the Garden of Eden. At the same time, we need continually to call children to commit themselves wholeheartedly to God and to the tasks to which he calls them. Knowledge is not neutral but will be directed either to the service of the one who is Lord of all or to the service of a substitute—what the Bible calls an idol.

Visitor: This is not the first time you have talked about idols—and I don't know that I agree that this a definition you find in the Bible! Be that as it may, it's not something that goes down well in this day and age—although at least one thing seems to have been learned from the New Age movement, and that is the reality of a spiritual dimension to life.

Principal: Yes, although I am afraid that our talk of holism and integrality has often made us sound like "New Agers" to other Christians. But I don't think that you can get away from Paul's injunction in Romans 12: the curriculum has to seek to lead children to present their whole selves as living, spiritual sacrifices to God. Worshiping God is not merely a matter of knowing the right doctrine or of having the right feelings; it is a matter of acting out our spiritual commitment in our bodies, bodies transformed by the renewal of our minds and hearts.

Visitor: So, spirituality is not about some realm floating above ordinary life or a matter of just getting in touch with your "inner self"?

Principal: Certainly not, and I think that recognition is another of the basic convictions undergirding our community. Our children must be exposed to real-life contexts. If their learning is to prepare them for discipleship in the real world, they must be taken out into this world to learn as much as they can of what it is like. The development of a Christian perspective on life is intended to equip us to be God's people in God's world. It is not for our own self-satisfaction, so that we can be sure we have all of the answers, dotted our i's and crossed our t's in some impervious system of doctrine, but to help us be servants. I, in fact, think that Christianity is the most down-to-earth faith there is, even though I also think that many Christian traditions have distorted this truth.

In my devotions the other day, I was looking at 1 Thessalonians and using a book called *This Is the Word of the Lord*. I wrote this down:

> The "day of the Lord" (the Lord's *parousia,* meaning "obvious presence") will be best prepared for by doing an honest day's work. The church is not to give up and freewheel. If Christians remain faithful, they will live with God. (Duckworth 1980, 13)

I remember someone else saying something quite similar, that we prepare best for the new earth by doing what needs to be done on the earth now.

Visitor: Well, I think that we've just about run out of energy! I'd really like to thank you for all of the time you have given me and for all of the food for thought. It's going to take me quite a while to digest it all.

Principal: Thank you for your interest. I actually quite enjoy talking about the school, because it has been a very exciting place in which to work, though not, as you would understand, without its fair share of frustrations and heartaches. But that would be a topic for another day—now, I think that it's time for a cup of coffee!

SECTION II

A Way of Wisdom

Wisdom is learned
    experientially
and expressed in ways of acting
    sensitive to context.

She is embedded
    in reciprocal relationships with the natural and
    social world,
characterized by care and love,
for the world is ordered and coherent,
turned not toward evil but
    fundamentally beneficent.

She is communal
    as well as individual,
recognizing the authority of an ongoing tradition but
    holding to this flexibly.

She rests in trust,
an optimistic view of life's potential,
    intimately linked with
commitment to a source of order and meaning.

She thus favors radical belief,
characterized by
    empathy,
    vulnerability,
    dialogue,
listening to what the situation
    says.

She recognizes a normative
        demand;
there is a way one ought to act in a given situation
        and not to do so
        is disobedient:
she is partial to justice and righteousness.

She revels in
        the dynamic character of life,
the challenge of
        the serendipitous and contingent.

She eschews logical control,
        knowing her own limitations,
favoring humility and submission,
a patient acceptance of
        the mystery at the heart of life.

She accepts there will often be puzzles, but
        does not surrender
        her optimism in the face of these,
because of
        an undergirding faith
        in the interconnectedness and
        reliability of all things.

— D.B.

3

What Is This Thing
Called "Wisdom"?

As soon as questions of will or decision or reason or choice
of action arise, human science is at a loss.

Noam Chomsky (1978)

What Chomsky means by "reason" in this quotation is obviously
something different from the theoretical reason ("Reason") that
is embodied in the sciences, human and otherwise. It is more of
the nature of what Aristotle described as "practical reason," the
domain of judgment, prudence, or wisdom.

I have suggested that an integral curriculum begins with the given
wholeness of experience, which has many sides in addition to the
rational. The goal of such a curriculum will not be, in the first
place, rational understanding, but wisdom, because wisdom is
concrete acting in a manner that does justice to this richness of
reality.

An integral curriculum locates learning in historical and cultural
contexts, rather than abstracting from them. In this respect, it
does make sense to talk about "real learning," as much as this
phrase is scoffed at as tautological, because what it is pointing to
is learning that makes a difference in the messiness of daily life,
and not only in the realm of abstraction. Certainly, the latter
also constitutes learning, but it is a subset and definitely not the
foundation—despite what has long been claimed.

It is, thus, time to say something more about what I mean by
"wisdom," for this is at the heart of my argument for a new shape
for schooling.

A Way of Going

We learn from an early age what it means to turn ourselves or something else "clockwise." But have you ever wondered what it is that makes a clock "wise"? Or even what entitles a *length* to this suffix? I confess that I had not until I began to do some etymological excavating. The *Concise Oxford English Dictionary* tells me that it indicates "a manner or a way of going." It shows the way (OE *wisian*—originally, to "make wise"), it points a direction. It is intriguing and also instructive that in this age of digital clocks and watches, the notion of doing something in a clockwise direction makes little immediate sense to many young people. I say instructive because a digital watch, by treating time as a succession of discrete moments, abstracts from the flow of movement that the hands on an analog clock face represent so well—in much the way that one assumes Chomsky recognizes that science abstracts from the flow of human decision making.

Although the dictionary distinguishes this meaning of *wise* from that of the quality we attribute to persons, it is not difficult to see that they are not completely separable. Indeed, wisdom is also a way of going, a manner of being, an established direction and pattern of living, as much if not more than a grasp of particular principles. Thus, when Jesus claims to be the way, the truth and the life (John 14:6), he is talking about a way of walking—the way of wisdom. (To complete the circle, so to speak, I may also foreshadow my later discussion of wisdom as "knowing *when*": by wisdom, we negotiate the flow of life in a timely manner—wisdom itself is "time-wise.")

In this light, *wisdom* may be construed as that which gives direction to what we describe in structural terms as knowledge. This would make good an apparent deficiency in English, in comparison on the one hand to the Teutonic family and on the other to Latin and the Romance languages. The German pairing of *wissen* and *kennen,* the French *savoir/connaître,* and the Latin *sapientia/scientia* each gives us in the former term access to a more comprehensive, personal, and thus implicitly value-laden term than is usual in English. It is not that the wisdom/knowledge dis/conjunction is not possible; it is rather that it is not usual. And this is nowhere more evident, perhaps, than in the fact that whereas there are pairings of *verbs* in other languages, we do not have a readily accessible verb form of *wise* to match the verb *to know.* We have merely the colloquial admonitions to "wise up," "get wise," or "put wise." How would one begin to conjugate *to wise*? "I wis" seems to have Shakespearean authority, though it is obviously archaic.[5]

How Many Stories?

According to Canadian educationalists Connelly and Clandinin (1994,

89), Chomsky's observation would be considered a profanity in Western culture (as indeed are many of Chomsky's musings). This is because he is contradicting a story so universal and taken for granted that they believe it may be described as "sacred." This theory-practice story proclaims that the way to flourishing and fulfillment in human life is by faithful application of the methods and findings of the academic disciplines to practical affairs.

A story of this overarching scope is what the French philosopher Lyotard (1984) had in mind when he spoke of metanarratives. He described these comprehensive stories about the meaning of life as authoritarian and "totalizing" and pointed to the violent effects that he believed they necessarily have. Because of these effects, he suggested that a stance of disbelief ("incredulity") toward all such stories is (appropriately) characteristic of our postmodern era. Looking back on a century in which "isms" of various hues have wrought destruction across the planet, we can no doubt sympathize with this view. We also wonder what the implications are for the Christian metanarrative (and return to these wonderings later).

The theory-practice metanarrative is not just an abstract academic fancy. Connelly and Clandinin (1994, 89) claim that it "creates a pervasive moral structure governing the actions" of people in our culture and, specifically, "the actions of university and school people"—and their purpose is to demonstrate that this structure is far from benign. Such a claim, if it is true, creates an immediate dilemma for Christian teachers. For what they are saying, without actually using the term, is that there is a "false gospel" at work in the world; moreover, that it finds its sharpest focus in educational institutions. Thus, whether I am working as a teacher in a government school or in a Christian school, I am going to find myself pulled in two directions. The story of schooling is that theoretical insight is the foundation for an abundant human life; the Christian story is that walking in the way of Jesus is truth and life. The challenge to the Christian teacher is how to be *in* the world of schooling while not being *of* it.

But in a postmodern era, it is widely believed that the priority of theory (or the "hegemony of Reason") has succumbed to a multiplicity of reasons. There is not now just the one story of inevitable human progress via the application of scientific knowledge (a story that has been characterized as "modernism"); there are many, each of which lays an equal claim to truth. For some, a large proportion of Christians included, this relativism presents the gravest danger, portending the death of reason and indeed of truth itself.

Modernism Rampant

I doubt that modernism's demise is by any means complete, however. Luther said, in characteristic fashion, that if we are not fighting the devil where he is actually attacking, the battle will be lost. We need to take note of this warning in the present context. In theory, the theory-into-practice paradigm is dead. In practice, however, it remains very much alive. For just as when the moon obscures the sun it becomes dangerous to look at the rays that escape around the rim, postmodernity witnesses in the partial eclipse of the modernist paradigm its intensification at the penumbra.

In this light, there are some who claim that "postmodernity" is not so much something that happens *after* modernity, but is in fact its high point and culmination (Saul 1993; Toulmin 1992). Indeed, the three legs of the modernist stool—scientism, technicism, and economism, the "idols of our times"(Goudzwaard 1984; Walsh and Middleton 1984)—are, if anything, more solid and the stool thus more stable, than before the New Age/Millennium dawned. The convergence of these three forces is seen no-where more powerfully than in the emergence of the "new economy" that is founded on information technology. Information, technology, econo-my—a veritable (putatively holy) trinity.

Thus, despite the presumed death of the metanarrative, that of the free market wields its invisible hand, promising to bring a heaven on earth to all humanity. The unimpeded operation of the laws of supply and demand, re-leased from the shackles of government regulation and national boundaries, will ensure that all will share in the wealth that belongs now only to the few.

Not surprisingly, the so-called "education industry" is to be a key con-tributor to this birthing of utopia, and it can only do so if it is made to conform to the corporatist model (Bates 1995; Marginson 1993; Pusey 1991). Far from the "factory model" of schooling being moribund, what we are now witnessing is an exaggerated attempt to rationalize it even further. Once again, the principles of scientific management are to be applied to ensure that appropriate techniques will guarantee the most efficient out-comes. Principals are no longer "educational leaders," they are CEOs, with hierarchical management structures edging out the small gains that had been made for collegiality, running schools as businesses and promoting them in an increasingly open and competitive market. And this despite the plethora of postmodern protests.

A Premodern Paradigm?

These voices of protest, too, seem to be converging, but quite para-doxically on a paradigm that is profoundly premodern. The voice that is emerging in protest is the voice of *wisdom,* but it is a voice from behind the veil of those "lovers of wisdom" ("*philo-soph-*ers") who, as Rorty (1979) has pointed out, ironically became pursuers of certainty. ("I know" supplants "I wis"?) Socrates and those identified as his forebears saw their quest as the right way of living; Plato and his successors pursued right *knowledge,* assuming that in the possession of this, virtuous living was guaranteed. But in the granting of priority to the way of seeing over the way of being, the split between ontology and epistemology was injected into the heart of Western culture, with consequences that have proved to be devastating, no less to the process of education. Although there have been perennial appeals to education of the "whole person," there has been a deep-seated prejudice that the body is no more than an umbilical cord to support the brain. A sound mind always had the privileged position over a healthy body—and bodily health was itself reduced to its physiological dimensions.

Certainly, there have been other voices, including that of Aristotle. But The Philosopher's salute to "practical reason" (*phronesis*) was buried within a system that had at its pinnacle a Divine Being who was "Thought thinking itself" (*noesis noeseoos*). In such a system, knowing would necessarily determine being. A healthy company of scholars—think of Alasdair MacIntyre (1984) and Joseph Dunne (1997), for example—has of late sought to rehabilitate "practical rationality" and "wisdom" in the Aristotelian mold, and their voices need to be heard. But the suspicion remains that in the philosopher who saw humans as "rational animals," imaging the god Reason, insufficient joy will be found.

Wisdom

The Bible is also centrally concerned with wisdom. As I have said, a large part of my purpose is to explore the implications of a biblical perspective on wisdom for teaching and learning in the formal context of the curriculum. More specifically, the Hebrew Wisdom Literature, because of its isolation from the way in which philosophical discourse developed under the influence of the Greeks, proffers a way of understanding how life should be conducted that is a genuine alternative to the theory-into-practice paradigm. It deserves to be rescued from the cloisters of the theological colleges to which it was confined by modernism, as another voice to be heard. I have given a concise overview of this perspective in the poem that opens this section; the dialogue of the next chapter provides more substance to the notion. In the present chapter, I wish to provide a link between the discussion of the integral curriculum in the preceding chapters and the discussion that follows.

My concern is shared with all educators: it is the promotion of schooling that will promote human flourishing. But the notion of what constitutes such flourishing is inevitably worldview-bound: this, too, we learn from postmodernism, if we had not already not learned it elsewhere. What is the world into which we have been thrown? What constitutes the good life within it? The ideological and ethnocentric dreams of the last century, which have issued in genocidal nightmares—one might rightly say, on every continent, though the "ethnic cleansing" has been perpetrated in more "civilized" forms in some places than in others—bear stark testimony to this influence of worldview.[6]

Though they will not generally appear in courses or texts of philosophy, the Hebrew sages, too, were philosophers—seekers after wisdom. It is their very down-to-earthness (so apparently paradoxical, in light of their belief in a transcendent God) that has helped to exclude them from the mainstream debate. But it is this mundanity (in which the apparent paradox is resolved, because their God was also invested in history) that makes them so profitable in the quest for an integral perspective on knowing and being.

An Integral Epistemology

The notion of an integral curriculum places an evident emphasis on "wholeness," whereas the "sacred story" of Western culture incorporates a dualistic division between theory and practice. My quest for a wisdom perspective is at the same time a quest for an "integral epistemology," an understanding of knowing that eschews the dualisms that have plagued the epistemological enterprise, in many respects since its birth: subject/object, fact/value, individual/community, mind/body, theory/practice, cognition/affect, science/metaphysics, public/private—and some would add, male/female and natural/supernatural. It eschews these dualisms in favor of an honoring of prior integrality.

To deny dualism is not to deny duality (or plurality) or to ignore necessary distinctions, but rather to argue that clear distinctions do not imply discrete substances (self-existing, nonrelational entities); as a corollary, neither is plurality denied by an affirmation of "wholeness" and "integrality." It is instead to advocate a more ecological epistemology, in which there is the attempt to recognize constantly that all things are part of one larger whole—God's creation (which others might call "Gaia"). Each of the terms in the pairs above depends in crucial ways on the other for its meaning; and in each pair, the second term is placed in a subordinate relation to the first. Rather, to the extent that we continue to require these terms, we should recognize their complementarity, in pursuit of a nonadversarial, both/and style of proceeding that John Dewey, *inter alia,* advocated. Or perhaps more boldly, in emulation of Derrida, we need to "take the side of the minor term and see it infiltrate the dominant, dismantling the hierarchy. At least, making it tremble" (Blake, Smeyers, Smith, and Standish 1998, 39). What tremors can "wisdom" cause to the edifice of "knowledge," which is equated with theory by the "sacred story" and, in large measure, identified with the privileged member of each of the above-mentioned pairs?

Hence, integral epistemology is a possible misnomer, for what is integral in experience are ultimately *being* and *knowing,* the designated fields of study for what the philosophers have termed *ontology* and *epistemology.* That these two fields are indeed interdependent is seen perhaps nowhere more clearly than in the field of subatomic physics, where the existence (or otherwise) of fundamental particles and knowledge (or ignorance) of them are inextricably linked. And it is of more than passing interest that Einstein's dispute with Bohr on this matter came down to a conviction that "God does not play dice with the universe"—a worldview commitment functioning as "control belief" for scientific research (Wolterstorff 1976). I cannot know what I do not believe to exist; and if I believe the ether or phlogiston to exist, I can only know in terms that they decree and may need to theorize (yes, quite legitimately, for theorizing is one mode of knowing the world) their nonexistence if understanding is to progress. And if I do not believe in the existence of God or in God's engagement with the world, I will not see God's hand at work.

The picture that the modernist paradigm gives us is of clear and distinct ideas only reached in abstraction from experience; such is the picture Descartes bequeathed, but with which Plato would have concurred. Theory might arise from reflection on empirical reality, but it must be framed at as great a distance as possible from concrete entities. The wisdom paradigm points instead to understanding-in-action, to the interrelatedness of all things in that experience.

"Experience" is, of course, a problematic notion. Since the time of the British Empiricist philosopher David Hume, it has been taken as virtually common sense that we encounter sense data in isolation from other dimensions of experience; so commonsensical, in fact, that *experience* itself is thought to be limited to *sensory* experience. What is hidden by this conception is that we can only distinguish the "sense-able" from its integral connection with all other modes of functioning of things by consciously thinking away these other modes or, in other terms, by focusing in an analytical, abstractive way on "sensations." But we are even only aware of particular "sensations" as subjective responses as we are able to distinguish them from sensations that are different. Such distinguishing requires analysis, even if only of the simplest kind. Further, we can only name such sensations by use of a language, and we (normally) encounter sensations only in proximity to that which evokes them.

An integral ontology of wisdom holds that we are able to sense, and there are things that can indeed be sensed. "Sensations" do not exist in abstraction, only in context; they are not merely subjective phenomena, but are evoked by the sense-able. Rather than a subject *over against* an object, separated by an unbridgeable divide, there are subjects in intimate connection with one another. This, I infer, is what William James (1977, 334) had in mind in his insistence that we are "coefficients" of the truth we seek to know, not alienated from or antagonistic to the world of which we are an inextricable part. And not only is there this integral relationship between knower and known—a wholeness to the field of experience—there is a wholeness to our response, whether in philosophical reasoning or in practical affairs: "the whole man within us is at work. . . . Intellect, will, taste, and passion cooperate. . . ."

The wisdom perspective does not entail a naive realism, however. What we "get" is not always what we "see," nor vice versa. As Thomas Merton (1989, 506) has said, "There is in all visible things . . . a hidden wholeness." This is where wisdom as discernment and judgment are so essential. It is thus that Brueggemann can assert that:

> The educational task . . . is to discern and to teach to discern, to attend to the gifts given in experience, to attend to the world around us. It is to read ourselves and that world in all its playfulness, to know that what immediately meets the eye is not all there is. (Brueggemann 1982, 75)

Wisdom does not assert a foundation in indubitables of everyday experience, for there are no such certainties. As I will explore in some detail, the wholeness of experience in which we are immersed is itself evocative of "problems"; a celebration of "wholeness" is by no means a denial that in experience we meet challenges, conflict, and, not infrequently, suffering. The Christian gospel is, of course, centrally concerned with how God has dealt with these, and how we in turn are to do so.

If ontological and epistemological beliefs have a mutual interdependence, it is *beliefs*—of varying degrees both of comprehensiveness and certainty—that are determinative of much of our experience. (Others would speak of the "theory-ladenness of observation" and "observation statements," but I wish to preserve a more precise sense for *theory*.) These beliefs are always of the nature of responses and thus are always fallible, always tentative.

Further, beliefs are not to be equated with intellectual inclinations or with propositions alone. I can seek to state what I believe, but these statements cannot encompass the fullness of my beliefs. This is true both because of the nature of propositions and the nature of the objects of my belief. For the latter, consider the limitations inherent in the confession "I believe in God the Father Almighty"—this but points to, and cannot comprehend, its "Object." For the former, consider that no proposition is self-contained, but always refers beyond itself to other terms and statements within the language—from whence do we derive the meaning of "father," what has been my experience of childhood?—and to an all-but-infinite range of things that are not intended as well as to what is consciously intended—is God not my Mother, can God be also a Rock? There are few terms that are not rooted in metaphors, no matter how long ago these ceased to be living.

If beliefs are constitutive (though not comprehensive) of our experience, we always function "world-viewishly." It is thus not only Christian or other kinds of overtly "religious" schooling that are education in a worldview; all schooling is rooted in a worldview. Education should teach students to be discerning of the worldviews that are operative, in the ordinariness of daily life as well as in more specialized activities like theoretical reflection, political policymaking, and economic programs. There are more than our beliefs and commitments at work, but there are necessarily these. I have noted, for example, that research programs are expressions of commitments, none more appropriate to mention in the present context than Einstein's conviction that the elementary laws of the cosmos can only be reached by "intuition, resting on sympathetic understanding of experience" (cit. Pirsig 1976, 107). For the Hebrews, a sympathetic understanding depends on commitment to God as the ground of experience; for others, the structure of experience has its source elsewhere.

One person's commitments are another person's prejudices. But it does not serve us well to deny our own prejudices. Some of these will be negative, as the common use of the term connotes. But some of these "prejudgments" will be benign; indeed, if *most* were not, we would be unable to function in the world. In any case, none of us comes to a text or a context devoid of these prejudices. We need to heed Gadamer's (1989) warning about the Enlightenment "prejudice against prejudices." The next chapter seeks to display some fundamental "prejudices" and their implications for the understanding of knowledge/wisdom in our culture and consequently, for the practice of schooling.

4

Speaking Words of Wisdom

I have noted that Israel took no part in the philosophical discussions of the ancient world. Perhaps this is true merely as a matter of definition: what the sages of Israel were interested in, and the way they went about exploring these interests, though it may exemplify a "love of wisdom," did not count as "philosophy" as this came to be understood in classical Greece. This is indeed what makes the Hebrew wisdom tradition significant as a source to investigate when we are seeking to extricate ourselves from the problematics that we have inherited from the Greeks via their modernist heirs.

Since the rise of modernism, however, there is another reason why the reflective tradition of the Hebrews has been deemed "unphilosophical." This is because it is so obviously "theological." Yet this separation between philosophy and theology is an artifact of modernism. It was not known to Aristotle, for whom theology was the "queen of the sciences," nor was it known throughout the whole of the medieval period. An interest in divine matters did not exclude anyone from a serious hearing right up into the modern period itself, not excluding Descartes, Newton, and Leibniz, to name just three of the most prominent early modern scientists.

If philosophy is characterized as a theoretical undertaking, it is true that the Bible does not provide us with, for example, a theory of knowledge—an epistemology. It is not a theoretical textbook of anything. But what it does do is to provide us with an alternative place to stand when looking at theoretical (and other) issues. It helps to map out a territory, a space to explore, giving us a range of nodal points between which to move back and forth. The Hebrew perspective (in both Old Testament and New) provides a different tradition from within which to explore the nature of knowledge. I wish to concentrate in what follows on what we can learn from the Wisdom Literature of the Old Testament—especially, but not exclusively, from a reading of Proverbs, Ecclesiastes, and Job. And I wish to do so by establishing a dialogue between sage and philosopher. Who better to represent these two traditions than Solomon and Socrates? Of course, as

I pointed out in the Introduction, they will to an extent be caricatures of the historical personages whose names they bear—though because they will be present with us in this conversation, they will be guilty of many anachronisms. To keep the search for a Christian approach to schooling in the foreground, I would like to introduce a third character into this discussion, an elementary teacher named Sophie. I am not wishing to suggest by her name, however, that she has a privileged position, though she has developed over time the wisdom of practice.

As I have said, my concern is not primarily philosophical, if this is meant to imply a discourse largely abstracted from the concerns of daily life and, specifically, the daily life of schooling. Graeme Goldsworthy, in his study *Gospel and Wisdom,* points to wisdom and its grounding in the relationships established by a Creator as the arena in which to find a solution to the search for a distinctively Christian curriculum. Behind the creation-evolution debate, he sees a more basic question, that of how God, humans, and the universe relate. He also suggests that "the doctrine of creation is an implication of what the Bible says about God's character as a just and redeeming God" (Goldsworthy 1995, 133).

Creation

Sophie: Solomon, I recall that Francis Schaeffer suggested that the story of creation in Genesis constitutes the "headlines" to the Bible, and that everything that follows is a fleshing out of what is broadcast there. Do you agree?

Solomon: Yes, creation is the starting point of everything, and not just in the chronological sense. Creation is not just an event that happened way back when, it is the constant framework within which we Israelites interpret all of experience. It is the backdrop to all that happens on the stage of life. Because the world is creation, everything is full of meaning. Creation is thus also the key to the biblical understanding of wisdom.

Socrates: Though I agree that some kind of craftsman was necessary to bring the world into its present shape, from the raw materials that already existed, I cannot accept that this tells us very much at all about the kind of world we live in, let alone how we should live wisely in it. As one of my esteemed colleagues has said, everything is in flux, the only thing you can count on is change—and of course, that means that there is not really much to count on at all, at least, not in this world. Rather than looking outward to the world, to our "experience," we have to look inward to establish if anything can be known for certain, to know what is of the greatest value in human life.

Solomon: Creation is the antithesis of chaos and the opposite of nothingness! God gave form to that which was formless, that which he had created out of nothing. The very fact that God chose first to bring the world into being and then to continue to sustain it moment by moment allows us to say that the world is of value, has value, is valu-*able*. Saint Francis was right to speak of "Brother Sun" and "Sister Moon," as he was to regard all creatures as worthy of respect and demanding to be treated with integrity. There is a call that comes to us from everything that is around us, a question (Fr. *demander*) that calls for an answer. It is not in the first place a matter of *deciding* what is of value, like a politician formulating policies by conducting an opinion poll, for example, but of responding aright to the *valuable*. The only way we can do that is by trusting our experience, not by mistrusting it.

Experience

Sophie: The place of "experience" in schools is probably one of the key issues that has been debated, not only by academics, but by parents, politicians, teachers, and school boards. How much of "real life" should we include in children's education? How "relevant" should it be? Many people argue that relevance is the enemy of academic excellence. If you are on the side of experience, you are on the side of Dewey, and that makes you a "progressive," the enemy of tradition and unchanging cultural and intellectual values. Most conservative Christians would opt for the tradition side of the debate.

Solomon: I think that many people—including, I have to say, our friend Socrates—suffer from a defective understanding of experience. They set it off over against something that is not experience. From my perspective, however, all that is around us, all that we are aware of, constitutes experience. There is nothing that is not experience. And the broadest context of experience is creation, in all of its diversity and interconnectedness. In answering the call of creation faithfully, value is realized, wisdom is at work. Turning your back on creation is foolish.

Sophie: I have to say that, save for your anchoring of experience in creation, you sound even more like Dewey!

Socrates: Well, I agree that we have to start with people's experience. It is by weighing up your experience against mine—the differences between our experiences of the world—that we are able to come to some clear concepts by which we can decide which is the most valuable. The clearer we get about our conceptual framework and the more indisputable it becomes, the more we are then able to leave experience behind. It is a staging ground only, something to jump off from, but definitely not the stage on which we want to continue to lead our lives. Surely you are wanting to do the same thing in your quest to get to heaven?

Solomon: I am not really very much interested in "heaven," at least not in the sense that you are talking of. If it is a place of abstract conceptual frameworks, of "philosophers" or "spiritual beings" who have left everyday life behind, I think that it would be rather dull—and in fact, downright disrespectful to God for bothering to make the kind of world he has only to want us to leave it behind. Wasn't it George Bernard Shaw who said that although dozens of people had written about spending a day at the beach, no one had ever written about what it would be like to spend a day in heaven?

Normativity

But at the root of this, and what I am most interested in, is the idea that it is by a process of rational calculation that we get most in touch with the real nature of things—that wisdom is basically a matter of rationality. I would rather want to say that, because of the diversity of creation, wisdom does its weighing up of situations under the lead of a host of different norms, those for rationality being only one kind. These other norms may be moral, but they may also be political, aesthetic, or economic. Rather than Socrates' image of wisdom being gained by somehow escaping from the complex richness of daily life, I would want to say that life is properly grounded when lived in faithful response to this complex creation.

Sophie: Do you mean to say that by "getting in touch with nature," we can get in touch with God? Isn't that really a pagan way of seeing things? It's the sort of thing that New Agers are trying to resurrect.

Solomon: No, Sophie, that's not what I'm wanting to say, though I certainly wouldn't leave the so-called "natural world" out of the picture. But we shouldn't think of creation as being restricted to the natural world.

Human life is part and parcel of creation—it's integral to it. That's why the Psalmist can point to the origin both of ordinances for nature and for humankind in God's creating fiat (Psalm 147:15–19). There is no dualism that separates social rules and the natural order (Wolters 1985, 16). Everything is a creature of God, even when it is shaped by human hands. Take marriage, for example: it is a creational ordinance that takes on a unique shape in each and every trothful bonding of a man and a woman. What is true of marriage is true of every human social arrangement. Marriage is a response to the norm of faithfulness, most importantly—but obviously not exclusively; the state is similarly a response to the norm of justice.

Sophie: All of this talk of norms, ordinances, and order carries connotations of unchangingness. I think that it is fraught with difficulties. It smells of rigidity and predetermined paths, as though some all-knowing Calvinist God had mapped out our lives for us in minutest detail. You must know that a theology of "order" was used to justify both Nazism and apartheid.

Solomon: Well, if that's a knockdown argument against me, I think that it also applies to Socrates, even if Plato did put words into his mouth (and not for the first time).

Socrates: You mean in *The Republic*? I do think that it follows that those who are capable of gaining the deepest intellectual insight into the structure of the world ought to be charged with leadership over those who are less able to extricate themselves from the earthiness of ordinary existence. It's not anyone's fault, it's just that some people have more earth mixed in with their nature than others. It doesn't mean they can't be perfectly happy by living in accord with their own nature.

Solomon: There is much more room to move than your conception allows, Socrates. I think, for example, of God's speech at the conclusion to the book of Job, which points us to the range of playful freedom that the order of the world allows to his creatures. Indeed, the book of Job resounds with the message that the rigid order of reward and retribution that the tradition—speaking through Job's friends—sought to maintain could not withstand the challenge of the God who is free to act as he chooses (cf. Crenshaw 1981, 125).

Sophie: I'm much happier with that way of putting it. I think that Brown captures what you're getting at quite well when he writes:

> It is out of gratuitous delight that Yahweh steps back and lets creation run its course, allowing the citizens of the cosmos the freedom to maneuver and negotiate their respective domains and lives. Far from being a divine tyrant, Yahweh is the gentle parent whose care extends beyond the maintenance of order and structure. God's love embraces each creature's individuality and unique role within the wonderfully complex network of life. (Brown 1996, 103)

Solomon: Thanks, Sophie. I certainly don't regard the law of God as either abstract or static: it is embedded in the dynamic, concrete interactions of ordinary experience, in the daily reality of parents and children or citizens and government as they discharge their offices before the face of the Lord.

Socrates: I don't see how you can possibly maintain that "God" addresses people in the messiness of daily life. Surely we have to sort out the gold from the dross, and the only way we can do this is by abstracting what is true and good from what is not by applying our powers of reason. We have to put everything under the microscope—slice it up and put it on a slide, as it were—if we are to sort out the objective truth from our own subjective delusions. It's a matter of seeing how things really are behind the veil of appearances.

Solomon: Rather than focusing on us as humans *seeing* the way the world really is, as though it is *over there* somewhere as an object for our perusal, I think of us as being responsible for *hearing*. The world—nonhuman and social—*speaks* to us constantly (cf. Psalm 119:89–92). And not only that, to hear it speak is to hear God speak (Job 38–41). In this respect, the world reveals God to us (e.g., Psalm 19:1; 145:10; 97:6). Experience—whether or not we have the ears to hear—is ultimately a response to God and his revelation. What is of value (be this truth, goodness, beauty, or whatever) is found in relationship, not as a subject standing at a distance from an inert object, but in a dialogue that is literally two-way.

God's speech to Job also serves to remind us that the interconnectedness—what some have taken to calling "integrality"—of life is central to the teaching of the Wisdom Literature, whether it is the structure of creation or the construction and maintenance of human community that is in view. As to the former, Job is called to marvel at the complex interplay of all that God has made; as to the latter, he is applauded for his refusal to allow a view of human life as organization to replace that of organic and vibrant interaction. He will not allow the "old answers" to stand in the way of the need to respond to what he is experiencing here and now, but neither will he abandon the conviction that there must be meaning to the occurrences of life if all of life proceeds from the hand of God.

Sophie: Brueggemann (1982, 86–87) observes that those wedded to the practice of technical reason are likely to jettison the belief in the interconnectedness of all things, but the "wisdom teachers abandoned the data in order to hold to the connection." I can see how the Mount Evelyn curriculum seeks to reflect this perspective. The emphasis on integrality is obvious, and the principal's explanation about creation is quite explicitly framed in "wisdom" terms. But as I said before, it seems to many like a progressive curriculum, with its emphasis on experience rather than on the academic disciplines or intellectual attainment.

Solomon: I think that the fact that you keep coming back to that dichotomy, with all of the negative connotations attached to "progressive," is an indication of just how much more successful than me Socrates has been in influencing Western culture! It's just as well Jesus is not in his grave, or else he would be turning in it.

Sophie: I don't think that you're in a position to be self-righteous, Solomon.

Solomon: Point taken, Sophie, but I was really trying to keep to the forefront my personification of wisdom, not my later lapses. But let me restate my argument to see if I can salvage anything for an experiential perspective.

If the creation is dynamically and organically structured—if change is just part of the way things are—true wisdom is attained not by denying this, but by being sensitive and responsive to it. Wisdom is approached historically and experientially, not above change, but in the very midst of it. Socrates and I agree that the condition of the world is one of change and growth—which also means the decay of one so that another might live. It's just that he (and many like him) believe that change has to be repudiated. At the same time, the experienced world is ordered, coherent, and intrinsically meaningful, but this is not because its inhabitants have their meaning in and of themselves—what some after Socrates referred to as "substances." Meaning is in the relationships, in the restless referring of one creature to another, in the inextricable interdependence of all things.

Sophie: You're saying that whereas the Greek philosophers tended to mistrust experience, the Hebrew sages believed that it is to be trusted rather than feared?

Solomon: Yes, because it is in experience that one meets God and his purposes for human life. Job clung to the experience of his own righteousness against all of the protests of his friends; God points him in the end to experience of creation as the final answer to his question, "Where is wisdom to be found?"

I know that talk of experience can be easily misconstrued; it has been overlaid with many different connotations as it has traversed the course of Western history. As I've already said, I'm using the term in a comprehensive sense: there is nothing in human life that is not experience.

Socrates: Hold on a minute, Sol, you're way off track. Are you suggesting that everything in human life can be reduced to sensation? That anything that comes to us comes through the senses? Haven't you read my Cave Allegory? Surely you know that no one horse is ever exactly the same as another horse, that all we can ever get from seeing hundreds and hundreds of horses is uncertainty about what actually makes something a horse? What we need is a clear concept of *horse.*

Sophie: "A horse is a horse, of course, of course . . ." I know the tune you're playing!

Solomon: One of the differences between you and me, Socrates, is your commitment to certainty. I, on the other hand, can live with ambiguity. It's one of the things that makes life most interesting—nuance, allusiveness, metaphor. . . . But far from what you think about me reducing everything to the sensory—I'll come back to this—you seem to suggest that you can think the idea *horse* without any sensory component at all, and I'm afraid that you are wrong. In fact, the so-called idea of *horse* clearly has a lingual or symbolic component to it. And I don't think that anyone can think of a horse without some image or sensory dimension to it. Plus, there is a numerical dimension, because you are thinking of one horse with four legs, and there is also a spatial dimension, because every possible horse is extended in some way. But I would go so far as to suggest that there is also at least a potential ethical dimension—a full idea of a horse would also have something to say about how a horse should be treated by its owner. And any idea of a horse has to include whether it is living. Finally—though even this will not complete the list of dimensions in which a horse functions—there is a confessional dimension, for you will ultimately have to assume something about how the horse came to be at all and to what power in the universe it owes its existence.

Socrates: Whoa, Solomon, you're running way beyond your resources. I am just talking about the *idea* of a horse, not any actual existing concrete horse. I am saying you can think away all of those other aspects when it is just the analytical concept you have in mind.

Solomon: And I am saying that unless you had seen a horse running, there would be nothing to "mind"—you wouldn't have any of the resources you need to be able to formulate the concept! My point is that all things function in all aspects of experience—lingually, ethically, psychically, biotically, and so on—though not all in exactly the same way. But the least I am claiming is that experience of anything cannot be reduced to its sensory dimension, and I think that Berkeley, following from Locke, showed clearly where you end up when you attempt to do so. Really, they end up the same place as your most famous student did—everything in the head and no contact with anything outside it at all. Descartes took a different route, but he reached the same destination: the self alone can be known and trusted. My hunch is that anyone who attempts to explain all of reality in terms of only one of its dimensions ends up a solipsist—left just with his or her own self.

Experience is not the preserve of "feelings" over against "intellect." Nor can we extract Reason and set it over against experience: thinking is also experiential, as are believing, trusting, hoping, and so on.

"The Fear of the Lord"

Socrates: I don't agree with Descartes, but it seems to me that you could argue that he held that knowledge of God and knowledge of self are inextricably linked. One of the things he was setting out to prove, even though he did start with the self alone, was the existence of God. So he was not really as locked inside himself (or even his stove) as you suggest. And I also find it fascinating that in this he was very close to Calvin, though Calvin, of course, started with the dependence of self-knowledge on the knowledge of God.

Solomon: Though we are by no means all Calvinists here, I don't suppose that you will find it surprising that I agree with Calvin, on this point at least. And the Wisdom Literature concurs that this basic question of human self-consciousness is religious in character.

Sophie: You're saying that where modernism would have us approach the world in a seemingly objective manner, standing as detached, singularly rational spectators, and postmodernism would counsel the celebration of our subjectivity, Israel hears a call to commitment and trust (Von Rad 1972, 67–68).

Solomon: Yes, that is why we say so often, "The fear of the Lord is the beginning of wisdom and knowledge"—but it is also its purpose.

Sophie: You know that that is a phrase we often use in Christian schools, almost as a motto or a slogan, maybe without thinking enough about what it really means.

Solomon: Perhaps you'll allow me to feel a little gratified, because I do think that this is one of the wisest things I ever said. And if I can help you understand its profundity, I will be even more pleased. The point is that wisdom is not merely or even primarily intellectual, and it does not seek indubitable foundations that are equally accessible to all.

Sophie: Which you think that Socrates, not to mention Descartes and Kant, were setting out to do. I have always been intrigued by the fact that Job does not have his question answered—you know, his question about where wisdom is to be found. Or rather, the answer he receives is one that burrows below the words in which he frames the question. It seems to me that God says to him at the end that the only way to a life of full flourishing, in which one has to learn not merely to *cope with* but to *live through* misery as a means of growth, as well as to revel in the joy, is to place one's complete trust in the Creator and his creation.

Solomon: Yes, face to face with God, Job can but be silent, in reverence and awe. And *this,* I believe, is the beginning of wisdom. So in a real sense, God does tell him the way in which he is to go about growing more wise. And it is a way of going, a journey, not an arrival.

Sophie: It is interesting that Job was not picked out for special treatment because he was a renowned theologian who had developed a perfect system of doctrine. We are told that he is "a blameless and upright man, who fears God and turns away from evil" (Job 1:8). The Adversary questions whether he really is a person of such integrity: maybe he fears God because of what he gets out of it, all of the blessings that God has bestowed on him. He wasn't to be challenged on an intellectual level, but in the realm of action.

Socrates: Well, I haven't read the Bible as closely as some have told me I should, heaven knows, but I have had plenty of time to dip into it here and there over the years. And what also struck me about the Job story was how it resonated with my early concerns. I wanted to find out what you needed to know to be able to act justly, piously, courageously—one could say, wisely. And so I asked the just man, the prophet, and the hero, but none of them could tell me. But the point is, I too started out with people's acting. It was only later that I (or was it Plato?—I can never be quite sure at this distance) thought that one had to start with theoretical principles for right acting. But the problem then was, how does one ever get from thinking to acting?

Sophie: Well, I wonder whether you have had the leisure to dip into John Dewey too. Perhaps you would agree that he was on the right track when he conceived of thinking as the deferral of action. Action is primary, and thought involves imagining and evaluating the possible paths one might take. But acting requires a choice, a commitment to a certain path. A suspension of questioning (Descartes' "methodological doubt") is necessary, and in its place, what Elbow (1986, 258–61) aptly describes as "methodological belief."

Solomon: Thanks for that, Sophie. Where you, Socrates, came to insist that action always be grounded in theory, we in Israel believed that action is ultimately a matter of faith. If we accept the definition of wisdom as the *realization of value,* this requires trust—though never devoid of risk. The necessity of commitment is what I think that Israel had grasped. I just happened to stumble on a nice way of expressing it—"the fear of the Lord. . . ." Actually, to give credit where it is due, I think that it was an *inspired* insight!

Sophie: I think that it is worth pointing out that the theory-into-practice paradigm is also a matter of faith. I know you won't like me saying so, Socrates, but it seems to me that the faith of the Hebrew and your faith—and the faith of the modernist, for that matter—are not functionally different: they merely have a different orientation—though how much this "merely" conceals! If for Solomon it is trust in the sufficiency of God, for you it is trust in the sufficiency of reason.

Solomon: Yes, one of the main things we Hebrews were trying to say was that belief is fundamental to human consciousness, that the vulnerability of belief—credulity—is what opens the channels of communication, even communion, with the world. Then not merely methodological, but *radical* belief is the beginning of wisdom, while Descartes' radical doubt can only, or so he thought, birth the intellect.

Our trust is in a living and personal Creator in vital interaction with his world, and not in abstract principles—I'm sorry, Socrates. This means that wisdom cannot be viewed as static and rigid. We are able to embrace the order of creation as dynamic, not only an active response to every word proceeding from the mouth of God but responsive also to the shaping activity of people. We meet the world not as subject versus object across an unbridgeable divide—an ontological chasm—but as partners created and sustained by the one God. We are already in relationship with one another, and thus we can know the other. This "belonging together," recognizing that we are fundamentally at home in the world, estranged not in our very being but only as a consequence of the curse that will itself be overcome, gives Israel's stance toward the world a very different tenor than that of nonbiblical traditions—perhaps especially yours, Socrates!

Humility

Socrates: Does this mean that you believe that we can eventually draw a detailed map of the world, one that shows us everything there is to know? That everyone can be a philosopher-king, holding audience with the Queen of Sheba?

Solomon: No, Socrates, I would never go that far. We are confident that some things at least about the world are knowable, else we would not attempt to chart its contours. But we are also profoundly aware of the limits to human understanding. God will not be put in a box. That somewhat pessimistic chap you know as Ecclesiastes (I wasn't him, in case you are wondering) finds all available tools for plumbing the depths of life wanting. Whatever the candidate for the meaning of life, the Teacher has pursued them all. Besides wisdom (and its counterfeit, madness), he has gorged himself on pleasure; courted happiness in wealth and power; dedicated himself to duty, altruism, social service, and honor; devoted himself to piety and religion—as well as contemplating atheism. Each of these toils under the sun he finds unable to deliver on its promise of fulfillment.

Sophie: Even so, it's important that, after it all, he affirms that ordinary life is not to be escaped but to be embraced, as the proper site of service of God. The future remains intrinsically unpredictable, because it is in the hands of God; better then to savor the pleasures and responsibilities of the moment that God gives into our hands, moments that C. S. Lewis described as "shafts of glory."

Socrates: He reminds me of myself in later life: it seemed that the more that I knew, the more I knew that I didn't know. At least he cannot be accused of having lived an unexamined life.

Solomon: Yes, Socrates, I think that here is one of the great paradoxes, which you know as well as I do: true wisdom consists in not considering oneself wise. Given the limits of human finitude, the necessary fallibility of the human condition, the proper counsel is humility. In the end, faced with his own incomprehension and face to face with God, all that Job can do is be silent. If I might be permitted to quote from one of my collections of sayings, there is ultimately "no wisdom, no understanding, no counsel" that is valid in God's eyes (Proverbs 21:30). There is a mystery at the heart of the universe.

Sophie: You're beginning to sound like a postmodern, Solomon. They would agree that we should pause at the threshold of grand generalizations, metanarratives, to hesitate at the promise of a "theory of everything." But of course, you go further, because in the end, our knowledge of creation does not depend on conquering it with our technologies—even, dare I say, the tools of philosophy or wisdom—but on submission to the one who is master. You're saying that we should subject ourselves to God as the condition of wisdom—is this "the fear of the Lord" again?

Solomon: Yes, and in a real sense, we should subject ourselves to God's world as well. This puts a somewhat different slant on the notion of the "subject" than that which is common in philosophy, though some feminists have been coming close to the same idea in recent years. We should allow the world to retain its constantly puzzling character. Instead of subjecting it to our schemes of domination, we should lay ourselves open before it, making ourselves vulnerable. We become its subjects, inviting it to correct us, rather than vice versa (cf. Von Rad 1972, 318). By all means, respect what can be known, for this is by no means trivial. But, at the same time, honor what is unknowable, remembering that ultimately it is God who chooses whether to give it into our hands. All knowing is a response to God's revelation to us, and what he does not lay bare, we should not seek forcibly to expose. You might say, Socrates, that if we steal fire from the gods, we will get burned.

Sophie: You rely on images of vulnerability on both sides of the "equation." This is so much more congenial than Francis Bacon's violent metaphor, of stretching nature out on the rack of science. And I like your gloss on revelation as "laying bare," which is the simpler Anglo-Saxon alternative to the Latinate "reveal." I like the echoes in the German word, "Offenbarung." And I also cannot help but hear a loud echo in what you say of the limits to human knowledge that God established at the very beginning, back in the garden. The creation story is a story of the boundaries that God has established within and around our existence—an existence as creatures. If the wisdom writers are guardians of a "creation theology," perhaps nowhere is this more evident.

Solomon: Yes, there are creational limits to growth in knowledge: the wise person accepts these in humility, which is a fruit of wisdom. This is the appropriate response to the hedge God has placed around human understanding.

Sophie: So as well as being its product, humility is the attitude out of which wisdom is born; it is what Schwehn (1992, 50) describes as a "precondition for learning."

Socrates: If that is your view, it is no surprise to me that you did not coin a term equivalent to "epistemology"—the "theory of knowing with certainty."

Solomon: Spot on, Soc! Like you, in many respects, we did not expect certainty *within* the bounds of experience, but only at the very outer limits. And this itself was more a matter of confessional certitude, of trusting that we were ultimately safe in God. Events are always ambivalent and puzzling: their meaning cannot merely be read off the surface.

Socrates: That is why I say that it is necessary to penetrate to a reality that lies beyond appearances! Yet you say that one cannot comprehend it in reason (as for Plato), nor conquer it in the power of human freedom (as for moderns), but only apprehend it in faith. This I find offensive!

Sophie: Well, Socrates, if you don't mind me saying so, the Apostle Paul said that you would. I have to agree with Solomon. While there is much we can know, we also recognize an inability to know. I like to think of this as a protective barrier against what Brueggemann (1982, 74) calls "a kind of *shameless scientism*," an attitude acknowledging no limits, bowing before no mystery, reducing all of life to a technique.

It strikes me that all of this talk about puzzlement, uncertainty, ambiguity, mystery—and yes, humility—might properly be at the heart of the approach our school has been trying to work with. It's what Freire (1972) calls a "problem-posing" approach to education. It should be quite different than even a problem-*solving* approach, which I think is fixated too much on an outcome, and which seems to guarantee that if the right technique is applied, then a solution will surely follow.

Socrates: Bah, humbug! What you have both forgotten is that there is only one right way to do things—if you understand the proper theory, then the appropriate outcome is bound to follow.

Solomon: You are one stubborn and recalcitrant dude, Socrates! But although you are certain that I must be wrong, I cannot be sure that you are not right. It's just that I think that it is preferable to keep open as many options as possible. And I am willing to keep open the option that in some circumstances, tightly circumscribed though they might be, theory might just be able to do what you claim for it.

Tradition and Community

Solomon: Although I believe wisdom is found in the specific experience of individuals—Ecclesiastes is the archetypal "lone seeker"—the reliability of the world means that wisdom is also intersubjective. As well as the immediacy of experience, there is a tradition that has been painstakingly constructed by the community living through history (Brueggemann 1982, 72). Indeed, I would go further—wisdom not only emerges in the community of teachers and students as they dialogue with each other and with the world, it has as one of its prime goals the building of community. One of the tests of wisdom is whether it strengthens relationships.

Sophie: I think that these days this might be referred to as an ecological perspective, so long as one recognizes that human relationships are integral to the web of relationships that constitute the cosmos.

Socrates: In my experience, seekers of wisdom can often fracture community. You can't say that my efforts—or those of Jesus, for that matter—ended up with "happy families"! I think that he and I both saw it as a major part of our role to call traditions into question.

Solomon: You are right about the fractures, sadly. Wisdom that is seeking what is just and true cannot avoid the reality of suffering and evil—nor can it eradicate the self-righteousness that characterizes many "true believers," when humility is forgotten. But let's look at how traditions develop. Dialogue is the key, as I am sure you will agree. A tradition develops through dialogue that stretches across time. A living tradition has within itself the resources for self-correction, because dialogue remains vital—full of vitality.

Socrates: Of course—I relied on dialogue. But it wasn't seeking the lowest common denominator of consensus. My purpose was that all of those who were worthy should come to see the one truth that was previously hidden.

Hearing and Doing

Solomon: Yes, here is another significant difference between us, which we have already touched on. You and your heirs favor a visual epistemology—you speak of seeing the truth, spectating (*theoria*), reflecting, insight, mirroring nature. Ours is oral and aural. It presupposes a two-way communication between a speaker and a hearer. This suggests a greater sense of immediacy and intimacy of contact between knower and known than your metaphors allow. Whereas something can be seen without seeing or without being conscious of being seen, hearing requires a speaker.

Socrates: The speaker is the rational person! It is his or her purpose to help others lose the scales from their eyes, to look through what appears to that which is illuminated by the true light of reason. There would be no wisdom without a rational discerning of the order that lies beyond.

Solomon: It seems that we return once more to our different assumptions about the stuff of the world. Creation is not just there, as passive object to be observed from a distance. It speaks to us, whether in human words or in what Seerveld (1980, 15) calls "creaturely glossolalia." It issues an invitation to be guided by its self-revealing. It is not a world to be "viewed," but a word that respectfully seeks a response, for only in conversation—intercourse—will the truth be known.[7]

Sophie: It seems important to me that you balance the focus on experience with attention to tradition. This would make the MECS curriculum look somewhat less "progressive" and more, shall I say, "traditionalist." Many people would be put off by a curriculum that only focused on the present experience of students and did not take into account the rich cultural heritage to which they are heirs. And, of course, you can never have an experience that is located outside any and every cultural context whatsoever. Experience is always encountered and interpreted within such a context.

Solomon: Just so! And it seems to me that Socrates would have us develop a contextless insight—yes, and insight is the proper word for what he advocates, just like Descartes and so many others, for it presupposes that we are viewing an inner theater of ideas.

But I think that I need to say a little more about what I mean by "responsiveness to the word." This is likely to be misleading unless we remember how we Hebrews thought of the *word*. For us, "word" (*dabhar*) was dynamic deed; as such, it could and would bring about change. The word not only *affects* but *effects* history. The word has power (Williams 1996).

Socrates: Whereas for us, as you know, *logos* referred to an abstract rational principle that gives order and stability to a reality that is fundamentally unchanging. Words are unable to have an effect on this reality, they only affect appearances. That is why I, and many after me, deemed history with all of its unpredictability to be largely devoid of serious intellectual interest (cf. Williams 1996).

Solomon: Yet we knew that God entered into history, and we lived with this in mind. Our very existence as a people depended on God's intervention—though I am not sure that this is quite the right word, as it suggests that God just "dropped in" from time to time. For us, history was written against a cosmic backdrop. We began not with our own local story, but with the story of the origin of the whole world. Arrogant, some would say, but if the history of creation was rooted in the Creator of history, one could expect to see the hand of the Creator at work in daily events. The *event* always took precedence over abstract ideas or generalizations. This emphasis is, of course, continued in the New Testament: it tells the deeds of God in space and time, of the Word become flesh for all to touch and to hear as well as to see.

What I have been trying to get through to you all along, Socrates, is that it is the happenstance, the serendipitous, the unanticipated responses that are the stuff of life, not the clinical world of algorithms and formulae. Our Wisdom Literature was not a collection of timeless truths, but always spoke to specific circumstances. Everything is open and fluid, and learning means deciding what is given and what is the appropriate response to it, from place to place and from time to time. "There is a time for everything under the sun," the Teacher said.

Sophie: I like the way Brueggemann (1982, 78) puts it: "What appears to work on one day may not be the choice on another day."

Socrates: How wrong you both can be! The Good, the True, the Beautiful, these are the same at all times and in all places. There can be no shadow of turning in the eternal verities. And neither can there be any variation in the way people grasp them. It is either raining or it is not raining. Surely you agree that no one can think logically without obeying the law of noncontradiction.

Solomon: You refute yourself there! Even the law of noncontradiction says that something and its opposite cannot be true *at the same time and in the same place* (cf. Clouser 1991). Time and place *are* important—even this "law" is not a purely abstract logical principle. And, as in your disregard of history, it is a lack of awareness of the importance of time—the importance of timeliness—that is most telling.

Socrates: Surely what is important is applying theory to practice, translating "knowledge that" into "know how."

Solomon: It sounds so simple! But how do you know *when* to apply *which* of your theoretical generalizations? Wisdom is (among other things) a matter of *knowing when,* of matching precepts to context, instruction to situation. In any case, in our wisdom tradition the precepts are not generalizations; they have a particularistic focus. It comes back to our understanding of the world as creation, meaning a world that is continually dependent upon and open to God—and what is the significance of supplicatory prayer if this is not the case? In such a world, there can be no formula that applies in each and every circumstance.

Sophie: I remember hearing Rob Walker explain in a Masters seminar at Monash a justification for the case study approach. Positivist researchers reject it because it does not meet their criteria for valid generalizations. He said something like, "What is necessary is not an instantiation of the general in the particular, but the recognition of similitude, the 'generalization' (by comparison) of my experience to the experience of another." That's a bit of a mouthful, but I think that he means that if I read a case study and see in it something that illuminates my experience, then I can learn from this description of a particular situation just as much, if not more, than I can from a generalization. And if you think about it, "Academic achievement is positively correlated with time on task" is about as trite an outcome of decades of research as I can imagine, no matter how many volumes of statistical evidence there are for it!

Solomon: Right, and that is much like what I mean when I talk about a wisdom methodology—though I hesitate to attach "methodology" to "wisdom." It seems like a contradiction in terms. Rather than look for how a universal principle is to apply in this or that instance, I am to weigh up my experience against that of many others, to see what matches and what is out of kilter. It is not like the application of a tightly worded legal statute, more like the careful sifting of cases in a common law jurisdiction, to see what is the same from case to case, but also what is different. Whether magistrate or jury, the call for judgment and discernment rests with the adjudicator. Of course, there is also the necessity for judgment in the application of statutory provisions, but I think that we can draw a distinction between the kinds of judgment involved.

Justice

Sophie: And what then is the connection between judgment and justice? Is it fair to say that wise action is also *just* action? Socrates, you would agree, wouldn't you—though no doubt not in quite the way I would explain it. I would say that just action is sensitive to the invitation of the world in its many and varied expressions. It hears the voice of God in the voice of the other. I remember reading in *Gospel and Wisdom* (Goldsworthy 1995) that the biblical teaching on creation is an implication of what the Bible also says about God as just and redeeming and, I guess one could say, vice versa. I had to think about that a bit, but I assume that he means that God continues to be faithful to all he has created because that is his character. And being faithful in a world that is not all it is meant to be will also mean bringing healing and redemption.

Solomon: Yes, Sophie, the wisdom tradition's commitment to community is certainly also a call to justice. How can there be true community when some members are allowed to suffer? The wisdom literature, in its very "secular" character—the absence of explicit reference to the covenant between Yahweh and Israel, the concern with the here and now—underscores that the people of God are to live out his glory in ordinary lives through faithful neighborly relations.

Sophie: Just like in the New Testament, where Jesus conjoins the two great commandments. As far as my study of Proverbs goes—and I hesitate to venture an opinion in your company, Solomon—I think that it is very much concerned with what it means to walk aright with one's neighbor. Ecclesiastes appears less so, but its account of an individual's exploration of what it means to live the "good life" expresses a commitment to seeking the way of human flourishing. I think that it has implications for how all people ought to be able to live, because he seems to be saying that anything that impedes a life of honest toil and enjoyment of its simple pleasures is implicitly to be combated. If these are "human rights," they are also "human responsibilities" for those of us who are in a position—or who are willing to put ourselves into the position—to do something about their realization. And when I look at Job, his story seems to me to be centrally a search not only for wisdom, but also for where justice is to be found under heaven. He agonizes over the fact that he in no way—in no wise!—deserves the fate that has befallen him. In the end, it is evident that justice is entirely dependent upon the grace and mercy of God.

Socrates: I am afraid that for me, as well as, I am sure, myriads of other people, the wisdom perspective is not easy to live with, as Brueggemann (1982, 80) says—there is too much "play" in it, "a slippage that cannot be overcome or explained."

Wonder

Sophie: But I would think that to be fair you need to complete the quotation: "to want more certainty is to crush the wonder that belongs to knowing." That's what is reflected in the book of Job—a crisis in the wisdom tradition, when this openness to wonder and preparedness for puzzlement has hardened into a rigid interpretation of the world as a virtually closed system of cause and effect.

Solomon: You're right, Sophie, and that's why Job's friends, bless their little hearts, are able to provide so little comfort. They have a simplistic doctrine of experience, in which you might almost say that wisdom has fossilized. They have forgotten it is *always* historically situated, that the passage of time presents "a series of life-opportunities to which each human being responds freely and creatively according to the needs and dictates of the moment" (Clements 1992, 51). Having made fixed general rules out of wisdom, they are incapable of dealing with the seeming contradictions experience presents. Though their words might be "true" as propositional forms, they just do not apply—they do not apply justly—to the specific case of Job (Goldsworthy 1995, 96).

Sophie: That reminds me of a friend of mine when I was a teenager. Annette carried *Living Psalms and Proverbs* with her everywhere. She used Proverbs in particular like a promise box, as though you could pull out an instruction for every situation at will. She read them as a series of specific instructions for right living, forgetting all of the time that she had already made decisions about which one was relevant, and in what way. I must say I found some of her behavior quite bizarre. And I remember someone else, who was looking for a house, and she read in Acts, "Go to Philip's house"—the trouble was, Philip wasn't interested in selling!

Solomon: Well, the proverbs do compress experience in symbolic terms, but often in the form of puzzles and by use of metaphor, so they need to be read *literarily*. Rather than telling you just what the wise thing to do is, they point to the way in which wisdom is to be acquired, as both gift and task. Creation speaks, and we are to respond. The proverbs don't resound like a voice from heaven crashing into and overruling our experience. They really impel us to seek out understanding ourselves, in the very thick of things, testing every encounter. Words can only go so far in articulating experience. Really, they never *capture* it, they *allude* to it. I struggle to explain my experience, to make it accessible to others, but in the end they have to discern the appropriate course of action for themselves. Judgment, discernment, responsibility—that's what living takes.

Sophie: If only our students could be really excited about that seeking and exploring of experience—or maybe we dull the edge of that urge by the way we school them; young kids seem so hungry to learn. I can see that if we were to take the message of wisdom to heart, we would have to give up all of our attempts at "transmission teaching," what Freire calls "banking education." We would have to raise a lot more questions—and encourage our students to ask a lot more questions themselves. I guess this is probably easier to do in some parts of the school than in others. I am inclined to think that very young children need a great deal of structure. Then, at the other end, there are all of the requirements of tests and college admissions to worry about. What's more, at all levels of schooling, there is this imperative to cover all of the content that the curriculum lays down.

Solomon: There are no simple answers, granted—but then isn't that what wisdom is all about? I would think—and I was surrounded by children of all ages!—that younger children are just so eager to explore, so full of wonder at everything that is new, that if we do not take advantage of this in our teaching, we are doing them a grave disservice. And what is really required for success in university study—isn't it the ability to be self-directed and to always search for your own answers? Don't forget, I have not been saying that the tradition is unimportant, that the knowledge that is embedded in the various disciplines, arts, and crafts is something to be ignored. By no means! But a dead tradition is one that does not have within itself the seeds for its own regeneration, that is content merely to repeat the truths of the past rather than to search for the truths of the present.

Sophie: I have a friend, a history teacher, who thinks that the Scholastics have received an unfair press. She says that they were much more innovative and creative than they are often given credit for. The caricature is that they were happy just to churn out the answers their systems provided, as though everything that could be said had already been said, and there was nothing new under the sun. This is what we mean these days by "schoolish"—doing everything by the rules, according to the textbook. And I'm afraid that, so often, this is not a caricature.

Socrates: You won't be surprised that I, too, think that the process of learning has to be much more creative than this. What we need is the cut and thrust of question and answer and counterquestion—the whole approach that I am so pleased to have associated with my name. If that's what you mean by "wisdom teaching," then I'm all for it!

5

The Realization of Value

In the Introduction, I noted Maxwell's (1984) characterization of wisdom as "the realization of value." He intends both senses of the term *realization*, as an *understanding* and an *implementing*, and I will explore this aspect of the definition in later chapters. But for now, I will focus on the element of *value*.

Value

I have encountered some resistance to the use of the term *value;* some people find it too nebulous and noncommittal. They assimilate it quite readily to "values," and these in turn are regarded as personal, subjective, and relativistic. Value, like beauty, is assumed to be in the eye of the beholder. But I think that value is a much more robust term than this—or at least, I seek to recover this robustness. Just as Pirsig (1976) set out on a quest for "quality" in *Zen and the Art of Motorcycle Maintenance*, I am suggesting that wisdom is the pursuit of that which is of value.

I am not proposing that value is something that exists in and of itself, independently of any human and cultural context. But if Herbert Spencer's question as to which knowledge is of most worth is a valid one for curriculum developers to ask, the question as to what is of (most) value has similar validity—it is, indeed, merely a translation of the former.

Richard Pring (2000, 158) argues that educational practice is "concerned with learning that which is judged to be of value—given what we believe to be of value in the cultural resources upon which the teacher draws and given what we believe to be a worthwhile form of life to pursue." Speaking specifically of educational research, he claims that:

> The object of research will necessarily be seen differently by different practitioners (and by different traditions of practice within which they work) as they select different cultural resources and different forms of life to aspire to. Educational research cannot avoid the systematic reflection upon the controversial values which pick out what is sig-

nificant to study, what constitutes an educational outcome, what is to count as value added. (Pring 2000, 158)

In commenting upon this passage, Michael Peters (2002, 359) says that there is "something fundamentally right" about Pring's position: "Can we simply say that all conceptions of education—and *ipso facto*, of teaching and learning—are both value-laden and essentially contestable?"

As Pring and Peters have observed, there will always be debate about what these criteria are. People's values will differ because they are a subjective communal response to what is of value—which implies not only human subjectivity, in the sense of individual and cultural variation of response, but that responses are *subject to* what is of value. Christians generally acknowledge the authority of Scripture over human activity—that the Bible establishes the normative frame of reference for life in general (though this, of course, works itself out in a great diversity of ways). My understanding, informed (not only) by the Wisdom Literature, is that this assumes a high view of creation, as that which is the primeval site of normativity. The Scriptures are then legitimately seen as a republication of creational revelation. Because God is confessed as the undivided source of both, any conflict between these two sources of revelation is assumed to be apparent only.

Normativity

I have noted that the term *value* can too readily be equated with what this or that person happens to value, a person's preferences or personal values. But wisdom has to be judged ultimately in respect to whether it is a realization in accord with the way in which the world is, as God's creation. If it is not, then realization is unwise: we do not need to appeal beyond the recent past to think of many figures of evil who not only had a clear understanding of what they wanted to achieve but sadly set out with great determination and attained a large measure of success in so doing.

I wish *value* to be understood as a synonym for *normativity,* an established standard of proper or correct behavior. This is a stronger philosophical term, having to do with what ought to be the case, with distinguishing the Good from the Bad (or Not-So-Good). Similarly, value refers to criteria that should be honored. I could countenance the notion that wisdom is the "realization of normativity," if the meaning of the latter were readily accessible. I might then from time to time use also the abbreviated form *norm,* having established that it is not average behavior nor a statistical mean that I have in mind.

Of course, both words are related to *normal,* but the ambiguity here, too, is obvious. In a fallen world, it is not what God establishes as normative for human behavior that is normal; what is normal or average—or even "standard"—behavior is descriptive of what most people actually do. In this context, where the normative directives for human life that God has established are gainsaid, descriptive categories are elevated to the vacuum thus created. Values do become "what most people value," and norms "what is normal for the population at large." A whole range of human life is reduced in the process: we are left with the categories of fact and description alone, those of value and normativity having disappeared. (This is, of course, the project that positivists and some analytical philosophers endorsed, but which has lately fallen into disrepute.) In such a world, terms like *ethnic cleansing* can be used as though they are devoid of ethical weight. It is no wonder that, in the values vacuum thus induced, being takes on an unbearable lightness.

Wisdom then is the "realization of normativity." Lest the singularity of this term also mislead, we need to note that normativity is not monolithic. Many Christians (and not they alone) tend to think of normativity in one- or, at best, two-dimensional terms. When considering involvement in politics, for example, the normativity of the political process—is it serving to promote public justice?—is frequently overlooked in favor of attention to the personal religious beliefs and moral standards of a particular politician. Admittedly, this is easier to do than to struggle with the question of which of two Christian brothers or sisters (and sometimes they may actually be siblings, as is the case with a couple of currently prominent Australians) of divergent opinions is holding to "the will of God" in matters political and economic. After all, "public values" are too often held to be separate from "private" ones, in the characteristic splitting of life into secular and sacred domains that the church has historically condoned, if not fomented.

But personal morality and spirituality do not by any means exhaust the range of norms that God has decreed. Thinking with logical consistency, speaking with clarity, interacting politely and sensitively, decorating with style—these and other dimensions of normativity may be added to the ethical, spiritual, political, and economic norms already identified. And all are matters of concern to God, who would have us present our whole selves as living sacrifices, seeking to honor Christ in all things, taking all of our thoughts and actions captive to him.

If wisdom is concrete acting in a manner that does justice to the richness of reality, it requires what has been described as "the simultaneous realization of norms" (Goudzwaard 1979, 65). In any given situation, there is a plurality of norms to consider—I like to extend the phrase in recognition of this and to speak of "the simultaneous realization of a multiplicity of norms"—and wisdom, judgment, discernment are required in weighing up each of them and seeking to ensure their "well-balanced harmonization" (Dooyeweerd 1953, II, 135–36). Action by its very nature must attend to all at once, for action cannot be at a distance (prescind) from any aspect of experience. If reality is that which we cannot avoid (cf. Taylor 1989), then we cannot avoid acting ethically, economically, aesthetically, sensitively, and so on—the significant question is whether we act in normative or antinormative ways in these dimensions.

Wisdom as Love

Wisdom is the realization of value. If beliefs are constitutive of experience and all people function on the basis of a worldview, we do need to acknowledge that people have differing subjective responses to value; they do have values that are often at variance with those of others. (This relativity of values, as I have said, underlies many objections to the use of the term *value* in the definition of wisdom.) Many of these variances may be contrary without being contradictory, matters of cultural tradition and individual preference that are a legitimate expression of human diversity at the communal and the individual level.

There is generally, however, a drive for coherence and consistency ("wholeness" or integrity) in people's value frame or worldview, which allows us to speak of an ultimate source of values that holds this whole complex together. Christians (and they are not alone in this) affirm that the greatest value is love.

In this perspective, love is not only a goal of wisdom, it is the means to its attainment. To be wise to the world is both to trust it and to know its love. Wisdom grows in an openness and vulnerability to the "phenomena" (in scare quotes because they are not mere objects), allowing them to enter into one at the same time as one enters into them. To trust someone is to place yourself in her hands; to believe in someone is to give yourself over to him; to love someone is to offer oneself as a willing sacrifice.

Wisdom, like loving, requires a playful intensity. There is both a lightness of touch and a seriousness of purpose about it. Its playfulness rests in its to-and-fro movement, the sense in which it has a rhythm and a dynamic structure. Love does not seek to master or conquer. It is a sense of belonging, an awareness that "I am my beloved's and my beloved is mine" (Song of Songs 2:16). It is empathy and sympathy, a dealing with the world in its integrity, meeting it and treating it as it presents to us. It is a standing in a right relationship with things, viewing them from an angle that allows the disclosure of their true meaning. It requires an attending and a focusing, in which the intention is not to see things through my eyes but to listen to things speak and to seek to hear their voices.

"The two become one," yet do not cease to be two. In love, the one is immersed in the other, without identities, however, being merged or lost. The Song of Songs helpfully rounds out a biblical view of wisdom as love:

> Something extremely simple yet incredibly mysterious is said in Song of Songs 2:16 and again at 7:10: "My beloved is mine and I am his." Love exchanges selves. When I love you, I no longer possess myself; you do. I have given it away. But I possess your self. How can this be? How can the gift of the giver be the very giver? How can the hand that gives hold itself in itself as its own gift? The ordinary relationship between giver and gift, subject and object, cause and effect, is overcome here. The simple-sounding truism that in love you give your very self to your beloved is a high and holy mystery. (Kreeft 1989, 128)

Though the impersonal objects of our acts of knowing may not be conscious of our attention, being in a right relationship with them is still a condition for our knowing them. The order of this relationship is better described by a spatial metaphor—like "under-standing" (standing under)—than in terms of a rational "grasp" of the essence of things. But it is also the relation of speaker and hearer: things "make a claim on us," call to us out of their integrity, asking us to listen to what they are revealing of what they are. Wisdom is (pro)creating, creating after and along with that which is known. It is not a creation ex nihilo, but a bringing forth of something that is nonetheless new and always miraculous. The birthing of wisdom, if done in love, is a careful and exciting undertaking.

Wisdom is, then, an active and interactive process. It emerges not primarily from contemplation, but involves imagination, will, commitment, and responsibility. It is a whole-bodied intercourse, in which the one presents to the other as a living sacrifice, and in laying down life, gains it. It is a breaking down of the boundaries, an acceptance, indeed an offering, of vulnerability, which is fully possible only in a relationship of trust. Wisdom is participating rather than acquiring, conjoining rather than conquering.

Feminist Voices

If we do take care to listen to the voices around and among us in creation, as wisdom counsels, there is a convergence here with feminist themes. Take the following example, from Lorraine Code's *What Can She Know?* (and pause to read/hear the title a few times, shifting the emphasis from word to word in turn):

> Extending to the natural world the model of knowing other people which establishing and sustaining a friendship requires could make possible a subject-object

> relation that is neither engulfing nor reductive, neither aggressively active nor self-deceptively passive—yet engaged and responsive, not neutral. (Code 1991, 155)

Indeed, this new "subject-object relation" would be much more akin to a "subject-subject relation," which is what Kreeft is seeking to convey (rather than "capture") in the passage quoted above.

As well as in Code's taking personal relationships as the model for knowing, yet another resonance sneaks up on me in her words. For in *A Vision with a Task: Christian Schooling for Responsive Discipleship* (Stronks and Blomberg 1993), we also chose the term *responsive* for our subtitle, rather than the then common use of *responsible*. But this additional resonance is no accident, of course, for it flows from the first mentioned one; though a friendship must be nurtured in a responsible, normative manner, responsibility is embedded in a free-flowing giving of one to the other, not out of obligation primarily, but out of continued choice and in recognition of mutual congeniality—born out of responsivity.

Male Models

Modernist epistemologies have been based on analogies with active male domination of the object of knowledge. A biblically informed epistemology will recognize that many of the qualities of Christ and Christ-like living are identified as feminine in our culture. Machiavelli is not the only one to revile Christian values for their "feminine weakness." Perhaps even more clearly, the understanding that wisdom in the Old Testament is personified as a female—at the same time as the New Testament writers identify Jesus as the embodiment of this wisdom figure—should give us pause to reflect.

I have noted that there is in modernism a raft of dualisms and dichotomies that an integral epistemology (and postmodern thought) seek to overcome. Many of these can also be seen to be inspired by images of masculinity. In the West, the male has been regarded as the embodiment of rationality, and the female as driven by emotionality (construed as the contradiction of rationality, which it need not necessarily be). Margaret Wertheim's (1997) fascinating study—*Pythagoras' Trousers*—demonstrates a number of interrelated theses that bear on this issue of male dominance, in the realm of the natural sciences specifically. Briefly, these are:

1. science has functioned as a religion in our culture;
2. a religion has to have a priesthood;
3. as in many other religions, this priesthood has been seen until quite recently as necessarily an exclusively male domain, and it remains predominantly so.

Her argument is compelling, and her anecdotes sometimes shocking, particularly in respect to the way that women scientists have been treated. That the natural sciences, which in their objectification of women and nature alike have served as the model for modernist thought, have in her view all of the trappings of religion, is deeply ironic. This observation may serve to strengthen the credibility of the overtly "religious" perspective from which I am pursuing my inquiries.

The Significance of Context

We have seen that wisdom is very much concerned with knowledge in context, with sensitivity to situations. Code (1991, 127) draws our attention to the fact that the illustrations used in discussing the standard Justified True Belief account of knowledge, utilizing the formula "S knows that p," are almost invariably decontextualized.

> Theorists assume that clear, unequivocal knowledge claims can be submitted for analysis only if they are abstracted from the confusions of context. Such examples . . . are commonly selected (whether by chance or by design) from the experiences of a privileged group of men, regarded as paradigmatic for human rational endeavour. (Code 1991, 127)

She further observes that (predominantly male) philosophers have characteristically assumed that an investigation of their own thought processes is sufficient to generalize to any and all human thought. In positivistic and twentieth-century empiricist perspective, the position of privilege is handed to a standardized observer (or to scientists).

> Their simple observational experiences comprise the primitive building blocks from which knowledge is made. A noteworthy feature of those observational "simples" is that they are caused, almost invariably, by medium-sized ordinary physical objects such as apples, envelopes, coins, sticks, and colored patches. Rarely if ever . . . is there more than a passing reference to knowing other people as an exemplary form of knowledge. The references that do exist are usually to recognition . . . that this is a man—whereas that is a door or a robot. With respect neither to material objects nor to other people do formally paradigmatic knowledge claims convey any sense of how these "knowns" might figure in a knower's life. (Code 1991, 128)

The upshot of this is "that apart from simple objects—and even there it is questionable—one cannot . . . know anything well enough to do anything very interesting with it. One can only *perceive* it, usually at a distance" (Code 1991, 128). By this means, most of everyday experience is excluded from epistemological discussion:

> [K]nowledge is not of concrete or unique aspects of the world or society. It is of *instances* rather than particulars: the norms of formal sameness obscure differences . . . and the idea that knowledge properly so-called must transcend or prescind from experience also place a knower—paradoxically—behind a "veil of ignorance." (Code 1991, 129)

Code argues that a feminist epistemology will be attentive to context, will take ordinary experience seriously, and will recognize that this experience is of the social world as much as it is of the natural world.

The importance of wisdom that arises from immersion in everyday experience of an encultured creation, and knowledge not just of instances but of particulars, are significant themes in my discussion. If these themes are also representative of a feminist epistemology, the convergence ought to be regarded as instructive (where some would be tempted to regard them as unfortunate).

Positions and Propositions

When Jesus proclaims himself "the way, the truth and the life" (John 14:6), he is indeed asking us to believe these words as a statement about himself. But he is asking much more than this, much more than assent to a proposition. He is asking that we believe (in) *him,* that we commit ourselves to him and to going his way—"Jesus-wise." The belief *that* is secondary to the belief *in,* the binding ourselves to him. He is asking us to take up a position in relation to him.

The English language makes this connection clear in the common origins of *truth* and *troth.* A pledge of troth in marriage is expressed in a form of words, but it is indicative of an intention to live a certain kind of life. The words are meaningless unless they are followed by a certain way of going—troth-wise, and the pledging of troth is not actually completed until the marriage is consummated; even then, of course, it is but the first step in a lifetime of recommitment, of continually positioning ourselves with and for our betrothed—"consummation" in far more than just its physical sense. The *Concise Oxford English Dictionary* definition captures this fuller meaning of truth: "Quality, state, of being true or accurate or honest or sincere or loyal or accurately shaped or adjusted."

Thus, on a model of knowing/wisdom as loving, even to know a truth that is embodied in a proposition means to be committed to that truth. It means to be willing to defend the virtue of that truth, to be loyal to it, to uphold its integrity. In the deepest sense, to know even a propositional truth is to do more than to give it intellectual assent. It is to recognize its power and thus humbly to submit oneself to it. Truth compels, knowledge impels.

This is why the true scholar comes to love her or his subject—because the scholar is actually subject to it in turn. Whether the subject is an academic discipline or some other realm of truth, it is indeed appropriate to think of a *subject-subject relation* as the model for knowing. As I have stressed, there is a two-way giving, a mutuality, an intercourse between partners in the act of knowing. There is a sensitivity and a carefulness that is required.

How different this is from the modernist paradigm. How different this is from the way in which Francis Bacon described the (male) scientist's relation to "nature" as one of placing her on the rack in order to force her to yield her secrets—though to be fair, he did have somewhat better moments, as when he suggested that "Nature can only be commanded by being obeyed" (cit. Peck and Strohmer 2000, 155). There may well be a certain tenacity required in wooing, but it must have all of the gentleness that a word such as *wooing* connotes; and there is always an element of risk involved in wooing (as in living wisely). There is no ironclad certainty that might equate to the conclusion of a syllogism in exercising judgment that is sensitive to the moment, that is at just the right time. And as in any normative relationship between lovers, the whole must be in a context of trust, in which the one has the freedom to make oneself vulnerable to the other at the same time as the other offers him- or herself to a partner.

A wisdom paradigm leads me to ask, "How might schools be places in which not only are personal relationships valued highly, but a love relationship is the model for all that transpires, in the curricular encounter with creation as well?"

6

Wisdom and Postmodernity

Where is the wisdom we have lost in knowledge?

T.S. Eliot (1971, 96)

Several years ago, I was visiting a number of Christian schools in New South Wales, on a promotional tour for the National Institute for Christian Education. In one school, the principal introduced me as someone who had been influential in determining the shape of Mount Evelyn Christian School. He described the school as probably the most innovative and progressive school in the Christian Parent Controlled Schools movement, and said, "It is good to have schools like that, that are willing to try something different." I managed to hide the smile that played within. Though I am sure that he was quite genuine in his comments, the subtext was that these things had not been—and were not going to be—tried in his school.

Not that I think that there is just one way in which Christian schooling can be done, of course. The school to which I just referred was deservedly respected, and the principal was a person of clear vision and integrity. There is no single blueprint that can be implemented without regard to historical and social context. Indeed, it is one of the significant features of wisdom that attention to context is given great significance. But at the same time, neither is wisdom served by an uncritical conformity to context.

In many Christian schools, the term *progressive* was certainly not an unequivocal term of approval—indeed, quite often the opposite. Today, much the same disapprobation attaches to the notion of postmodernism. And just as Mount Evelyn sought to distinguish itself from the progressive education movement, at the same time as it sought to learn from those features that comported well with a biblical perspective on schooling, so one could imagine a concern to distance itself from the "excesses" of postmodernism—as well as to learn from its insights.

This dual concern sets the context for what follows. A large number of the staff are involved in postgraduate study: a commitment to professional development has been part of the Mount Evelyn school ethos from almost the beginning. The board has mandated involvement in further study, balancing this "stick" with the "carrot" of study leave and salary increments. Staff are encouraged to share the resources and projects from their study with others, and one of the staff meetings each month is set aside to consider broader educational issues. The theme for this term's meetings is postmodernism. This discussion commences with an article from that week's newspaper, which had been photocopied and placed in staff members' pigeonholes the day before.

Leave a Boy in School but You Won't Make Him Think
Success should not be equated with university admission scores

Christopher Bantick

Australian schooling equates success with university admission. TAFE [Technical and Further Education] colleges continue to remain second best in the minds of many boys and they do not carry the status of a university degree. The problem is that too many boys—ill-suited for higher study—stay on at school in the post-compulsory years....

The 1997 report by the House of Representatives standing committee on employment, education and training—*Youth Employment: A Working Solution*—had this to say about the relevance of school and pointed to a reason for the drop-off in boys' participation. The report noted: "The decline is highly likely to be related to curriculum content."

Boys are often bored by school and as a consequence muck around. What boys in years 9–11 say about school, in a recent study by Malcolm Slade of the school of education at Flinders University,

is damning. A common response from years 9–11: "We just mess around in class because we're not learning nothing . . . the teachers won't teach us . . . it's not interesting."

There is a simple solution to the boredom and alienation many boys feel about school. This is to lower the leaving age and encourage boys who are not interested in or suited to the post-compulsory years to leave and find work or training elsewhere. But this is not so easy in a knowledge-based and services-dominated economy that calls for increased qualifications.

Any teacher who has taught boys will testify that there are some boys who should not be in school beyond the compulsory leaving age. They are wasting their time and make the lessons for everyone a miserable experience. Challenge a lippie male adolescent over behaviour and teachers are liable to be given a mouthful or worse. As uncomfortable as it might be for warm and fuzzy educational theorists to hear, some students—and boys far outweigh girls in this regard—are unteachable. Inclusivity does not mean improvement.

In a recent article in *The Spectator*, foreign editor Andrew Gimson pithily argued that the one education cut the Blair Government needs to make is in the number of pupils in English government schools. It is a point that transfers readily to Australia.

Gimson said: "Comprehensive schools are clogged with children who neither want nor ought to be there. By the age of 14 it is clear both to the staff and to the pupils themselves which of them are suited to an academic education."

It would take a brave federal government to advocate that fewer, not more, students should stay on to Year 12 level. Yet for some boys, this is exactly what needs to happen. Australia has the clever country millstone around its national neck. But the clever country is an ideal that is based on quantity, not quality.

Boys who do not want to be at school should be given practical training and encouragement to find what they are good at and develop it. This is not a boy problem but a systemic one, a problem governments at national and state levels, together with schools and industry, need to solve urgently. Surely it is time for jobs for the boys.

THE AUSTRALIAN—Tuesday, 17 July 2001, 15

George: Perhaps Bantick is right—schools are not the place for some, maybe many, people to be. I think that it is clear that a large number of people in our community would agree with him that a main reason for this is that schools are oriented too strongly toward university admissions.

Susan: So, is it time to give up on schools altogether?

George: Not quite—or, at least, not yet! If Bantick is also right in saying that the problem is a systemic rather than an individual one, then perhaps we first need to see whether we can change the system—even if this means only one school at a time. After all, the various pressures for adolescents to stay on in school are not likely to disappear overnight—including the pressures of systemic unemployment, as Bantick also concedes. Even if schools have for some students what is largely a custodial function, then we need to ensure that this is as much a matter of care as it is of control.

Kerry: It occurs to me that in his proposal to deschool at least some students, Bantick may be seen as merely reflecting the spirit of the age. The idea of the school as a total institution—one that encompasses the total lives (during defined hours) of a total population (of a defined age)—is one that is out of step in the postmodern period.

George: I know that it could very easily be said that MECS is itself a postmodern phenomenon. There are indeed many similarities between our style of education and approaches to schooling that might be regarded as "postmodern." I find that this is at the same time both perplexing and promising.

It is perplexing, because Mount Evelyn Christian School sees itself as operating within a biblical tradition, which has obvious premodern roots. Perhaps the school community is deluding itself: what if it has merely imposed a postmodern reading on the biblical text?

Susan: Well, I know that for some people, and perhaps especially for many Christians, the very label *postmodern* is sufficient condemnation.

Kerry: If postmodernity is either an attack on modernism or the condition attendant upon its demise—or both—then a modernist has every right to be disturbed. And if one happens to be a Christian modernist, a postmodern critique can all too readily be regarded as an attack on Christianity itself. It seems such a simple step from "All you need is love" to "Imagine there's no heaven . . . . Nothing to kill or die for, no religion too." Even *World Vision* used Lennon's song in a commercial!

George: But this is what is also promising, because the Christian community has to be responsive to the times in which it lives, without by any means being conformed to these times. And perhaps postmodern critiques of and contributions to educational practice have something to teach us. It is my conviction that this is indeed so, for one of my guiding principles is that all people are made in God's image and live in his world and cannot help but bump up against the structure of that world—though it leaves me with the further perplexing question of how this is as true of modernism!

Susan: Let's stick with postmodernism for the moment. If, for good or for ill, we are living in a period that can legitimately be described as postmodern—and the frequency in which the term appears in book titles is at least circumstantial evidence that something is going on—then it seems wise to explore how we are located in this context.

Alison: I think that it is fair to say that one of the features of the world in which we find ourselves is just in the freedom that it gives for us to speak self-consciously (in the positive sense) as Christians into this context. For one of the major contributions of a postmodern perspective is that it acknowledges the inevitability and hence the legitimacy of perspective. It's the notion of "standpoint epistemology": what I can know will depend on where I position myself to survey the territory. I cannot leave my "self" at the door to my study, and I had better be as open about who that self is as I possibly can, if I am to do justice to my discussion partners, whatever their own perspective might be.

What Is This Thing Called "Postmodernism"?

Stuart: But *postmodernism* itself is such a slippery concept. I recall one book on the subject that started out by listing six different definitions.

Mary: I guess it's in the nature of the term. You would have to know what you meant by *modern,* first, because what you are taking a stand over against would pretty much define what you are. And there is by no means agreement on what *modernity* is. *Postmodern* is not a positive term in itself, but a parasitical one. Way back in 1982, Stephen Toulmin (1982, 254) wrote that it was necessary to reconcile ourselves to the idea "that *we no longer live in the 'modern' world.*" But he also suggested that there was as yet no definition of what our postmodern world *is,* in any positive sense, but only in the negative sense of what "has *just-now-ceased to be.*"

Susan: I found Wanda Pillow's (2000, 22) comment intriguing, to the effect that we cannot just understand postmodernism "as simply against modernism or after modernism; rather, postmodernism is best understood for how it exists alongside modernity (Ilter, 1994; Schmidt and Wartenberg 1994)."

Colin: And, just as it is seemingly impossible to indicate an agreed definition of postmodernity, it is, as one would therefore expect, impossible to pinpoint the time of its birth. That is especially so if it does indeed exist *alongside* modernity. One favored moment is 1962, which marked the publication of Thomas Kuhn's *The Structure of Scientific Revolutions.* I find it deeply ironic that this book was published as part of the project for an "International Encyclopedia of Unified Science," under the editorship of logical empiricists (or positivists) such as Otto Neurath and Rudolf Carnap, for there is no publication that has done more to shatter the dream of a seamless scientific enterprise modeled on physics than this one.[8]

It is to Kuhn that we most directly owe the notion of "paradigms" and thus also that of "paradigm shift." He described the development of science not as the steady accumulation of objective facts, but as a competition between differing models of the world. These models were as much sociologically defined as they were scientific: their survival depended upon the adherence of a supporting community. They were perhaps more subjective than they were objective, in that Kuhn likened the move of an individual from one paradigm to another to a religious conversion. It seemed that power and faith—not the cold and calculating intellect—were the realities at the root of scientific progress.

Alison: I would say that, historically, the implosion of World War II may well mark the collapse of confidence in the power of the modernist project to deliver on its promises, though this process was certainly well under way at the time of the Great War. At least in the West, however, the 1950s were something of a plateau period, during which there was a nostalgic clinging to established intellectual, social, and moral values. There was, after all, a new enemy to combat during the Cold War, and traditional standards seemed to provide the best safeguard against the threat of an atheistic and presumably valueless "evil empire" (if the anachronism may be pardoned). In 1960, Kennedy was elected, a knight in shining armor emerging from his castle—"Camelot," no less!—to do battle with the forces of conservatism within his own country; in 1963, he was assassinated, and his death to many symbolized the death of a dream. Vietnam proved that the dream was really a nightmare.

Kerry: Personally, I don't think that we should forget that Dylan was already singing, and The Beatles released their first single in 1962. We can't separate postmodernism as an intellectual phenomenon from everything that was happening in the broader culture in the 1960s. Indeed, I think that one of the features of postmodernity is the breaking down of the barrier that had traditionally existed between "high culture" and "folk culture." The fact that the revolution in the West was sexual, that "Make love, not war" and "If it feels good, do it" became the slogans of a generation, can't be ignored. The Beatles went East, and thousands upon thousands followed them, at least metaphorically. Hippies, yippies, and Students for a Democratic Society called into radical question the values of their parents' generation. The bourgeois revolutions of 1848 were in 1968 those of the students, though both led to the collapse of governments.

Susan: And Daniel Bell thought that their victory was so complete that there was no longer an avant-garde, because there was no one on the side of order and tradition anymore over against whom an avant-gardist could locate him- or herself. "There exists only a desire for the new." He observes that what has ensued is a "psychedelic bazaar" (Bell 1976, 53). The Baby Boomers have taken over the asylum!

Mary: Yes, and not long after, Jean-François Lyotard (1984, xxiv) introduced the phrase "incredulity toward metanarratives" as a descriptor of "the postmodern condition."

Stuart: I guess the phrase itself is enough to tell you that he was a French philosopher! What in the world is a metanarrative?

Mary: According to Lyotard, a metanarrative is an overarching story or paradigm, which purports to encompass all of the other stories within its pages. It is an ultimate story of the meaning of the world, promising to make sense of even our own individual stories. As Kuhn's picture of competing successive paradigms might suggest, there can no longer be any confidence that there is one greatest story to be told, world without end. Instead, there is only skepticism. This is what he means by "incredulity": people are loath to believe in grand tales anymore.

It is this admittedly sloganlike phrase that many seize upon to trumpet their opposition to postmodernism. However, I think that one needs to distinguish between this as a descriptive and a prescriptive statement. If taken as the latter, Christians rightfully regard it as a challenge to the claim of the biblical story to provide the overarching framework for human life.

Susan: Exactly! What is the story of creation, fall, redemption, and consummation but a metanarrative, the frame within which all other stories, including the story of each human life, are to be interpreted?

Mary: In the hands of some, this incredulity certainly is wielded as a weapon. But even so, it is worth remembering that it is also a weapon against such stories as that of Marxism or the liberal ideal of inevitable human progress, as much as it is deployed against Christianity or any other explicitly religious explanation. It is in opposition to all of those totalizing tendencies that Christians, too, ought to oppose, when these take one human institution (including the institutional church) and exalt it to a position of dominance over all others—a position of hegemony.

101

Absolute power corrupts absolutely, as Lord Acton said, and a totalitarian institution will necessarily do violence to those who oppose it. We are called to be on the side of those who are in fear of being crushed by such power. I believe we ought to recognize that the authority of all institutions—the state, the business enterprise, the church, science, even the family—is limited in a mutually constraining fashion. Only God has ultimate and supreme authority.

Susan: So you are saying that, in this respect at least, Christians should share an incredulity toward metanarratives, for each and every one will in some way compete with The Greatest Story?

The Appeal of/to Narrative

George: But a paradoxically related feature of postmodernity is indeed its fascination with story and narrative—or rather, with the many stories that can and must be told as a condition of human cultural embeddedness. There is a recognition of the traditioned and contextualized character of life, that in itself stands over against the notion that the truth about anything can be found in impersonal, decontextualized, abstract forms—as modernism would have it.

Stuart: I seem to recall that one of the first contexts in which the term *postmodern* was used was that of the visual arts and architecture.

Mies Is More
Richard Lacayo

EVEN PEOPLE WHO HATE modern architecture—all those featureless skyscrapers bunched along heartless avenues!—can have a soft spot for Ludwig Mies van der Rohe, the most steadfast modernist of them all. In his later years, he proposed variations of the same building for every purpose. For office towers and museums, a black steel-and-glass carton. For symphony halls and convention centers? Ditto. For houses? O.K., for houses, something more domestic—a steel-and-glass carton in white. . . .

Now Mies is back, in a big retrospective that has opened at two New York City museums. "Mies in Berlin," at the Museum of Modern Art, covers the years when he and other European Modernist pioneers, especially Le Corbusier and Walter Gropius, slashed away at the history of architecture until they arrived at Platonic refinements of geometric form.

Two simultaneous shows are a lot of exhibition, especially for the man who said, "Less is more." But there couldn't be a better time to look back fully on Mies, 32 years after his death and two decades after Postmodernism rose up to proclaim that less is a bore. The last big Mies show, 15 years ago at MOMA, happened during the heyday of Postmodernism, when Mies and his followers were charged with hostility to history, to imagination and to What People Really Want. Now it's Postmodernism that's in trouble. For anyone tired of whimsy, streetscapes modeled after the Magic Kingdom and office towers topped by medieval crenellations, the dry pieties of Modernism are looking good again.

TIME—23 July 2001, 74–75

Kerry: Yes, postmodern architecture repudiates what it regards as the sterile formalism of modernism and substitutes for it allusions to many different styles, incorporating these into wholes that would be best described as "organic" rather than "mechanical." For a typification of modernist architecture, one cannot go past Mies van der Rohe, while Frank O. Gehry's Guggenheim Museum in Bilbao is perhaps the best known of most recent buildings in the postmodern style. (It is said to be the only reason one would want to visit Bilbao!)

Susan: For supporters of a postmodern perspective, what Bell pejoratively named the psychedelic bazaar is more positively viewed as that which literally builds upon the past. It draws it forward into itself, revels in allusiveness and eclecticism and celebrates multiple layers of interpretation (Jencks 1987)—if not multiple interpretations.

Mary: You will recall that Toulmin (1982, 254) suggested that postmodern science will eventually issue in postmodern philosophy and theology. I think that we might confidently assume that it will lead also to postmodern education. In 1993, William Doll wrote a book called *A Postmodern Perspective on Education*. He is probably a good commentator to start with. He argues that "our curricula should be multifaceted, mixing the technological with the human, the proven with the innovative, and the serious with the playful." He thinks that our work should be infused with irony and parody, "lest we become so wedded to any one tradition or narrative that we deify it" (Doll 1993, 8).

George: It's interesting that Doll would, even if in a metaphorical tone, warn against deification of a tradition—what we know as idolatry. This is a strong message that Christians should heed; it is a message that comes

103

through loud and clear in the book of Job, where the protagonist's friends offer him only the cold comfort of a moribund tradition.

Mary: Yes, and Doll goes on to claim that "this is what the Marquis de Laplace did to Newton's ideas, what the followers of Marx did, what the social scientists did to the doctrines of the natural sciences, and what the Tyler rationale did to the simple task of setting goals" (Doll 1993, 8).

George: But I would also draw attention to the exhortation to playfulness and related attitudes. This, too, is something to which the wisdom tradition calls us in our living in and coming to know God's world.

Stuart: *A Vision with a Task* regards this as so important that they include it as one of three moments in their curricular rhythm of "play, problem-posing, and purposeful response" (Stronks and Blomberg 1993, 193–218).

Susan: But as soon as one refers to *play*, there is the danger of being dispatched to the postmodern wastebasket, and we know that is the kiss of death for many Christians. In another book of Toulmin's, *Cosmopolis* (1990), he puts an interesting argument, which is in brief that the modern period is something of an aberration in our history. He thinks that we have returned to what are really premodern questions. We are recovering an interest in the concrete, the local, the timely, and the particular that characterized Montaigne, Machiavelli, Erasmus, and Shakespeare, but was abandoned by Descartes, Galileo, and their heirs—the ones that Saul (1992) called "Voltaire's bastards." And those concerns were much more continuous with the medieval period that has its roots not only in Greek philosophy but also in Christian tradition, no matter how mixed the two became.

Stuart: So you are suggesting that postmodernity, rather than being a turn away from the Christian tradition, is in some respects a turn toward it, a *re*turn?

Susan: Playing with words, Stuart? Could be dangerous! But yes, and also that Toulmin's idea about a postmodern theology itself ought to be seen not as a repudiation of orthodox Christianity, but as the possibility of recovering a more orthodox form, before the Church became consumed by the modernist project. Patrick Slattery has written a book on

Curriculum Development in the Postmodern Era that contains a chapter with the intriguing title, "Postmodern Schooling, Curriculum, and the Theological Text." Slattery (1995, 67) claims that "postmodernity seeks to restore the prominence of theology and spirituality in the curriculum discourses and practices of the 1990s," and that a "postmodern vision of curriculum as theological text is emerging." He says, however, that "these postmodern educational proposals are vociferously opposed to proselytization and denominational sectarianism."

Stuart: Well, you certainly have me intrigued! Just what is Slattery talking about with this reference to "theological text"? It was never mentioned in any of the courses I had in my training. In fact, theology was ruled out of any discussions at university.

Susan: Naturally! But, as Alison said earlier, that's one thing, at least, that Christians have to thank postmodernity for, the chance to talk about religious issues in public again. Slattery (1995, 67) explains that his motivation is to "address the hopelessness, poverty, injustice, violence, and ecological devastation that plague the entire global community and contribute to the decay of the social milieu of schools."

George: So he agrees with Catholic curriculum theorist David Purpel (1989) that it is necessary to focus on the moral and spiritual crises in society, rather than merely attacking the symptoms?

Susan: Yes, and he proposes to use the term *theology* to distinguish the moral and spiritual issues of interest to postmodern curriculum development from sectarian religious debates (Slattery 1995, 68).

Stuart: Well, the question that I would want to put to Slattery is how is it possible to take a stand against the evils he denounces without erecting an edifice of ideals—a fortress, perhaps, from which to mount an attack? How indeed can anything be declared evil without criteria for making such a judgment? How can one be vociferous in opposition without strongly held convictions? And if one holds these convictions to be on the side of good rather than of evil, why wouldn't one wish to win others over? Isn't such a cluster of convictions in itself a form of sectarianism—though it may not have the name of a traditional denomination? Doesn't even eclecticism require a basis for selection, of sorting what is evil from what is not evil? And when all this is put together, aren't we suspiciously on the way toward formulating a metanarrative, albeit a secular one?

Susan: Slattery makes clear that what he has in mind is definitely a *postmodern* spirituality, one that is to be distinguished from closed systems of doctrine with their own internal logic—which may be said to be imbued with the modernist spirit. The kind of spirituality he is espousing shares many features with that of the New Age, though it is certainly not identical to it.

George: I should hope not! New Age spirituality has more to do with the self-awareness and self-actualization that comes by communion with forces encountered through the rituals of nature religions. It's got nothing to do with an encounter with the personal God revered by people of the Book. The restlessness of the self is not to be satisfied by finding its rest in God revealed in Jesus Christ—which is how Augustine so aptly described our human need. And though this New Age spirituality may well counsel asceticism, this is not to be confused with the self-denial that Christ enjoins upon his followers. Where Slattery (1995, 75) urges schools to resist "fundamentalist calls to retreat to premodern religious practices," Christians who believe in Christ's authority will demur, even when they would not identify themselves as fundamentalist. But Slattery is probably casting this net sufficiently wide as to catch John Paul II in its mesh! That's what this pan-everything spirituality tries to do.

Susan: No doubt, George, and I know you feel these things strongly. But I would also suggest that our demurral will need to be nuanced. Indeed, I think that you will find it is for Slattery himself, who goes on to argue for the preservation of "ancient religious traditions in the social context of contemporary spirituality and theology." Although he notes that this is a huge task, he nonetheless counsels those who believe education in its essence must be religious—as Whitehead said—to consider that there are valuable lessons to be learned from contemporary curriculum discourse—that is, if one is committed to postmodern curriculum development (Slattery 1995, 75).

Stuart: But we always need to remember Jesus' injunction—we might be *in* the postmodern world, but we ought not to be *of* it.

George: Okay, in certain important respects, Christians who are seeking to be biblically authentic will be committed to a *premodern* perspective, because that is what the Bible is. With Slattery, we will also wish to preserve something—a great deal, I would think—of what is ancient in our own tradition. But only, I suggest, in certain respects. Thus, while we will not aspire to schooling practices that are driven by the spirit of postmodernism, we are nonetheless called to exercise our faith in a postmodern context. In this sense, at least, we must be postmodern Christians. We, too, affirm that "the essence of education is that it must be religious"— even more, that education is *necessarily* religious, whether or not this is explicitly acknowledged. Remember our confession, that "human life in its entirety is religion"?

Stuart: Yes, but the question remains: how well do the insights deriving from a postmodern perspective comport with those deriving from a premodern, biblically informed perspective? If we are indeed called to be not of the world while yet we are in it, how are we to make our way?

Kerry: I find British theologian Tom Wright's (1991) analogy of the five-act play helpful here. The final scenes of the last act of the play have been lost, but we are professional actors who have studied the other four acts and the few remaining scenes well. We know our characters, and to a certain extent we know our playwright's intentions, as these are embodied in the earlier acts and in her other plays. We take the stage without a script, but we are called to follow the characters and the plot through to a conclusion that brings a believable resolution to the story, one that is faithful to what has gone before.

We have a manuscript—the Bible—that is complete, but its conclusion points forward beyond its own pages. We are sent out into all of the world by our Lord to continue his work. We do this as a community, and we take many opportunities to workshop the developing play before we continue, as we are called together for focused times of worship and fellowship. We do this in the power and seeking the direction of the Holy Spirit, knowing that Christ has sent him to be our Counselor, and that through him, Christ is in our midst; he is with us always.

Stuart: So, our task is this—how to be faithful servants of Christ in a postmodern world, a world that remains his world, but one that is very different from the world in which the Word was incarnated and inscribed?

Susan: Yes, and for this, we require wisdom. And as one might anticipate, Slattery also sees a prominent role for wisdom:

> Postmodern curriculum promotes the exploration of this mystery of eternity, and the return of theology to its authentic place as queen of the sciences, not in the premodern sense of an authoritarian monarch to be feared or in the modern sense of an antique barren goddess to be displayed in a museum, but rather as the postmodern benevolent and nurturing Sophia, goddess of eternal wisdom. (1995, 75)

Stuart: I must say that I find that image of "an antique barren goddess" quite compelling.

Susan: Yes, but I would point out that just as Christian theologians adopted and adapted Aristotle's notion of the "queen of the sciences," so Slattery in turn has rung his own changes. For his "Sophia" is evidently mythical as well as mystical, a symbol manufactured as rallying point, much like that of Liberty storming the barricades in Revolutionary Paris in that painting of Delacroix's. Admittedly, though we all know wisdom when we see it (we would like to think), we find it very difficult to define. And maybe seeking the one precise definition is just what we should not do. Maybe this is a modernist trap. Probably for this reason, Slattery wisely goes to a poet in support, and I have the poem here—though I did have to dust off my copy, literally!

> The endless cycle of idea and action,
> Endless invention, endless experiment,
> Brings knowledge of motion, but not of stillness;
> Knowledge of speech, but not of silence;
> Knowledge of words, and ignorance of the Word.
> All our knowledge brings us nearer to our ignorance,
> All our ignorance brings us nearer to death,
> But nearer to death no nearer to GOD.
> Where is the Life we have lost in living?
> Where is the wisdom we have lost in knowledge?
> Where is the knowledge we have lost in information?
> The cycles of Heaven in twenty centuries
> Bring us farther from GOD and nearer to the Dust. (Eliot 1971, 96)

George: That sure is a great poem, and worth pondering. But Slattery is hardly fair to Eliot's Christian faith. I think that we can safely assume that Eliot's appeal is to the God who is revealed in Jesus Christ—his reference to "twenty centuries" makes this clear—and not to a mere ideal of wisdom personified.

Susan: Yes, but by the same token, it is again only fair to Slattery to note that he continues his discussion by citing sources of wisdom in many different religious traditions. As I have said, his Sophia is a useful myth, suitable to synthesize what he holds to be the essential truths at the core of all religious traditions—or, if "essential truths" be too modernist a phrasing, then at least all of those notions that rival metanarratives may be held to have in common, a sort of touchstone. Such "wisdom" may be the philosophical core of these otherwise competing stories, once the accidents of their histories have been stripped away.

Mary: The problem for Christians with this sort of approach is that we regard Jesus of Nazareth not just as one expression of wisdom, but also as in a unique way its exemplar, its incarnation.

Susan: Certainly, so that even though I agree with Slattery that wisdom is to be our aim, this is going to have a different meaning for me than it does for him. I confess myself to be constrained in ways that he is not—and I have no doubt you feel the same! But let's see where else Slattery takes us. He identifies three important elements of a postmodern vision for schooling:
- Schools will be cooperative communities rather than competitive organizations modeled on the practices of business.
- They will eschew reductionism in favor of a "holistic process perspective."
- The curriculum will be multilayered and interdisciplinary, with "spirituality and theology" integrated into "every dimension of the educational process." (Slattery 1995, 93–96)

Kerry: Well, I can certainly go a long way with him on these points. My conviction is that Christian schooling—which, I take it, is *normal* schooling, or what schooling ought (*normatively*) to be, even if without the confessional language (cf. Fowler 1990)—must be committed to a cooperative ethos. And, of course, we are also committed to a holistic or integral curriculum, in which instruction and content are merged. Does that make our school postmodern?

George: Just because we arrive at the same conclusion as someone else doesn't mean that we have taken the same route to get there. Our starting point is with the whole world as God's creation and with God himself as community, three persons in one.

Susan: I can also affirm these first two points, Kerry, and I think that the second one spills over, with certain modifications, into the third. Slattery explains this further and seeks to justify it in the following paragraphs, which I think are worth quoting at length:

> [I]t is no longer assumed . . . that the best way to study a problem . . . is to do so in terms of one of the traditional disciplines, subdisciplines, or courses. A new understanding of knowledge in conjunction with a vision of interdependence, spirituality, and wisdom rather than the values of the modern engineer, scientist, and economist is emerging. The curriculum as a theological text provides expanded opportunities for students and teachers to explore alternative solutions to the ecological, health, and economic problems of the world today. The traditional behavioral-technical curriculum . . . is seen as outmoded and inappropriate for all school systems. . . .
>
> Because the very nature of postmodern schooling is eclectic, ecumenical, and inclusive, the first and most important lesson . . . is that [it] will not simply add a new course in theology to the curriculum in order to pacify religious interest groups. Rather, the nature of schooling will change to reflect postmodern values. . . . [T]he discussion of curriculum as theological text has presented insights into the evolving milieu . . . which is understood as reverent, reflective, inclusive, cooperative, just, holistic, and caring. (Slattery 1995, 95–96)

George: From Slattery's juxtaposition of the values of "interdependence, spirituality, and wisdom" to those of the "modern engineer, scientist, and economist," through to his conviction that curriculum should be "reverent, reflective, inclusive, cooperative, just, holistic, and caring," I cannot help but say "Amen!" Certainly, I say this from a distinctively biblical and thus premodern standpoint, whereas his is explicitly eclectic and postmodern—but the confluence of values, at least in formal terms, is evident. I am somewhat flabbergasted!

Kerry: By "eclectic," I take it you mean that he seems content to pull bits and pieces together from all over the place, from different religious traditions.

George: Yes, and the problem with that is that he must be operating with some set of criteria, even if they are implicit, to decide what is worthwhile and what is not.

Susan: Well, I think that he is quite explicit about his values, but he appeals to them almost as givens that anyone would accept. In addition to the "postmodern values" he has already mentioned—reverence, inclusivity, cooperation, and so on—Slattery (1995, 96) lists the following: "flexibility, critical literacy, ethics, autobiography, ecumenism, global interdependence, ecological sustainability, narrative inquiry." He says that postmodern schools will encourage questioning, reflection, investigation, and meditation. The boundaries between the school and the community will be broken down, as students move outside the classroom walls to explore community resources and to become actively involved in projects of service to the community.

George: Once again, without necessarily endorsing the particular content that Slattery gives to these values, I find myself affirming most of these as well—though probably in respect to my presumably "fundamentalist" take on the ecumenicity issue, Slattery would find me an unwelcome companion.

Susan: Well, precisely in that respect, you would no doubt find it interesting that in concluding the chapter, Slattery (1995, 97) cites Mark Schwehn (1993), who is an alumnus and now faculty member of a denominational university. So maybe you're doing Patrick an injustice! He draws on Schwehn's study of the role of religion in American academe in support of the view that connecting to spiritual virtues—faith, humility (piety), charity, self-denial, and friendship—is essential to the process of genuine learning and meaningful teaching.

Stuart: "And all the people said . . . !"

George: Do you think that it is possible, then, that conservative Christians can indeed come to a rapprochement with postmodernism? That the themes that we have identified as emerging from a biblical wisdom perspective and as having their resonances with postmodern themes are not tarnished by this association? Though this would not be to advocate a synthesis of biblical and postmodern perspectives, it would allow us to approach the growing postmodern literature on education with a positively critical stance, rather than in rejectionist mode. The gold of Egypt, as Augustine argued, is in the end the gold of God.

Mary: And it was that in the end because it was God's in the beginning! Remember, the Egyptians gave gold, silver, and clothing to the Israelites

111

willingly (Exodus 12:35–36). I, for one, would certainly like to explore this possibility of convergence further, but in a spirit of receiving gifts rather than of plundering. I've been reading a book by William Doll, which I quoted earlier. I'm writing a paper on the postmodern curriculum, and I thought that it might be helpful for our discussions if I were to give everyone a copy of the notes I have made on his book. Maybe we can use this as something to bounce off in our next Study Meeting?

George: Good idea, Mary! Can you get a copy of it to us by the end of the week?

Premodern, Modern, and Postmodern Perspectives

Susan: Before we finish, I thought that I would hand out a table that Slattery (1995, 84) includes in the chapter we've been looking at. Of course, his framing of the categories is from a self-consciously postmodern rather than Christian perspective—as we've all been at pains to point out! It is in many respects provocative, but you might like to consider what description you would provide in the column I have added, headed "Curriculum as Christian text in the postmodern era." I'd be interested in seeing your feedback!

THEOLOGY AS CURRICULUM TEXT	CURRICULUM AS TECHNOLOGICAL TEXT	CURRICULUM AS THEOLOGICAL TEXT	CURRICULUM AS CHRISTIAN TEXT IN THE POSTMODERN ERA
PREMODERN	MODERN	POSTMODERN	
DENOMINATIONAL	SECULAR	ECUMENICAL	
TRANSCENDENT	ANTHROPOCENTRIC	ANTHROPOMORPHIC	
AUTOCRATIC	INDIVIDUALISTIC	COMMUNITARIAN	
MYTHOLOGICAL	TECHNOLOGICAL	ECOLOGICAL	
DEPENDENT	INDEPENDENT	INTERDEPENDENT	
PAST TRADITION	PRESENT EVENT	FUTURE HOPE	
METANARRATIVE	CARTESIAN DUALISM	INTEGRATED WHOLE	
DOGMATIC	SCIENTIFIC	SPIRITUAL	
FUNDAMENTALISM	POSITIVISM	PROCESS PHILOSOPHY	
"GOD IS ABOVE"	"GOD IS DEAD"	"GOD IS AHEAD"	
FAITH IN THE CANON	FAITH IN HUMANITY	FAITH SEEKING WISDOM	
LITERACY/READING AS COMPREHENSION	LITERACY/READING AS DECODING	LITERACY/READING AS RUMINATING	
CULTURAL LITERACY	FUNCTIONAL LITERACY	CRITICAL LITERACY	
NATURAL LAW	BEHAVIORAL GOALS	*CURRERE*[9]	

SECTION III

What Is This Thing Called "Curriculum"?

When I first undertook postgraduate studies in education, one focus of my work—according to the project's title—was "the development of curriculum." I had not yet been a teacher, but I had had more than fifteen years' experience of schooling on the "receiving end." I read as many books about curriculum as I could find. But I can remember saying to myself at one point, in quite palpable confusion, "I have less idea what curriculum is about than when I started!" Why should such an obvious feature of schooling be so difficult to pin down? I think that one reason is our confusion about what "part of speech" curriculum is, and Chapter 7 calls into question the assumption that it should best be construed as a noun.

It will not be surprising that postmodern discourse is similarly skeptical about the objectification of curriculum and Chapter 8 engages primarily with William Doll's seminal contribution to this discussion. It is only as we break with the view of curriculum as a body of knowledge to be transmitted (as "information") by the teacher to the student that we can embrace a vision of schooling as the formation of character, or the "getting of wisdom." Within this frame, academic excellence is only one of the excellences to be pursued, the academic disciplines only one kind of contributor to full-orbed discipleship. This is the argument of Chapter 9.

7

What Kind of Word Is "Curriculum"?

Not theory, but acting in wise ways with one's students, is key.

Curriculum as Noun

I know that a common perception among teachers, parents, and students is that the curriculum is a course of study to be followed, a scheduled sequence of activities and lessons culminating in some form of assessment. The curriculum is something external and relatively objective, to which teachers and students are subject(ed) in the classroom. It is a *thing*—hence, a noun, and not infrequently, a proper noun, such as "the Grade 11 Biology Curriculum."

Nouns may also be either concrete or abstract, and curriculum is generally considered the former. As a set of prescriptions, it is identifiable, tangible: not just a force but also an object to be reckoned with. Teachers feel its effect in varying degrees, but no more so than the substitute teacher, who comes in for a day or a week to execute someone else's lesson plan.

Recently, a teacher's sudden illness left me in charge of a Grade 10 class, with her notes laying out for me step by step just what I had to do. This could be considered a relief (for the "relief teacher"?), but I experienced it as a burden. I could see from the outset that the class had little interest in the activities that I was to lead them through, but I was forced to carry on regardless. When at the end of the lesson one of the more recalcitrant students chose to say in my hearing, "Doesn't he know we find this boring?" I was almost inclined to speak up in agreement. But it was neither my place nor my curriculum.

On the positive side, the specification of the curriculum makes it public and open to scrutiny. This is obviously one of the requirements for communal engagement with the curriculum, an engagement that is necessary if teachers are to break out of the isolation and self-perpetuating cycle that is often their lot.

On the negative side, it is a hardening, an ossification of the judgments that have been made *in situ*. As with Job's friends, the tradition of the community becomes impervious to the experience of the individual teacher and classroom. The judicious selection of segments and timing of the transitions between them is supplanted by a schedule. The process of curriculum enactment has become reified—"thing-ified," turned into a thing. In instances such as these, it is evident that the prescribed curriculum determines not only the content to be covered, but also the very character of the relationship between the teacher and the class. It tells me how I am to *be* with, be *present to, present* myself to students. It can too readily become a script to be followed, rather than a conversation in which to engage.

I am sure that every teacher has had the experience, not once, but many times, of teaching a lesson a second time to a different class. So often, though it may appear to be a more polished presentation, there is a failure to connect with students in the same way as on the first occasion. The digressions and witty illustrations that seemed to go so well, this time fall flat; the explanations previously devised seem not to address these students' concerns. Even the logical structure of the lesson seems somehow to have lost its coherence.

Curriculum as Verb

The curriculum as it is actually experienced is always a *process*—or, if that also is too reifying, it is always a *processing* by students and teacher. Teachers and students are inevitably *doing* something. Even at the extremes of curricular imposition, when the teacher merely dictates "content" for students to transcribe, the curriculum is not an encyclopedia on the shelf, but a tool in the hands.

The etymology of *curriculum* is often traced to the racecourse, the rails that keep the horses on track. As such, and as noun, its objective and constraining nature is emphasized. Woe betide if students "go off the rails" (to mix the metaphor). More recently, in the Reconceptualization movement and postmodern discourse in particular, there has been a welcome emphasis on the verb form, *currere:* it is the *running* of the race that then comes to prominence, the active participation of the student in learning (Pinar 1994; Pinar and Grumet 1976; Schubert 1986; Slattery 1995, 56–57). This parallels Dewey's argument that *mind* ought to be regarded as a verb rather than a noun. Mind is an active reaching out of the organism into the world: it is not a thing—a blank tablet, a receptacle, a sponge—but an orientation and an intentionality.

It is this active dimension that I have sought to capture (Blomberg

1995) in the metaphor of the curriculum as "worm" composed of a series of segments and of artful teaching as consisting of sensitive segués between segments. In this respect, I see teaching and curriculum as two sides of the same coin: teaching is curriculum enactment; curriculum is a plan for and a record of teaching. The normal division in college programs between "Curriculum" and "Instruction" may be organizationally useful (though I am not fully persuaded), but the two cannot be separated in practice (cf. Walker and Soltis 1986).

A Classroom Vignette
"Think of any number.
"Now double it.
"Now, take away three.
"The answer is eight.
"What was the number?"

The basis for this exercise is contained in a Grade 8 mathematics textbook. Many in the class were bemused by it. As an observer, so was I.

The teacher's instruction to "think of any number" was misleading (though quite unintentionally so, of course, and I am sure there is no teacher who has not erred in this way on many, many occasions; this is just part of the uncertainty attendant upon teaching). Only one number would give the correct outcome. But the textbook had earlier provided a definition. "Any number" was actually a code term for a pronumeral, n. Any number could indeed fill the place it was holding—but only if the answer had not been specified.

Many of the students thought of it as one of those guessing games; indeed, this is how the teacher had presented it to them initially. "Think of a number," he said, then took them through the routine and asked a number of students to tell him their answer. Then, by "backtracking," he was able to tell them the number they had thought of (except in those cases when a student had been unable to perform correctly the operations described). So when it came to the exercise described above, his "advance organizer" had set many of them up for failure.

The lesson had begun with definitions of an "equation" and an "inequality," each hanging respectively on the meaning of the = and < or > signs. The definitions were to be duly copied into the students' books. Rather than grounding the activities in contexts of use, they were seen to be meaningful only within an artificially circumscribed field of school study. They were concerned with what was true in all times and in all places, but with absolutely no reference to what was true at this time and in this place. "Think of any number . . ."—but not just any number would do.

I thought that it might have been helpful to provide some context for the notion of a pronumeral. "When would you ever use it?" one student asked. "How often do you use pronouns?" I asked. "Hardly ever." "You mean you rarely use 'I' or 'me' or 'they' or 'she' to refer to someone without actually naming them?" "Oh, no, I use them all the time," she replied, somewhat grudgingly. "Well," I ventured, "it's the same with pronumerals." She remained obviously skeptical.

When I talked to another student about the problems she was having, she responded that her father had told her that he had never used any of the algebra that he had been taught at school. It was unlikely that this girl was going to listen to the exhortations of a teacher as to how useful algebra could be. I explained how I had used algebra just that week, in working out the dimensions of materials for a gate I was building. I also told her how useful it was for calculating currency conversions when traveling. She remained unpersuaded.

What I have been describing in this episode is the curriculum at work, the enacted curriculum. The example demonstrates, among other things, that whatever the curriculum—in this case, a textbook—mandates, it is what the teacher and students actually do together that they will learn (to echo somewhat the famous words of Ralph Tyler). Though there are many different levels of curriculum, from the most general (national and even international prescriptions) to the most specific (the curriculum as we see it playing out in this particular lesson), it is the latter that ultimately determines what learning will occur. It is the way in which teachers and students interact to achieve prescribed goals. As such, it is not an object but a process, not a noun but a verb—a "doing word."

Once again, we see illustrated, I think, the inadequacies of the theory-into-practice model. While the curriculum might be thought of as a general or "theoretical prescription" for teacher practice, and it might be made as "teacher-proof" as professional curriculum developers can manage, what remains is the exercise of the teacher's judgment, his or her identification of what is most significant and salient—of most value—in leading students in learning. There can be no escaping the priority of wisdom on the teacher's part, no substitution for the teacher's discernment in deciding what will contribute to the realization of educational value.

Curriculum as Preposition

I have explored the significance of construing *curriculum* variously as a noun or a verb. Now I wish to suggest that it ought also to be understood as a preposition. Prepositions, of course, indicate the relation of one thing to another—pre*position* (from the Latin for "place before")—and in this respect, I wish to stress that curriculum is very much about relationship.

The curriculum constitutes the frame in which a teacher relates as a professional, in other words, in the office of teacher to students. It is analogous to the way in which the norms of a medical consultation frame the relationship between doctor and patient in the service of the latter's health; those of a trial frame the manner in which lawyers, judge, and jury relate to a witness in pursuit of reliable evidence; or those of a family oversee how parents orient themselves to their child in seeking his or her comprehensive well-being. Obviously, none of these frames is rigid or deterministic. They do not decree one and one only course of action, nor do they exclude different modes of relating in other contexts, such as that of friendship, citizenship, or church membership. But each relationship has a particular or peculiar *quality* that identifies it as just that kind of relationship and not another. In this sense, a relationship can be said to be *qualified* by that mode of relating (in much the same way as an adjective qualifies a noun).

The purpose of the teaching office is that others might learn. If a person is willing to declaim without consideration for learning efficacy, this may constitute oratory, it may even represent a desire to communicate, but this is still at least one step removed from teaching. There must be a sustained sensitivity to what will promote learning on the part of those with whom one is engaged. There must be pedagogical intent.

This notion of pedagogical intent is already implied by the very designation of people according to the offices they currently hold, namely, those of teacher and student. And it follows that the curriculum as experienced/ enacted is a relationship in time between teacher, student, and pedagogical intent.

I use the term *pedagogical intent* advisedly. It seems to me that the conception of curriculum as noun is so powerful that the question of the link between curriculum and subject matter is begged from the outset; that is, it is tacitly assumed that curriculum is to be defined by reference to certain subject matter, thus importing all of the connotations of "school subjects" that pervade the traditional system.

Rather than subject matter, it is subject *manner* that should be our concern in respect to teaching, for as Goodlad (1990, 280) has observed, "Pedagogy is not something *appended* to subject matters; nor is the reverse the case. They become one in the teaching of, for example, mathematics." Shulman (1987, 7) considers it a defining mark of the teacher that he or she is able to "transform understanding, performance skills, or desired attitudes or values into pedagogical representations and actions."

All relationships have a subject matter. It is assumed that in an intimate personal relationship, this subject is the other person, the "thou" to my "I." This, of course, cannot be all that there is to the relationship, all of the content that it contains, but commitment to the other will give these other subject matters a particular focus. So it is in a pedagogical relationship: any and every subject matter is to have a pedagogical intent, or the teacher is abusing authority over/for the student. Content or subject matter is by no means irrelevant, but it will be selected to serve identified pedagogical goals. This, not any particular subject matter or subject matter in general, is what defines the teaching task (cf. Blomberg 1999).

In recognition of the importance of personal relationships, Christian teachers argue that schools should be above all places of care. Unfortunately, the significance of "care" can be too readily *restricted* in its application to personal and pastoral relationships. But the teacher-student relationship is not in the first place a friendship relation. Noddings (1992) takes this "above all" to mean that the curriculum should be structured around "centers of care." In other words, she takes the issue of care into the heart of schooling, the teacher and student in relationship—as teacher and student. If, as Noddings seems to agree, it is the curriculum that describes this relationship, we face the question of what curriculum structure would most likely make this also an embodiment of care.

This question, I believe, is among the most important questions that any school faces. Its importance was reinforced for me recently in a conversation with a middle school teacher; like me, he was substituting in the senior school for a teacher on extended leave. "You guys are much more concerned about curriculum up here," he said, "whereas our focus is on relationships." This seems to me to get it wrong from both ends—from one end, because the curriculum is a relationship, from the other, because the teacher-student relationship *is* the curriculum.

I am by no means denying the importance of interpersonal values, for teaching remains a personal relationship. It is impossible to overemphasize the importance of trust and respect in teaching. This does *not* require that students have a personal liking for the teacher, as helpful as that would be. It *does* mean that students are willing to give the teacher (more than) "the benefit of the doubt," to accept the authority of the teacher, and to assume that the teacher is working not in opposition to them, but is motivated by their best interests. In addition to the normal ethical criterion of "respect for persons," this will require a recognition of the *office* of teacher, a recognition that it is in the first place a relationship of authority. (This is, naturally, not to be confused with authoritarianism, for the proper exercise of authority is in itself a matter of service to those for whom one has responsibility.) Although respect and trust that have been lost are very difficult to regain, they ought not in the beginning need to be earned. Similarly, trust and respect for students in their office as learners is required of the teacher.

Curriculum as Adjective

In concluding this parsing of curriculum, I wish to suggest that it ought to be regarded properly as an adjective as well. For curriculum is also and always a *description* of the world. As the embodiment of communal wisdom, it conveys a worldview. This is true not only of the *substance* of curriculum, but also of its *form*.

While many Christian schools do recognize that education should be (among other things) worldview education in respect to its *content*, they can at the same time overlook that curriculum *structure* itself carries a worldview. What schools need to acknowledge is that the structure of the curriculum might work against the worldview that they are seeking to convey by its means. A significant implication of my present investigations is that *form* might fight against the intended *function*. Once again, we must confront the question of what curricular structure would most likely make it also an embodiment of love.

Al Wolters (1985, 2) defines *worldview* as "the comprehensive framework of one's basic beliefs about things." The curriculum is also a "comprehensive framework," and it certainly embodies in its structure some quite "basic beliefs about things," such as what kinds of learnings are going to promote a flourishing human life. But "basic beliefs" are also central to what we understand by religious convictions.

I have suggested elsewhere that teaching can be conceived as "articulate artisanship" (Blomberg 1995): teachers are those who articulate or conjoin various learning segments into a seamless sequence. The notion of teachers as artisans is, of course, linked to a view of teaching as craft and, more specifically, a "moral craft" (Tom 1984). Van Brummelen (1988), to bring the broader horizons of normativity into the picture, has espoused the notion of teaching as a *religious* craft; Slattery (1995), in his conception of curriculum as "theological text," has something similar in mind, as we saw in an earlier chapter. Maxwell, writing, like Slattery, in opposition to any narrow or sectarian conception of religion, defines it as follows:

> According to the philosophy of wisdom, academic inquiry is concerned fundamentally with religious ideas and problems. If "religion" is characterized in a broad way as "concern for what is of most value in existence" then academic inquiry . . . is essentially a religious enterprise. If "God" is characterized in a sufficiently open, unrestricted way—as it ought to be according to many religious traditions—as that unknown something that is of supreme value in existence, then inquiry . . . has as its overall goal to help us to realize "God." (Maxwell 1984, 76)

The *Concise Oxford English Dictionary* is hesitant about the derivation of *religion:*

> **réli´gion** (-jn), n. **3.** One of the prevalent systems of faith & worship . . . . **4.** Human recognition of super-human controlling power & esp. of a personal God entitled to obedience, effect of such recognition on conduct & mental attitude . . . . [f. L. *religion* perh. connected w. re(*ligare* bind).]

Acknowledging the hesitancy, I think that the proposed etymology is at least suggestive in the context of the present discussion. Teaching segments are "articulated" into a whole, but what binds them together? What are the ligaments or ligatures? My understanding is that what melds the parts into a meaningful whole is, as Maxwell suggests in the preceding quotation, "concern for what is of most value."

Interestingly, to *analyze* is to "loosen up the connections," and thus works in the opposite direction. If the outcome of analysis is disconnected, so-called "brute facts," then wisdom moves counter to it. It moves in the direction of seeing how everything has its meaning in its connection to other things, ultimately, to everything else.

Of course, what is regarded as of most value is perceived differently by different traditions. Slattery and Maxwell are hopeful that traditions can be transcended. My perspective is that each one of us can only begin with the traditions with which we are identified—or better, with which we have chosen to identify. As Gadamer (1989) has reminded us, there is no prejudice-free starting point; to think that there is, is in itself a prejudice.

The "ties that bind," providing coherence to the experience of learning and teaching, are religious. Religion expresses itself in interaction with experience as worldview. It does so in respect to the two inseparable dimensions of curriculum, the *what* and the *how* (or subject *matter* formed as subject *manner*). If curriculum may be described as *the selection and organization of experience for pedagogical purposes,* the criteria for selection and organization must themselves be considered *values.*

A major justification for insisting upon structured educational settings is that they promise to provide more efficiently and effectively for the development of students than would occur by leaving this to chance: rather than leaving children to the vagaries of circumstance, schools ensure a carefully arranged sequence of experiences that will "guarantee" socially desired and individually desirable outcomes. But what is desirable is itself contestable between value perspectives.

Thus, as a *selection* of experiences, the curriculum will necessarily construct a particular view of the world for students, by what it excludes (Eisner's [1979, 83ff.] "null" curriculum) as well as by what it includes. Does it include dance, drama, and drumming or only physics, physical education, and physiology? Is spirituality pervasive, putatively confined to Religious Education or consciously repudiated? Choices such as these are not merely choices of subject matter; they are also choices of subject manner, of certain ways of being in and relating to the world. They open up certain possibilities at the same time as they close down others. Selection is inevitable, but what criteria are thought to apply?

The curriculum is a painting of the world in miniature, as well as the world viewed from a certain number of preferred standpoints. What is selected for attention and how it is organized will provide students with a particular map with which to chart their way. For a number of centuries, the favored map of the world has been the Mercator projection. In recent years, it has become more widely recognized that this projection distorts the spatial relationship between the countries of the generally wealthier North and the South, showing a preference for the status of the former. Simply moving the line of the Equator so that it is in the middle of the map—which is where one would reasonably expect it to be—rather than closer to the bottom, allows this distortion to be corrected. But it is a telling illustration of the power of the maps by which we have learnt to live that the resulting shapes look so wrong to us!

The disjunction between fact and value, and the presumed exclusion of the latter from the project of schooling, has long been accepted. It is a disjunction that I have, of course, been questioning throughout, in the conviction that schooling ought to be in pursuit of wisdom, which requires the realization of value. In this context, I wish to mention an independent evaluation of the Australian Values for Life (VfL) program offered by Care and Communication Concern (an organization headed by evangelist John Smith, of Christian bikers' "God Squad" fame). It was conducted by Graeme Withers, Senior Research Fellow with the Australian Council for Educational Research (who identifies himself as non-Christian to allay any suspicions of bias). He writes:

125

> I firmly believe . . . that public money spent on this VfL enterprise
> would be a judicious and powerful expenditure of social capital. Young
> people . . . are led into a situation where they are given not just in-
> formation about social and moral development, but strategies for un-
> dertaking this development themselves. They are powerful strategies,
> educationally and ethically respectable, and they stick. Put quite sim-
> ply, every young person needs them—the more who get the contact,
> the better for the country. And the less it will have to spend later, I
> believe, coping with the homeless and disaffected, on juvenile justice
> cases, and cleaning up after the suicides. Yes, I think it's that good.
> (Withers 1997, 56–57)

This is a ringing endorsement indeed. And, as Withers suggests, the pity is
that such a program is not an integral part of the school curriculum, but a
supplement that has to be bought in from outside. A wisdom curriculum
would be one that makes "values for life" its central concern.

Nationalism, Rationalism . . . or Wisdom?

I will have more to say later about curriculum structure. I will at this
point address briefly the issue of worldview and curriculum content. I do
so with the conviction that the presumed exclusion of values and evaluative
frameworks from the modernist curriculum is itself a myth. All curricula
are value-laden; all presume a set of criteria or "basic beliefs" that constitute
a worldview.

To make the influence of worldview more concrete, I tender in evidence the 2000 epic, *The Patriot*. Not itself curriculum—though I suspect,
given the prevalence of "video instruction," that it will be shown in many
Social Studies and History classrooms, and that even if it is not, it will constitute for many the content of their historical understanding—it neverthe-
less illustrates processes at work in the construction of curricula.

The film has been criticized by many non-American reviewers (and
by some Americans as well) for a view of the Revolution that is often consciously distorted (e.g., the exclusion of slavery, the invented mass murder
of civilians in a church) and mostly one-dimensional ("goodies" vs. "bad-
dies," erstwhile cowboys opposing red-coated Indians). *TIME*'s critic, Richard Schickel (2000), however, has only the following mild caveat to offer in
his otherwise glowing report of the movie (though he must at least be con-
gratulated for recognizing—if you will pardon an historian's intrusion—
that the Revolution was indeed a civil war): "What's not to like about *The
Patriot*? Well it certainly suffers from irony deficiency. It is four-square for
democracy and decency, and this, of course, will cause a certain amount of

superciliousness among the postmodernist swells."

In a film in which Loyalists and British soldiers alike are demonized, any plea for a more nuanced account is dismissed, if I may paraphrase, as postmodern prattle. The story told is one of the courageous victory of rational men fighting for freedom—the victory of modernism, the triumph of Reason over the tyrannical *ancien regime,* of nationalism over imperialist aggression. Any challenge to this story is regarded with contempt.

Though not, as I say, "curriculum," there are curricular analogues. For this story is the one that is told within American high schools (despite American protests about Japanese textbook distortions of World War II) and that has only rarely been criticized, in books like *Lies My Teacher Told Me* (Loewen 1996; cf. Loewen 1999) and *A People's History of the United States* (Zinn 1980). The challenge of postmodernity is that alternative stories be told that recognize the pervasiveness of evil, supported as this is by totalizing narratives: what we have in *The Patriot* is the story of the beginning realization of the American Dream, where all of the evil is on one side and all of the good on the other. Christianity would offer a challenge similar to the postmodern one, confessing that there is nowhere in creation where sin has not had its effect, while adding, however, the recognition of the presence of God's grace in even the most depraved circumstances.

This movie purports to be an historical narrative. And indeed, Schickel seeks to draw some object lessons from it. For one, he cannot help comparing "the brutal reprisals the British take against the families of the men fighting with [our hero, played by Mel Gibson] . . . with what we have been horrified to see, the day before yesterday, in the Balkans. Civil wars—which America's Revolution was—are even more relentless and unforgiving than other kinds of wars, Rodat and Emmerich insist." All very well—but the "brutal reprisals" depicted are the invention of the writer and director he names!

If the film is shown in classrooms, we cannot hold the filmmakers responsible for the use that will be made of their production. In the hands of a skillful and honest teacher, however, some quite valuable lessons about historiography might be learned.

The criteria for selection in the curriculum as well as in films are informed by "basic beliefs about things." There is another element to the film which, though more covert, is instructive in our present climate. It affirms the belief that in freeing the ruggedly individualist American from imperial and mercantilist control, the Revolution allowed the birthing of that spirit that holds our hope for the future—the spirit of economic rationalism.

In thrall to this spirit—or paradigm, if you will—governments throughout the Western world (and elsewhere) are demanding curricula that will promote explicitly economic ends. Further, they are also seeking to ensure that form will follow function, in encouraging the privatization of educational provision, or at least partnerships between businesses and schools that allow the businesses to capture the loyalty of new customers early.

Privatization has some beneficial outcomes for those who are seeking to develop alternative models of schooling, including Christian schools. However, we cannot agree to accept what is inevitable on this model: the free marketing of education will lead to a much higher standard of schooling for some, but a much lower standard of schooling for most. Government-supported public education, with equal opportunities for people of all faiths, is another thing entirely than a privatized market of unbridled competition.

If we live in a postmodern era, this reliance on the market may be seen as but one of its defining features, insofar as it allows for the breakup of state hegemony in schooling and the celebration of the choices of individuals. The irony is this: economic rationalism is itself another metanarrative, one that trusts that out of the unconstrained (and part of the myth is that there can indeed be such) choices of individuals, the collective good will emerge. There is no shortage of the credulous in respect to this grand story.

This story needs to be challenged on at least two levels. The first is the contention that economic goals in life are the primary ones to be pursued. The second is the belief that in freeing economic life completely from the shackles of government control, a more fair and just society will emerge. Neither of these are values that we would wish to see embodied in our curricula.

Economic rationalism—what a telling term! What would economic *wisdom* entail (or perhaps better, *ecological* wisdom, because both are terms that direct us to stewardly care of our "household," the earth)? The hypothetical "rational man" makes choices that are always in his own best interests, these then mystically accumulating to serve the best interests of all. The (perhaps similarly hypothetical) "economic wise person/wizard" makes choices that seek the realization of value, and not economic value alone, but the realization of a multiplicity of norms. All then converge on normativity, not their own interests: can one not then more reliably expect the best interests of all to be served?

The economic rationalist worldview is taken by many to be merely descriptive of the way the world is, not an ideology at all. In the same way, worldviews in general might be regarded as objective, relatively passive "things," which one learns by absorption; indeed, this is one legitimate ground for criticism of the notion as an organizing idea for Christian schools.

Alternatively, and preferably, a worldview ought to be considered an active *viewing*, attending to and acting: a way of seeing, but also a way of *being* and *doing* in the world. It is not knowledge delivered once and for all, but *knowing in ongoing process*. It is not then just a perspective that one takes *over against* the world, but a way in which one continually and dynamically repositions oneself in relation to other things. Thus, if there is a limitation in Wolters' (1985) definition, it is that it is susceptible to interpretation as primarily a *conceptual* framework—and "framework" itself is insufficiently flexible a metaphor for our purposes. It is as though people should come to a situation and try to fit it to their own categories, which carries the risk with it of insensitivity to particularities, rather than the gift of openness to the newness that all living brings. Thus, worldview and curriculum alike, and their inevitable intertwinement, ought to be understood in active and relational terms, as verbs, prepositions, and adjectives, rather than as nouns.

Curriculum Traces

Worms leave traces in the tunnels and castings they create, and so do teachers in the classrooms they leave behind. It would be remiss of me to ignore, in my critique of the curriculum as noun, another experience of curriculum that is common to teachers. This is as a collection of documents and materials, to be found in filing cabinets and stacked in cardboard boxes on storeroom shelves, perhaps including teachers' lesson plans and worksheets. When a new teacher is appointed, he or she may be lucky to have a brief introduction to these resources from the person being replaced; more often than not, novices will be left to sort their way through these materials in an exercise resembling an archaeological dig. This leaves a much more subjective view of curriculum than that of the imperious noun and, in fact, evokes appropriate sympathy for the latter standpoint.

It was in part to smooth some of the heartache of this transition that Mount Evelyn Christian School undertook a curriculum documentation project, which I have described elsewhere (Blomberg 1991). There was a concern to inscribe the "oral tradition" in a more accessible and reliable form, to ensure continuity and stability in the school's program—and in turn, to nurture a more articulate community of curriculum artisans. This is the positive side of making the curriculum public, and I have explored in the article cited the extent to which this was actually a teacher development project.

But the resulting documents are, I suggest, despite my large personal investment in the project, no more the curriculum than the plan for a building is the building. Now, if one is building, it is obviously useful to have a plan, and the more complicated the project, the more detailed the plan needs to be. My wife and I are currently talking about adding a room to our house; at the moment, we are tossing ideas around, but if we want to translate these ideas into an actual building, we are going to have to employ a draftsman. But even the resulting blueprints will not yet be the new room. The curriculum documentation project approximated this blueprint phase, but it is the next one—the actual building of the room—that is crucial and that carries the real cost.

How much detail can go into a plan? How many things are assumed? If one assumes that nothing can be assumed, there is no end to the detail that is required, no end to the writing of books. But in reality, many things must be taken for granted.

Several years ago, we did add a small extension to our house—it is obviously a "work in progress"! Fortunately, I was employed close to home and tended to drop in at some point during the day to see what progress was being made. On at least three occasions, I had to ask that a major piece of work be redone. The first of these had to do with the part of the project that involved adding a new entry area to the existing living room. The builders had removed the old front door and windows and boarded up the resulting cavity. Working on the other side of this partition, they had then laid particleboard as flooring. The problem was that the floor of the room that this was to enlarge had pine floorboards. When I pointed this out to the builder, his response was, "Oh, I thought you were going to carpet the room." A reasonable assumption? Perhaps, but it was not our intention.

The builder was correct when he pointed out that the plans did not specify pine flooring—it was something that I had taken for granted, probably had not even consciously thought about. Be that as it may, plans can never be so detailed and specific as to exclude entirely the exercise of judgment, the necessity of interpretation.

Theory into Practice Again?

Is this analogy with a building project an example of "theory into practice"? It will be no surprise when I suggest that it is not. I am sure that the draftsman does not regard his drawings as theoretical: they are very practical plans for a very specific and concrete project. They are not "theory," but a mode of practice isomorphic to the practice of building. They are an attempt to represent building values in graphic form, according to the values of drawn objects. They are "imaginings," perhaps, but they are an attempt to *realize* beforehand what the completed building will look like.

The plans draw on general principles—walls should be vertical, corners should be square—but these are not abstracted from the particular context and are indeed amenable to modification; one of our windows was, in fact, to be on a 45 degree angle to the side wall (and an architect working on the design of a Steiner-Waldorf school will know how even the most taken-for-granted conventions can be subverted, right angles being avoided not occasionally but as often as possible). The plans are focused not on Buildings in General—the "BIG" picture—but on this one and only building in particular.

This capacity for reflecting on events before they happen, for considering possible courses of action, possible and valued outcomes, is a crucial human ability. Thought, says Dewey, is deferred action. But it is not, in most cases, theorizing. The theory-into-practice paradigm is a misreading of the thinking/acting (and when we are acting, we are still thinking) rhythm of human life. And while acknowledging the element of deferral in thinking, it must also be said that thinking (and theorizing as one type of thinking) is itself an activity, a practice, with often very practical goals in view, and practical tools in use. The formulating of intentions and decisions as to which of the many possible courses of action to pursue is an essential ingredient of thoughtful (which also means caring and careful) living.

Similarly, it would be a mistake to regard a recipe as a theoretical *prescription* guaranteeing success (or for that matter, a doctor's prescription as a pharmacist's theoretical recipe). Any cook will know that there is a long way between a recipe and a gourmet meal, and that even the best-laid plans can go awry. Yes, in a loose sense, a recipe is a theory—an idea—for a dish; more precisely, a recipe is a description of "best practice," and such a description—just like the description of the Battle of Borodino in Tolstoy's *War and Peace*—is no more theoretical than a Mother Goose nursery rhyme.

"In theory, theory and practice are the same. In practice, they're different," said America's practical philosopher, Yogi Berra. But the baseball player at the plate, visualizing the bat connecting with the ball, is not theorizing. He or she is imagining—picturing an image of—action that is to come, in a very specific and concrete way. Nothing could be more practical than this. What would be totally impractical would be focusing on Newton's First Law of Motion, even though this is indeed an accurate theoretical articulation of what will happen if the bat does connect with the ball. (In fact, it will also be an accurate explanation of what will happen if the bat does not connect with the ball, which makes Newton's law—and possibly any theoretical law—in this case *practically* useless.)

In any concrete context, there will be many laws that are operative.

One cannot "think them all together," and if one tries to think them in succession, the ball will already have passed by. There will be psychological laws that apply to the batter's and the pitcher's confidence. There will be physiological laws that apply to their movements, nutrition, and fitness. And there will be a myriad other physical laws that apply to the flight of the ball and its contact or noncontact with the bat, in addition to Newton's first. There are a great number of things that have to come together at once if the batter is to hit a home run (cf. Chalmers 1982).

So much for buildings and baseball—"back to the basics!" Even if the syllabus were a theoretical prescription, it could not be determinative of action. There are many things that have to come together at once in the classroom. In one respect at least, it's all in the timing—a matter of knowing *when*. In another respect, it all comes down to the teacher, in realizing what is truly of value for his or her students.

Not theory (n.), but acting (v.) in wise (adj.) ways with (prep.) one's students is key.

8

Playing with Doll:
Exploring a Postmodern
Perspective on Curriculum

The only avenue towards wisdom is by freedom in the presence of knowledge.

Alfred North Whitehead (1967, 30)

Though consolidating his reputation as a mathematician of the highest caliber in the three-volume *Principia Mathematica,* coauthored with Bertrand Russell and published in 1910–1913, Alfred North Whitehead moved in the 1920s to Harvard, as Professor of Philosophy. In many respects, he then left the certainties of abstract mathematics and logic behind him in pursuit of a more romantic view of the world, in which the concrete and the particular are to have priority, though certainly not in isolation from one another. Indeed, in his philosophical work post-*Principia,* he rejects the bifurcated Cartesian-Newtonian world, with its array of static substances, in favor of a world in process, in which all is subjectivity, all is connected to everything else (which echoes both the biblical view of creation—see e.g., Colossians 1:15–20—and a remark by Vladimir Ilyich Lenin!). He termed his perspective a "philosophy of organism," which in turn gave birth to "process theology," in which God is above all the God of possibilities.

Whitehead made a significant contribution to reflection on education, which he describes in terms of a rhythm of romance (play), precision (mastery), and generalization (abstraction). He suggests that the conception of education prevalent in his time tends to restrict it to the second stage of the process, rather than attending equally to all three. He contends that "Education must essentially be a setting in order of a ferment already stirring in the mind. . . . We are concerned alike with the ferment, with the acquirement of precision, and with the subsequent fruition" (Whitehead 1967, 18).

There are marked parallels between Whitehead's perspective on education and the critique and conception elaborated herein. It will be no surprise, then, to find the MECS staff, gathered for their next Study Meeting, exercising their minds with Whitehead. They are to discuss the notes for a paper that Mary is writing as an assignment for her Master's degree.

Ferment and Freedom

Mary: Thanks for being willing to discuss this with me. I hope it will be of help not just to me, but to all of us as we think about postmodernism and education. At this stage, I've basically got a summary of some of the things that Doll says that I think are interesting, and I would be really thrilled to have your feedback and criticism.

I want to start with a reference to what Whitehead said about education having to do essentially with "setting in order a ferment already stirring in the mind." I think that when he says that we can only become wise by "freedom in the presence of knowledge," he gives us something important to ponder about the relation between wisdom and freedom. But I hope that we'll come back to that.

Anyway, in commenting on "setting this ferment in order," Doll (1993, 148) observes that rather than dealing with the ferment, the "Tyler, Taylor, and behavioral movements" have totally ignored it. On the other hand, "Schön's *messes,* Prigogine's *chaos,* Dewey's *problems,* Piaget's *disequilibrium,* or Kuhn's *anomalies*" are attempts to face it head on, recognizing that here lies the basis for all learning and, indeed, for life itself. He agrees with Whitehead (1933, 157–58) that "recognizing 'the radically untidy, ill-adjusted character' of actual experience...'is the first step in wisdom....'"

Susan: There's a reference to "wisdom" again! What does it have to do with the messiness of ordinary experience? It contrasts so sharply with where we would locate the beginning of wisdom—in the fear of the Lord.

George: Maybe it does, and maybe it doesn't. Isn't it the messiness of experience, over against the neat and tidy system of his interlocutors, that cements Job in his fear of the Lord? And didn't the Teacher follow a similar path? Whitehead is saying that we need to *recognize* the messiness, come to terms with it, not treat it as the final word. Fundamentalisms of all kinds—secular or religious—overlook it, thinking that their systems map the world neatly, without excess.

Linear versus Complex Curricula

Mary: I'm sure that becoming wise does have a great deal to do with learning to tolerate ambiguity and to live with uncertainty. But I need a little time to set the stage.

We noted last time that if we are to understand postmodernism, we need to locate it in relation to modernism. The modernist perspective presupposes a step-by-step, logical, linear progress toward understanding. This is reflected in contemporary approaches to curriculum design, in which "materials are so structured that the 'learning' students do is framed not in terms of their own self-organizing processes—which will have 'gaps'—but as the result of following others' pre-set, logically designed, simply ordered sequential steps" (Doll 1993, 76). It is the same commitment to logical sequencing that we see in Frederick Taylor's time-and-motion studies, the scientific efficiency movement, B. F. Skinner's operant conditioning, and Madeline Hunter's "Seven Steps." As an ally in his opposition to this modernist paradigm, Doll (1993, 76) quotes Dewey's (1938, 48) assertion that "Perhaps the greatest of all pedagogical fallacies is the notion that a person learns only the particular thing he is studying at the time." *That* is to deny the messiness of experience.

Doll (1993, 76–77) suggests that this "particularist perspective" contradicts what we know about how the brain normally functions. He cites Leslie Hart (1983, 60, 76), who writes that the brain is "an amazingly subtle and sensitive *pattern-detecting* apparatus," designed or shaped "to deal with *natural complexity,* not neat 'logical simplicities.'" A curriculum that enhances the brain's abilities, bringing forth "higher order thinking skills," will be "rich in natural complexity and delivered in a manner sensitive to the brain's pattern-detecting devices." In Doll's view, few, if any, curricula have taken this as an explicit goal.

Alison: Actually, I think that all of those books on "brain-based education" (e.g., Caine and Caine 1991; Jensen 1998; Sylwester 1995) are trying to get teachers to recognize the same thing.

Technical Rationality

Colin: Mary, you've already mentioned Donald Schön (1983), and for me he seems to have been one of the most influential writers in helping to develop an alternative to the theory-into-practice paradigm. He uses the term *technical rationality* to describe the view that knowledge is linear, reductionist, scientific, and taxonomic. *Practical* knowledge from this perspective is no more than the *application* of theoretical knowledge. From this, obviously "modernist" standpoint, the knowledge of the expert is generalized and systematized knowledge.

Not so, says Schön: the knowledge of the professional practitioner—

indeed, that of the ordinary person—is precisely *experiential* knowledge that has been refined and reflected upon, but that is often tacit. Problems are approached as unique, personal instances rather than as exemplars of generalized theory. Surprised or puzzled by something, confronted with "uncertainty, instability, uniqueness, and value conflict" (Schön 1983, 50), the practitioner uses intuition, analogies, and metaphors—not universal rules—to help frame or situate a problem. *Frames* are the assumptions and connections in which a problem is ensconced. "When a practitioner becomes aware of his frames, he also becomes aware of the possibility of alternative ways of framing. . . . He takes note of the values and norms to which he has given priority" (Schön 1983, 310).

Susan: There's an interesting clue here. If wisdom is the "realization of value," and there are a variety of evaluative or normative frames available, then wisdom will present itself in varying modes. There is not merely one correct way of framing a problem, such as the theoretical, but a number of different "ways of wisdom." And that also means, as you said before, Mary, that there is a *freedom* involved in the exercise of wisdom that is not possible if our actions are truly constrained by a theoretical framework. Wisdom requires situated understanding, not knowledge abstracted from context. And contexts are always value-laden (though postpositivists tend to say "theory-laden").

Mary: Yes, and this implies, as Doll (1993, 46) points out in his discussion of Schön, that it is not just the practitioner's means, but his or her ends as well that become subject to public scrutiny. Then we can—and should—inquire, just what kinds of value are being sought?

Colin: It's interesting that one of the ways in which Lyotard (1984) characterizes postmodernity (as high modernism) is that it is an addiction to what he calls "performativity." He intends by this a concern with means rather than ends, with efficiency and effectiveness rather than the significance—the value—of the goal being pursued. It is as though the performances of actors are to be valued above the quality of the play in which they are acting. While in certain respects, this is valid—when the focus is indeed legitimately, for example, on casting an actor for a role—an actor's performance in itself cannot replace judgments about which play is more worth staging. Yet this is what Lyotard contends characterizes the postmodern condition.

Mary: Well, plays require dialogue, and it's interesting that Doll (1993, 46) suggests that a third aspect of Schön's practical methodology concerns "dialogue," as though the practitioner is "listening for 'back talk'. . . from the situation and employing the language of metaphor in discussion with the situation. Such an open dialogue—with oneself, with others, with the situation—is key to developing a reflective methodology." It follows from this that while a practical methodology need not become reflective (if dialogue is absent), all reflective methodologies have their origins in practice.

I find this likening of "reflective practice" to a conversation reminiscent of the biblical wisdom perspective, with its emphasis on *hearing* instead of *seeing*. And it seems to me that we can extend this perspective to learning wherever it occurs, not only in the professions. Unproblematic practice is a playful engagement with the situation, but once an anomaly arises, a puzzle presents itself, a second level of reflectivity needs to be entered into.

Kerry: Yes, a notion of "dialogue" breaks through the rigid subject-object dichotomy—the presumed distance between actor and acted upon—seeing them rather as actors together in the one unifying drama. It points toward what we might term a "subject-subject" conception.

Mary: It's interesting that you should put it like that, because from what I understand of Whitehead, he saw the world as a collection of subjects as well. But I think that it is also worth noting in this context what Doll (1993, 184 n. 5) sees as missing from Schön's concept of reflection. This is the process of *distancing* oneself from one's thoughts and actions.

George: "Distancing"—isn't that what *A Vision with a Task* (Stronks and Blomberg 1993) identifies as the second step in coming to know, which they equate in curricular terms with problem-posing?

Alison: You're right, but I wonder how that would fit with Schön?

Kerry: Well, despite my loud applause for a break with a rigid subject-object dichotomy, I think that we have to acknowledge that it contains the germs of some truth. There is a time when we meet a certain resistance in the materials we are dealing with—a stubbornness, obduracy—and that's when we experience a distance. We are no longer, I think, fully immersed in the situation. It can happen in ordinary conversation, as well: things are flowing along nicely, and someone drops a clanger! There is an awkwardness that intrudes, a rift that has to be healed. It is still part of the conversation, but at the same time it stands a little apart from it. I must say that I find the relationship between the straightforwardly practical and the problematically practical, problematic in itself.

Mary: We will need to revisit that, because I agree that it is very hard to pin down. I'm not persuaded that *A Vision with a Task* has succeeded, either. I just want to point out that in Schön's work on "reflective practice," we see the beginnings of what Munby and Russell (1989, 71) call an "epistemology of practice," which "conceives of knowing in terms of the process of 'becoming,' not in terms of the discovery of 'being.'" I think that captures the notion that we are in an ongoing, developing relationship with "situations," rather than the idea that we can achieve an absolute grasp of their essence. It's a more humble, relational view of knowing—much more a "wisdom" view. Schön emphasizes the importance of problem-finding or problem-framing, what Freire terms "problem-posing," whereas technical rationality focuses on problem-*solving*. I agree with Doll (1993, 46–47) that the former are more important than the latter in "our contemporary and rapidly changing world," though my hunch is that it has always been thus.

Susan: That's probably true, but in a postmodern world, the condition of relativity certainly makes the choice of ends—deciding what is actually a problem, and deciding out of a range of problems which one it is that we want to pursue—all the more urgent. But I think that we agree that the choice of ends is properly the province of wisdom, and that this in turn is rooted in a worldview or values framework.

Disequilibrium

Mary: Yes, indeed. We will take a look later on at what Doll says about the importance of "self-organization," and I think that links in quite closely with what we mean by wisdom. But I want to look briefly at Piaget, as we all know how prominent he was in our training, even if his work seems to have sunk from sight somewhat these days.

Doll (1993, 82–83) points out that in Piaget's model of learning, disequilibrium plays a key role. "In trying to overcome disequilibrium—here perturbations, errors, mistakes, confusions—the student reorganizes with more insight and on a higher level than previously attained." (Doll comments on Piaget's assumption of "a sense of Enlightenment progress" in this depiction—in other words, that Piaget is still basically a modernist, and I think that I agree.) He also underscores "that this disequilibrium must be deeply felt or 'far-reaching.' The disequilibrium must be one that is structurally disturbing before reorganization will occur." Piaget believes that organisms, of which students are but one example, will continue in established patterns (equilibrium) as long as possible. If change (learning) is to occur, the perturbations must arouse genuine concern, asking the student "to doubt in a fundamental way the procedures being used and assumptions being made."

George: It seems to me that the discussion so far is pointing us in the direction of the significance of "problem-posing" rather than "problem-solving" in learning. I am not sure, however, in the light of what you have just said, and in terms of a biblical view of the world, that we should agree with Whitehead's characterization of "actual experience" as "radically untidy" and "ill-adjusted." This is a more Hegelian, even Heraclitean, view of a world fundamentally in tension. If Piaget is correct, and organisms will continue in set patterns as long as possible, then it seems as though disequilibrium is not a constant feature of experience, but something that has often to be introduced into it if learning is to occur. Teaching would then be—at least in part—a program of problem-posing. We have to "stir up the ferment" in our students' minds.

Mary: Yes, but there is an important counter to this, which I have been reminded of from time to time when I have talked in terms of "unsettling students." We have to be concerned with establishing a context of security and stability for students, especially in this day and age. So as well as promoting disequilibrium, the teacher is responsible for establishing constraints and providing a framework for learning, otherwise it will result in "unbridled disruption." I am sure that you would agree that the task of classroom management is a much greater practical problem—and hence also, a much greater theoretical problem—than it is for Piaget (Doll 1993, 83).

Kerry: You're telling me! What about that Grade 12 student yesterday who wanted to use the computer when middle school students were having a class—she said she "had a right to," and when I said that they were shared facilities, she told me to stick the computer . . . well, you know where!

George: We know Mandy too well, Kerry. She left my Monday class ten minutes early, skipped the Tuesday class, and then took clippings from a newspaper all through the next one! Sometimes I think that we are too tolerant.

Mary: And the point is, that sometimes students are too "disequilibrated"—and not just intellectually! Although disequilibrium is "the driving force" in development, the crucial factor is in the nature of action itself. I mean, not just any action will do—or should I say, it's not just activity, signs of life, that we want to see in students, we want to see certain kinds of action, satisfying particular criteria.

As far as Piaget is concerned, every transformation or reorganization is an internal reconstruction of external givens (cf. Bringuier 1980, 114). (He does recognize that there is an order and structure to the world, so that in that sense he is not a radical constructivist.) Learners have strategies that come into play not merely to overcome perturbations but because their very nature is to be active. They actively pose problems to the world, not just respond to problems posed. For Piaget, action is the defining characteristic that permeates change throughout all of the developmental stages. Action— "concrete operations" or "concrete experience" in particular—is not just a matter of doing things with the hands, acting on material objects. This is a superficial understanding of what Piaget has in mind: he is always more concerned with actions involving intellectual restructuring. As Doll (1993, 83–84) goes on to say in his discussion of this point, "Such a restructuring and transforming of reality is . . . the teleonomic end of all education, intellectual growth, and personal development."

Kerry: Well, I certainly cannot approve of how Mandy wanted to "restructure reality"! But it strikes me that "restructuring and transforming reality" is pretty much what we have in mind when we talk about "the realization of value," about promoting "purposeful response" in students, though our phrase helps us to keep the value-dimension much more clearly in view and thus not to limit change to the intellectual dimension. I agree with you, Mary, that Piaget is still caught very much within a modernist paradigm, Schön's "technical rationality." But what on earth does Doll mean by "teleonomic"?

George: *Telos* concerns "end" or "purpose"; *nomos* means "law." So I guess that he means that the lawfully regulated purpose of all development is restructuring and transformation.

Self-Reflection

Mary: Well, we should probably see the Mandy episode in positive terms—she needs to learn to respond in ways that take into account the values of respect for the needs and rights of others. That is as much our goal as intellectual development. I think that it helps to remember that Piaget always saw himself as a *philosopher* engaged in the project of "genetic epistemology." He was concerned to abstract these personal structures and build them around forms of logical organization.

Although Jerome Bruner was certainly very much influenced by Piaget—Doll (1993, 83–84) notes that he shares with Piaget "the concept of challenging or pushing personal structures so they are transformed to higher, more comprehensive levels of organization . . ."—Bruner differed from him in particularizing these "to *an* individual within *a* culture. . . ." In other words, he recognizes the situatedness of cognition much more than Piaget did—until, that is, Piaget's later years, when research findings prompted him to acknowledge the importance of individual interest and specialization in cognitive development (see Peterson 1996). Consequently, Bruner places much greater emphasis on the self and self-reflection than Piaget. We can't just look at Mandy in the abstract as an eighteen-year-old: she is Mandy in all her "Mandy-ness"!

George: Madness, more like it! One of the younger teachers asked me the other day if kids had changed much since I started teaching twenty years ago. I said I thought they were pretty much the same, but I do think that I would have to admit that there is much less respect for authority—no, just less respect for persons—these days. Of course, I recall that that's what my parents would have said, too!

Susan: Does that have to do with "incredulity toward metanarratives"? If there is nothing beyond my own experience that is validating, why should I take anyone else's word for it?

But I think that what we are talking about here is another important feature of a wisdom (as well as of a postmodern) paradigm. One certainly gets the impression from Piaget that there is an immutability about cognitive development, as though the cultural context is largely irrelevant. I don't see how we can ignore the particular situation in forming judgments, and an important feature of our situation is that kids live in a world where there are few certainties, few values that are not up for grabs.

Mary: That's all the more reason we have to encourage self-reflection, to help students to step back from their actions and to evaluate their own behavior. I think that has to be an organic part of our understanding of curriculum. I hope that you don't mind another technical term, but more recently, Bruner has written about "recursion theory." *Recursion* is a word that derives from the Latin *recurrere*—"to run back"—which is linked to *curriculum* through its verbal root form—"running the course." By this he means that:

> each statement or proposition is re-examined in terms of re-looking at its original foundational assumptions . . . as one steps back or "distances one's self" from one's creation. A hermeneutic reflection where "the mind turns around on itself," creating both a "summary of its capacities" and a "sense of self" (1986, p. 97), is one where new possibilities emerge, where transcendence occurs. (Doll 1993, 123)

In fact, I heard someone at a conference recently suggest that for Bruner, recursion is a central human characteristic. If I link that to Bruner's seminal involvement in *Man: A Course of Study* (Bruner 1966), where the focus was on what it means to be human and how one "can become more so," there are some interesting lines of thought to follow up. I guess we are more familiar with the notion of "metacognition" as a way of describing the process he is talking about.

George: Yes, and there's that notion of "distancing" again. And Van Brummelen (1988, 50ff.) takes up the idea of transcendence in his book, where he describes it as the final stage in the rhythm of learning.

Mary: You're right, and like Van Brummelen and in a significant way, Bruner builds transcendence into his conception of curriculum, because that should not just be a fixed structure, something given once and for all. It should also "turn around on itself"—it should "spiral"—for the same concepts can be revisited many times with profit, at increasing levels of sophistication, which is what Hilda Taba used to say all curriculum should do.

Narrative and Metaphor

Bruner believes that the act of meaning-making, a "push to organize experience," is innate to humans. He regards this as a "*radical thesis*," the radicalness of which consists in the assertion that we do this "narratively," not logically (Bruner 1990, 79). Logical thinking, as favored by Piaget and the positivists, *succeeds* rather than *precedes* the narrative, which is more natural and less formal; he thus speaks of a "narrational" search for meaning (Doll 1993, 128–29).

Colin: I would think that this "push to organize experience" is what we mean by *religion*, at least in part. Humans are meaning-making creatures, because we are made in the image of God. Perhaps meaning-*finding* would be better—creation already is meaningful, we don't make it so. And meaning involves looking for coherence, seeing how things are related to one another and hang together, what order there is in the world. Wasn't Viktor Frankl (1963) on about this in his logotherapy?

Alison: There is an interesting thought here in what Bruner says about narrative. Of course, an emphasis on story seems to be one of the characteristics of postmodernity. I think that he is hinting at something *other than* the rational, but it is, in fact, a different kind of "rationality." We might even call it "narrationality." Is it not the case that we are nurtured in stories of various kinds from the time that we enter the world? Does not the language that we speak embody a particular way of seeing the world? More specifically, does not the language of our family circle shape our way of seeing the world? There is a "logic" to this way of seeing and being that cannot be reduced to a formal logical level. I think that that is where Piaget so often went wrong, in assuming that children's explanations were not logical, when really they embodied a different form of rationality, their own internal logic. Why shouldn't trees be drawn growing outwards rather than up from a mountain? That's the way they look to kids standing on the ground.

Mary: Well, Bruner certainly regarded the narrative—or "humanistic"— as a mode of knowing in its own right. He felt that it comprises *multiple perspectives, presuppositions*, and *subjectifications* (Bruner 1986, ch. 2), drawing "its meanings from the heuristics of metaphor not from the validity of logic. . . . Here, meaning is personally created and historically generated, not just empirically discovered and validly proved." As different as the narrative and analytical modes are, they are complementary, and "Bruner believes they should be integrated, producing a curriculum that utilizes both the methods of hermeneutics and the canons of logic. Such a curriculum would encourage us to think of knowledge in a new light" (Doll 1993, 124).

George: Again, that resonates for me with *A Vision with a Task*. They talk about a rhythm of immersion, withdrawal, and return, and a curricular rhythm to match it of play, problem-posing, and purposeful response. I don't think that one could map Bruner onto that precisely, but I think that there is something there about going with the flow of everyday experience—maybe its narrative structure, its timedness—as well as standing over against it from time to time to take stock, though not necessarily in only a logical manner. I would think that the logical would be only one mode of distancing, in their schema of multiple ways of knowing. It's like Schön says about bringing different frames, different value positions, to bear in formulating a problem.

Mary: I think that the idea of narrative ties in with what Doll (1993, 110) says about the significance of metaphor in our day and age. He suggests that a "more liberated use of metaphor is one of the key features of post-modernism." It is another expression of the impulse to escape systematic, unequivocal, one might say one-dimensional, typifications of experience that are characteristic of modernism. One—if not the—key metaphors of the twentieth century is "'turbulence' (Hayles, 1990), a focus on which may require not only new mathematical and scientific concepts but also new epistemological and metaphysical ones (Kitchener, 1988) . . . ." (Doll 1993, 90).

Alison: It strikes me that that is what metaphors themselves do—they introduce turbulence into our otherwise stable systems of meaning, into our taken-for-granted concepts (which, paradoxically, are themselves so often dead metaphors!). They are problem-posing devices. Postmodernity is itself a shaking up of the accepted categories that constitute the modernist frame.

A Postmodern Curriculum Paradigm?
Mary: From Doll's viewpoint in 1993 (and his manuscript was obviously completed much earlier than this), a postmodern curriculum paradigm was still in its infancy. Interestingly, because somewhat paradoxically, he suggests that "[n]o coherent *theory* has yet emerged to unite the disparate trends—constructive and deconstructive—inherent in the paradigm"— and note that I emphasize *theory,* which is where I see the paradox. Not that he thinks that such coherence will be easily won, for it is the very genius of a postmodern paradigm that it does seek to incorporate rather than to repudiate these divergent trends. As far as he can see, one of the greatest hurdles that traditional education will have to surmount is just this utilization of "paradoxes, anomalies, indeterminacies" (Doll 1993, 128).

Doll (1993, 110) believes that a postmodern perspective leads to a more open view of education and curriculum, in which nonanalytic (Oliver, 1989), metaphoric, and narrative modes can find their rightful place. If he is correct, then I think that there are exciting possibilities for what we can achieve here, in the provision of alternative learning pathways, such as those our Vocational Education and Training program has begun to address, but by no means limited to this. And an approach to education that embedded paradoxes and anomalies at the heart of its process would help a great deal in breaking away from a modernist—and I have to say, nonbiblical—view of learning.

Kerry: Well, if one of the effects of postmodernity is to bring about changes in parental expectations, as well as in government requirements, we have cause to be hopeful. I wonder, however, if I will be around long enough to see this happen! It seems to me that education is still very much in the grip of modernist assumptions.

Mary: Insofar as these assumptions include a view of knowledge as being concerned solely with assessing how accurately our ideas mirror reality, I think that you are right. What we will seek in its stead is to develop an understanding of knowledge as *generative,* "that 'endows our lived experiences' with meaning." This "will deal not merely with truth but with playfulness, paradox, complexity and indeterminacy. . . . This will be a hermeneutical, not a positivist, epistemology" (Doll 1993, 110–11). I presume that what he means by *hermeneutical* is an emphasis on the importance of interpretation, rather than the idea that one can just read off the face of the world the way things really are.

Susan: Thanks, I was wondering! But "playfulness, paradox, complexity, indeterminacy"—these are all aspects of life that we also say need to be honored if we are to take the biblical perspective on wisdom seriously. I like it! And I can see why you would need to emphasize the importance of interpretation in the context of such ambiguity.

Self-Organization

Mary: I am glad that in all of these technicalities I have been able to stimulate at least a modicum of enthusiasm. But Doll does have one more thing to say that I think is important, if you will bear with me a little longer. He believes that *self-organization* is the feature that most distinguishes the postmodern from the modern paradigm. Not surprisingly, then, he also regards it as the characteristic with the greatest implications

145

for curriculum, and notes that for Piaget "self-organization is the essence of life itself"; it underlies both assimilation and accommodation, and one without the other is inevitably destructive. It is only through their interactions that "growth, maturity, and development occur" (Doll 1993, 158).

Just as for Piaget, equilibration brings contrary tendencies into balance, postmodernism calls into question "the rigid dichotomies" deriving from Cartesianism. Doll (1993, 158–59) contends, however, that a holistic perspective will not encompass a "bland and entropic equilibrium, where everything meshes into everything else"—a kind of gruel or overcooked stew, in which the individual flavors and textures have been lost. I guess that by *entropic*, he means a running down and loss of the energy that comes from the tensions between contraries. He talks rather of a "transformative union" resulting "from differing qualities, substances, ideologies, selves combining in new and (thermo)dynamic ways." And he thinks that self-organization is what underlies this transformation. As far as he is concerned, the only alternative to considering self-organization as an essential quality is the "assumption that all being changes from its present state only through external force," as formulated by Newton in the First Law of Motion (Doll 1993, 158–59).

Alison: Your mention of Newton, and earlier of Descartes, reminds me that Toulmin (1992, 108) describes the Cartesian dichotomy as "the chief girder in [the] framework of modernity," and then he goes on to list a dozen other dichotomies supported by this central one. One of these is the belief that "the material substance of physical nature is essentially inert" (111). This belief continued virtually, though not entirely, unchallenged into the twentieth century, when John Dewey was one of the first philosophers to recognize the significance of Heisenberg's quantum mechanics for overturning this view of nature as a giant machine (147).

Mary: Yes, Doll's take on this seems to point similarly to the effect of the New Physics on the postmodern worldview.

Colin: It's that hoary philosophical question about freedom and determinism that we looked at in Philosophy 101—and I failed my only essay ever! But without going down that road again, it looks to me as though Doll is grappling with what Whitehead said was necessary if we are to approach wisdom: "Freedom in the presence of knowledge." I think that human freedom is ultimately the ability to *value* one thing above another, to make choices and decisions about what is most or more important in life. It is "response-ability." And one is then *impelled* by a commitment to it, rather than being constrained by robotic knowledge that *compels* a certain course of action, and one course only. Wisdom requires the capacity, the space—capaciousness!—in which to choose, not so that we might act arbitrarily, but so that "obedience to truth might be practiced." The seeming paradox in this notion of *obedience* is that valuing is always a response to what is of value; we are creatures defined by responsibility.

Mary: It's like the quotation from Schön (1983, 310) that I read earlier. Let me just dig it out again. Here it is: "When a practitioner becomes aware of his frames, he also becomes aware of the possibility of alternative ways of framing the reality of his practice. He takes note of the values and norms to which he has given priority." I think that I have learned from my reading of Doll that wisdom requires the freedom to self-organize according to deliberately chosen norms.

George: I remember being at an Australian College of Education conference in Sydney in 1988, at Saint Joseph's College, and hearing a keynote by a psychologist, Wilf Jarvis. He pointed out the fallacy in Abraham Maslow's (1950) hierarchy of human needs that put "self-actualization" at the top of a pyramid, on the assumption that one could only "self-actualize" when one's more basic needs had been met. He told the story of addressing an audience one time in which a wheelchair-bound Vietnam veteran vehemently disputed this claim, saying that the drive to self-actualization—to the realization of that which one holds to be of value—is the most basic human impulse, that indeed, he had been willing to lose his legs to save the lives of his mates—and he didn't regret it, nor did he feel that he was any less of a person as a result—on the contrary!

Kerry: I can remember even further back than the Bicentennial, George, to when I was at university in the sixties—"self-actualization" was all the buzz. If Doll is right about self-organization, I think that I have been surrounded by postmodernism for most of my life! But I know that even Descartes would agree with Calvin that self-realization is impossible without some realization of God.

Alison: And that seems to me to bring us back to the confession that the fear of the Lord is the beginning of wisdom!

9

The Getting of Wisdom

Wisdom is supreme; therefore get wisdom, though it cost you all you have. . . .
Proverbs 4:7

Bob Clifford is a leading engineering entrepreneur who was a dunce. He did not pass the test for entry into the public high school, so his parents enrolled him in a nongovernment school. He proceeded to fail everything there, too, including woodwork. He copied most of his homework from friends and, not surprisingly, failed the Schools Board Examination. Yet from his boatyard in Hobart, Tasmania, Clifford runs a large and efficient organization that turns out some of the world's most innovative aluminum car ferries, which he himself designed, and which are sailed across the globe to ply the waters of the Baltic Sea or north to the cities of Asia (Mant 1997).

Who Are Schools For?

Bob Clifford is a prime example of the maxim that schools are poor predictors of success in later life, except in those areas that are homologous to schooling, especially academia. This should be no surprise, as academics exercise an influence on schooling that bends it to the model of knowledge and the person that they favor. Of course, their intention is not insidious; but they too often forget that the demands of the professions and of the disciplines for expert practitioners are not the same demands that face schools, which must seek to ensure that all are educated to their fullest potential.

Hence—and sadly—one of the concrete realities of schooling in Western culture is that it is academically elitist. As Pring comments in the English context:

> Success eludes too many. Of the 25 per cent of 16-year-olds who embark on "A" level courses ("the jewel in the crown," "the gold standard" of our educational system), over 30 per cent will either drop out or fail in any one subject. Of the 75 per cent of 16-year-olds, the majority will terminate their education at the first opportunity, having experienced little but failure in the attempts of the school to initiate them into "the conversation of mankind." (Pring 1993, 57)

Bowles and Gintis's (1976) classic study demonstrates the sorting function of schools—some are selected for the managerial elite, others are destined by their failure to be workers at lower rungs in the employment hierarchy—even in that supposedly most democratic and classless of all societies, the United States. But as Mant (1997, 161) says, if "natural capacity is not uniform, then the uniform school is by definition unfair to those who don't fit the mould."

It is my conviction that we cannot continue to live with this unfairness. Schools (and the society that supports them) have a responsibility to those they currently "sort out"—the connotations of recrimination and exclusion being foremost here. A wisdom perspective promises an approach to schooling—pluriform, rather than uniform, and oriented to character rather than focused on intellect—that would address this current inequity.

I am motivated by concern for those whose obvious talents go unrecognized, unrewarded, and which indeed, are often denigrated by schools. The Bible's teaching on the gifts that God has given to each and every one goes hand in hand with its central injunction to seek God's Kingdom and justice, for justice requires that everyone be given his or her due, that all people be respected for whom they are, and that all people be treated with integrity. And justice is one of the prime values that wisdom seeks to realize.

Thus, the shape we choose to give to formal education, whether at the level of system, school, or classroom, is fundamentally an issue of justice. It is a matter of dealing fairly and equitably with the lives of people who are compelled to submit to a regime imposed upon them, in the first place, by the state and, in the second, more and more by economic necessity and structural unemployment, because it is supposed to do them good. If it does not indeed do the bulk of them good, how can its continuance be justified?

The "Duran Rule," formulated in a management context, suggests that where there is a problem, 85 percent of the time it is in the system, and only 15 percent of the time is it with the worker (Hough and Paine 1997, 184). If we were to put the question to the schooling system in the case of Bob Clifford, a man of obvious breadth and depth of ability, who failed? Was it the worker or the system?

You are perhaps familiar with the episode of *Yes Minister*, in which the Rt Hon. James Hacker—a "Secretary of Administration," in American terms—was taken to view a new hospital (Lynn and Jay 1982, 11–40). His hosts were proud, for it was a model of efficiency: the administration, catering, cleaning, and maintenance staff, a complement of doctors and nurses, rows upon rows of neatly made beds—but no patients! While the Minister was rightly appalled, the hospital itself illustrated the self-justifying and self-perpetuating nature of many bureaucracies and professions (epitomized also in the Circumlocution Office of Dickens' *Little Dorrit*). There was no mess here, least of all the mess of operating tables.

As is true for so many episodes of the series, this satirizing of the bureaucratic mentality, of technical rationality run rampant, is telling. With the Minister, we are shocked by the waste of all of these resources that are meant to be helping to heal the sick. Effective hospitals are those that deal compassionately and expertly with real, live—and dying—people. At their core, they are messy places, because the patients that present to them arrive often with ill-defined problems requiring sensitive diagnosis and tactful treatment. Unfortunately, we all have our horror stories of people left to suffer hour after hour in the corner of emergency rooms because they cannot be accommodated within prescribed routines.

Similarly sad to say, many schools have been exemplars of this bureaucratic syndrome. They are places in which the world has been cleaned up and neatly packaged, and woe betide students who are not appreciative of the gifts with which they are presented, their own gifts notwithstanding. If modernism is out of favor in certain cloistered quadrangles, it remains the dominant paradigm in most professions—and in politicians' programs for them. Thus, despite the best intentions of individual teachers, teaching is still conceived by many as a knowledge industry in which the demands of the disciplines take precedence over the needs of students. In the words of Richard Bawden:

> our entire formal education system has been grounded in belief of learning as the pervasive accumulation of preserved quanta of knowledge, generated from experience often long forgotten and certainly remote to the contemporary student. The model forges an awful reliance on both the aggregation of specialised and selective packages of second-hand information and on those who disseminate it to us in the name of teaching. (Bawden 1985, 44)

Properly conceived, teaching, like medicine, is a "helping profession," one in which the intention is that students might learn. Teaching is a task oriented to an achievement. No matter how one decides curriculum content, unless it can be effectively learned, it is of no use. All teachers teach *something,* and they teach it to *someone,* and perhaps one would not like to argue for the priority of either. Nonetheless, a thorough academic grasp of a subject is insufficient to make a good teacher: the notion of teacher subsumes both dimensions. The mark of good teachers is that they are able to promote learning (though it is, of course, central to my argument that not just any kind of learning will suffice).

If the teacher's concern is first and foremost with the grasp of a body of knowledge, students can only be measured in terms of whether they attain it: knowledge is seen as a possession, and some have more of it than others. But if we take the nurture of the child as our central concern, then we will be interested first and foremost in the ongoing learning of this or that child, rather than seeking to ensure that some absolute standard is attained (cf. Kelly 1986, 114). The question of methodology then is not just a question of *how* one teaches the *what*. Teaching and learning are always of or about *something*, but that something is—in a qualified sense—secondary. There will certainly be things that are more worth learning than others, but the qualification is that there is no point in deciding that children should learn something if they are—for whatever reason—unable to learn it. I am not counseling a "comfortable curriculum," one without effort, struggle, and plain "hard work." But just as sports medicine can help to determine the particular activity to which an athlete is best suited, the field in which he or she is most likely to reap the rewards of blood, sweat, and tears, curriculum and pedagogy must be tailored to the gifts of the child.

In schools as in hospitals, I reiterate that this is an issue of justice: the curriculum must be inclusive, attending first and foremost to what will promote the most effective learning on the part of all students. If doctors were more concerned with those patients who gave them the opportunity to practice their favorite therapies and ignored or gave minimal care to those whom they knew required different, perhaps less medically "interesting" treatment, we would be rightly dismayed. How much more so ought we be by those who might not destroy the body but snuff out the inner life!

Many people are, of course, aware of this. The following editorial locates this discussion in contemporary political debate, echoing Bantick (whom I quoted in Chapter 6), but broadening his critique beyond a concern for boys:

> There is no reason to doubt that Education Minister Alan Carpenter is well intentioned in his proposal to raise the mandatory school leaving age to 17, as he is in his willingness to fund a shortfall in parent school fees.
>
> Although both propositions are likely to attract some community support, they are also likely to prove to be troublesome over time. In particular, few people would dispute that keeping all youngsters at school until they are 17 is a fine ideal, but in practical terms, it would lead to more discipline problems.
>
> The point is that students leave school at 15 or 16 because they don't like it. They don't believe it offers them what they want or need— it doesn't seem relevant to their immediate concerns. Perhaps some also

resent the imposition of rules and routines when they are impelled to assert their independence and individuality.

To compel such students to attend school is to ask for trouble. Schools already know the difficulties dealing with some students who would rather be somewhere else—in some cases almost anywhere else.

Mr Carpenter says that allowing children to quit school at 15 in the 21st century is criminal. This might be an overstatement, but his drift is right.

Ours is an increasingly complex society and most young people need to master a range of relatively sophisticated skills to survive, let alone flourish. The chances of 15-year-old school drop-outs finding rewarding jobs and building fulfilling lives diminish rapidly as the world around them demands more advanced skills.

The solution, as Mr Carpenter implies, is more (and better) schooling. But the way to achieve this is not through compulsion. Youngsters will attend school in what are the present post-compulsory years if they can see that is has something of value to offer them.

The challenge for schools is, or should be, to provide the type of courses and teaching styles that deliver value for young people whose natural strengths are not in academic pursuits—and to be seen to be doing so. Of course, schools have been changing along such lines for some years.

But the retention rate in the government sector for upper-level high school students of just 61 per cent (compared with 75 per cent in private schools) suggests that more change is needed. If Mr Carpenter has an enthusiasm for reform, this is where it should be directed. ("Make Schools More Responsive" 2002)

The author could not have better summarized my central contention: "The challenge for schools is . . . to provide the type of courses and teaching styles that deliver value for young people whose natural strengths are not in academic pursuits—and to be seen to be doing so." Delivering value—seeking its realization.

With the author as well, I acknowledge that schools have seen significant changes in the required direction for some time. However, I believe that the ideology underlying institutionalized schooling needs to be challenged radically and a viable alternative portrayed, if these changes are to be sufficiently thoroughgoing.

The "Sacred Story": The Hegemony of Theory over Practice

Though the term *ways of knowing* is relatively new in academic discourse, the attempt to differentiate knowledge is as old as human reflection.[10] In the main, however, the concern has been with a differentiation of "real" knowledge from what only masqueraded as knowledge. The classic example of this is Plato's "divided line," but his most telling image is contained in the Allegory of the Cave (Plato 1955, 274–286). It would be anachronistic to suggest that the meanings that he gave to such terms as *metanoia* and *parakletikon* carried the same meanings as they do in the New Testament (viz., *repentance/conversion* and *counselor/advocate*, respectively), yet it would be similarly so to suggest that the meanings are unrelated. As we have earlier seen, what Plato thought learning entailed was a turning away from appearances to face what he regarded as reality, a conversion *from* the concrete and particular *to* the general and abstract. The counselor that was to help with this transformation of the mind was none other than arithmetic.[11] The pre-Socratic, Platonic, and Aristotelian conviction that the only true object of knowing must be eternal is a further indicator of the religiosity of knowing, as the quest for that which will never let one down, that of which one can be certain and on which one can always rely (cf. Rotenstreich 1977, 4–9).

I have previously noted Connelly and Clandinin's (1994, 89) claim that there is a story so universal and taken for granted in Western culture that it can legitimately be described as sacred. According to them, the "theory-practice story . . . creates a pervasive moral structure governing the actions" of people in our culture and, specifically, "the actions of university and school people." This story then is not merely an issue of how we think, because it concerns how people should and do relate to one another: *it creates a pervasive moral structure*. And this, of course, is the story that has come to be known as "modernity."

A trenchant and accessible critique of modernity is found in John Ralston Saul's (1993) *Voltaire's Bastards: The Dictatorship of Reason in the West*. In characterizing modernity, Saul writes:

> [R]ational structures, moral beliefs and representative government have been confused as one in people's minds. . . . [W]hile structures reign supreme, man's sense of right and wrong is in frenzied confusion. . . .
>
> None of this would have been possible had the people themselves not been seduced by the religion of reason . . . accept[ing] that such things as expertise, administration and efficiency were irrefutable values. . . . (Saul 1993, 247)

It is not Voltaire but his illegitimate children whom Saul holds in contempt, those who have defaced what Voltaire bequeathed. Where Voltaire epitomized rationality in pursuit of moral ends, these children have exalted structure and methodology, rational planning and systems to the be-all and end-all of human behavior, devoid of all attention to values other than these.[12] There is no overarching normative framework, no larger encompassing story, no metanarrative—except, that is, the value of Reason. It matters not what script one is enacting, it is how well one performs that counts: "performativity" is key. And Saul charges that education systems, at all levels, have been designed to further this "religion of reason," to reproduce and reinforce the values of the "rational class."

Thus, in a specifically educational context, one form this story has taken is Piaget's project of genetic epistemology, which theorizes that as children mature they move from concrete to formal operations, from the merely here and now to the abstract and theoretical. This unilinear development, though supposedly mirrored in moral and faith development (Fowler 1981; Goldman 1968; Kohlberg 1984), decreed a vertical differentiation of students, sorting out the artisans from the philosopher-kings. Propositional knowledge or formal operations, the level of the most generalizable, is the goal to which all are called, but for which few are chosen.

I would once more emphasize Connelly, Clandinin, and Saul's claim: we are dealing with a pervasive value framework, though one that pretends to be altogether free of values. And these authors indicate the religious character of this framework.

Lovers of Wisdom or Acquirers of Knowledge?

Like Saul, Wolterstorff (1983) has rightly chided Western philosophy for considering rationality in the abstract, whereas it is always embedded in a context. Where Saul focuses on the value-laden context of human action, this is an instance (though one of great significance) of the more general understanding that what is rational depends on the conditions to which a person in a community is responding. Whereas the logic of the proposition demands that all swans are white, at a certain point it becomes not only rational to believe, but impossible not to acknowledge, that there are black swans—or, for that matter, egg-laying, duck-billed mammals.

Educational researchers have explored the notion that cognition is not only situated in an environment but also distributed across it, so that we share our understanding with the tools that we use (Brown, Collins, and Duguid, 1989). Watching a potter at work at the wheel is a vivid reminder of how connected to a context cognition can be: there is strenuous bodily thinking at work here. Watching myself at work preparing this chapter is a further timely reminder that I labor with a language, I wrestle with the previous words I have written, and I work with what so many others have had to say on related topics.

155

The Timed Bodiliness of Wisdom

The notion of situated cognition resonates well with the biblical wisdom tradition, which presents an alternative to the "sacred story" (cf. Blomberg 1997, 1998). I wish to focus here on the historical-experiential nature of understanding, its timed bodiliness, to which this tradition points.

Melchert (1998) points out in his study of the implications of the Wisdom Literature for education that the Western tradition has had a strong tendency to regard the physical and the sensual as less worthy components of human experience. This has the pedagogical corollary that the concrete is of lesser value, and the greater the level of abstraction from the particular the better. But as I have argued in many ways already, in conscious repudiation of Descartes and all who are his heirs (including "Voltaire's bastards"), knowledge comes from looking outward, not inward. It comes from recognizing the connectedness that one has with one's environment, from being connected to start with. It is only by thinking away these connections, primarily by thinking away one's bodiliness and turning one's inner eye on the ideas within,[13] that one is faced with the problem of escaping from the discomfort of this disconnection. The normal human response to the smell of smoke is, "What's burning?" and we look immediately for its source. The fact that we might be mistaken, and thus find no fire, does not delegitimize the search: responsiveness to our environment is no guarantor of infallibility, at the same time that our fallibility is not a contradiction of our connectedness.

It is to the Pragmatists that general philosophical discourse owes the recognition that the subject-object dualism is an intellectual imposition and that concomitantly, skepticism is parasitic, not primal. Rather than standing over against, we start in contact, in touch with the world, not from a position of estrangement and doubt, but from one of engagement and trust. From the time that we were knit together in our mothers' wombs, we are immersed in a world from which we only gradually and only ever partially individuate.[14]

We can blame it on Descartes, but over him looms the figure of Plato. For Plato, the goal of human life was *escape* from immersion, from the merely human existence of the Cave, to meet the Good and participate in its nature. Rather than recognizing the connections implicit in our incarnateness, he would have us *re*-cognize the eternal truths with which we were acquainted in a previous ex-carnate existence. This is his way of resolving the dilemma of the *Meno,* that we cannot seek to know what we do not already know, and yet, we do come to know new things. But if this *re-*

cognition is of what we already know through concrete experience, of that with which we are already in touch, but of which we as yet cannot speak, the dilemma is resolved much more parsimoniously.

And it is, of course, Plato and his heirs who also cast a shadow over the *theologizing* of Christianity, the transformation of Christian faith into a system of theological thinking. The history of Christianity would have been quite different if the incarnation of Christ and his and our bodily resurrection—and indeed, Adam and Eve's *knowledge* of each other—had been treated with full seriousness. If it had been taken to be saying something fundamentally different about the nature of the world and of our relation to it than the stories emerging from the groves of Athens, an incarnational epistemology of not just embodiedness but bodiliness would have alerted us to the fact that being has many different modes, of which seeing (*theoria*) is only one. And this means, of course, that it would take history, the daily changing experience of the material world in which we live, seriously.

In wisdom perspective, bodily existence is not something to escape from, but something to revel in. And it is the fact that we are bodily that brings with it the necessity to choose, not merely to contemplate; in this respect, though a purely spiritual being might *choose* to choose—one presumes (contra Ockham) that a sovereign and omnipotent God did not *have* to create the world—we are *compelled* to do so. In my mind, in my dreams, in my waking fantasies, I can be anywhere or anyone I like. In my body, I can only be one thing in one place at one time: moment by moment, I confront the need to choose who, where, and when this will be. Thus, the problem with Plato's philosopher-kings was how to entice them to return to the Cave to do their political duty, how to coax them back from the "real world" of the Forms to the world of appearance, the world of change and human action. You may recall Rorty's (1979, 61) claim that the philosophers had given up the quest for wisdom in exchange for a quest for certainty. How true is this of schools also?

The quest of theory is certainty in all situations; that of wisdom is context-sensitive judgment. As Jerome Bruner observes:

> While meanings relating to intentional states, to human actions and its vicissitudes, and to cultural normativity can, within limits, be translated into the propositional forms of a logical calculus . . . they risk degradation in the process. For although propositional translation always works toward the decontextualization of meanings, intersubjective, actional, and normative meaning making remain stubbornly context dependent. Construing the meaning of the condolence "I know how awful it feels to lose a close friend" is no mere exercise in propositional

calculus. It requires pure "psychologism." Its meaning lies in its appropriateness. And its appropriateness is context bound. Its context, moreover, is the story into which it can be fitted. (Bruner 1996, 97)

Although the educational literature is replete with references to rational autonomy, it is not the intellect in abstraction from the world that is the source of human autonomy, but bodiliness; reflection is the weighing up of possible alternative *actions*.[15] We cannot be certain of the outcome; indeed, many of the outcomes of human action are essentially unpredictable, because we cannot in our finitude account for the all-but-infinite variables. We can only exercise our best judgment. Learning is in this (Popper's) sense, trial and error-*correction*.

The weighing of actions takes precedence over the validation of propositions. Plato's model for knowing was propositional, whereas the biblical wisdom model is personal; rather than a correspondence relation between propositions and reality—where the very nature of correspondence remains "mystical" (Putnam 1995)—to know something more intimately is to be in the right (just, ordinate, lawful, appropriate) relation to that thing. Plato's model was logical, whereas the biblical model is religious. Thomas Aquinas's perspective on faith as "assent to propositions" betrays the extent to which Hellenistic notions of truth infected the Christian faith. Truth is essential to knowledge, but truth (like troth) is a matter of faithful relationship. In this respect, we understand what it means that an arrow flies true to its target, a dog is true to its nature, a blade is true, and a person is true to form or to character, to him- or herself.

Instantiating Values

Our best judgment is wisdom, the instantiating of values in action (Aspin, Chapman, and Wilkinson 1994, 50). Wisdom is a characteristic of actions before—indeed, always more than—it is a property of propositions. We value this course of action in preference to that one: it is out of the need to choose that values emerge and are identified. Values (subjectively considered) are higher order beliefs, ones that are accorded and in turn help to determine priority amid the otherwise "blooming, buzzing confusion" (though I echo James with tongue in cheek). We notice the smell of smoke and focus our attention, search our environment for its source. This search takes on importance for us, it directs our bodily energies. All noticing is e--*value*-ating, a judgment as to the significance of that which we confront. It is noticing that constitutes beliefs, responses to states of affairs that are not just undergone but of which note is taken. Epistemologically, then, the distinction between facts and values is one of their relative significance, for both alike are framed within a web of belief and underdetermined by the data.

It is in confronting choices that much learning occurs. Experience poses problems to us, and we pose problems to experience; as we act, we are acted upon. An appropriate metaphor for this interaction is that learning is coming to be more in touch, in contact. It is not so much a matter of possession as it is of participation (cf. Sfard 1998; van der Hoeven 1995; Van Manen 1991). It is coming to be in a more intimate relationship with things.

Intimacy respects the integrity of that with which one relates. "The real host values are, particularly, the trio of truth, respect and justice, all . . . acknowledgments of the independent value of objects of experience" (Walsh 1993, 107). It does not violate or oppress the other, but sensitively seeks out its core, entering into it empathically. It is a relation of mutual giving, rather than of standing over against. In this intimacy, the other discloses or reveals itself to us and we respond (if we are acting normatively) in appreciation, not mastery or possession. Wisdom is not stolen from the gods, it is freely given. In the words of Thomas Berry, the world is a communion of subjects, not objects.[16]

Learning is thus not singularly of propositions; in this, Plato was correct. It is being in relationship with the True.[17] To be more intimate is to be in the right relation to something.

Co-responding in Complexity

There is indeed something mysterious, if not "mystical," about the relationship that I am trying to portray. In a world turned toward us as revelation, speaking with the voice of God, we are indeed talking of a *co-responding* relationship. This is what Dooyeweerd (1953) was seeking to describe in terms of an *integral subject-object-relation,* a two-way responsiveness functioning in all aspects of experience. This co-responsiveness is in place of *correspondence,* the attempt by the knowing subject to capture in analytical-symbolic terms the fullness of functioning of the to-be-known object. On this view, learning does not *reflect* experience, it remains immersed within it; "reflection" as a metaphor introduces too great a distance.

What is "right" is the achieving of valued (properly, valuable or *normative*) goals. Among these are theoretical objectives (such as the solving of quadratic equations), economic objectives (using one's limited resources wisely to meet one's family's needs and to save for future requirements), lingual objectives (formulating a sentence or a paragraph to communicate one's intent clearly), and so on. In each of these and similar cases, the test of achievement is intrinsic to the task: it is the test of completion, when one can move on in pursuit of other goals. Extrinsically, it is the test of growth, when one's capacity to deal with other problems has been expanded. This, too, acknowledges the historical (and responsible) character of human experience.

Valuing is a variant of loving, of acknowledging the worthiness of the beloved. "One learns to know only what one loves, and the deeper and fuller the knowledge is to be, the more powerful and vivid must be the love, indeed the passion" (Goethe 1963, 83). In loving, one enters into relationship—or responds to the demands of an existing relationship hitherto unrecognized—and is called to the task of fidelity in this relationship. What it means to value properly or appropriately is decreed by the particular relationship, and according to the character of that with which or whom one is relating.

I ought to love my wife in a manner different from how I love anyone else; but similarly, I ought to love my children in a manner befitting their special relationship to me. But this does not mean that I will love each of my children in exactly the same way, without respect for their uniqueness, nor that another husband will love his wife in just the way that I love mine, without regard for the differences between the four people. Though today we find his first phrase grating and would prefer a phrase such as *to treat with integrity*, the Puritan John Durie has nonetheless captured what I am talking about here when he said that the purpose of knowledge is "to make use of the Creatures for that whereunto God hath made them" (cit. Taylor 1989, 232). Aristotle had something similar in mind when he wrote (in the *Nicomachean Ethics*, 1953, 6) that, though it is easy to be angry, it is by no means easy "to be angry with the right person, to the right degree, at the right time, for the right purpose, and in the right way": "rightness" is a measure of appropriateness, aptness, to the person, situation, and purpose to hand. It is a matter of according them the value befitting their unique station, a normatively purposeful response.

As the examples of family relationships could well demonstrate, there are many different factors that enter into the decisions that we make. Judgment is required as much in weighing up these different values as it is in identifying the other complexities of the situation. In this respect, one can say that actions are always overdetermined: there is never just one thing going on. Thus, when a person is heard explaining their actions to someone, and the explanation differs from the one he or she gave to you, there is as often as not no deceit involved, but a different calculus of salience operative, a different way of measuring what is relevant to that person in comparison with what was pertinent to you. The four gospels, each with their different purposes and different audiences, are paradigmatic examples of this principle; we are willing to assume that contradictions are apparent only.

In any particular situation, a multiplicity of norms, of creation's call and invitation to us, is at work. Each action is an attempt to simultaneously realize this complex of values—to satisfy as many demands (pressing questions) as one can, with respect to their relative priority. If we were to revise his pragmatic utilitarianism by a creational understanding of normativity, we may understand the realities that William James is addressing when he writes, "Since everything which is demanded is by that fact a good, must not the guiding principle for ethical philosophy . . . be simply to satisfy at all times *as many demands as we can?*" (McDermott 1977, 610–11).

The significant question in determining value and priority is, which beliefs one would be least willing to give up. These constitute one's core values and, fundamentally, one's religious commitment. These value-beliefs comprise a worldview, the frame within which all else is judged.

Grounded Normative Dispositions

In place of the "Justified True Belief" account of knowledge, with its conviction that truth resides in propositions and that learning is "the accumulation of preserved quanta of knowledge" (Bawden 1985, 44), I am proposing an alternative depiction of wisdom (in which knowledge is subsumed). In relinquishing the quest for certainty in favor of context-sensitive judgment, I have been developing a view of wisdom as Grounded Normative Dispositions:

- **Grounded,** because firmly rooted in and responsive to an historical-cultural *context;*
- **Normative,** because there is a multiplicity of norms to which we are *accountable* in any given situation;
- **Dispositions,** because we should be most concerned with how we *tend to act,* not with what we think or say we will do.

Wisdom's interest is in tendencies to act in normative ways (cf. Wolterstorff 1980), not mainly in the ability to enunciate what the principles of proper action might be. It is these tendencies toward action that betray what we ultimately believe. As Dewey averred, beliefs are *habits,* the fabric in a person's life that constitute "character."

These three features of wisdom suggest three modes of *realization of value.* I will discuss these in the final chapter in their application to curriculum, under the rubrics of *play, problem-posing,* and *purposeful response.*

Formation or Information?

It might well be regarded as a commonplace: wisdom is a response to normativity. It is about how we ought rightly to *act.* My conviction is that schools should commit themselves to the nurture of wisdom, as a spirit permeating the development of knowledge. A wisdom paradigm will enable schools to help form students of character. And just as important, such a pursuit of wisdom will enable this goal to be achieved not just for the favored few, but for all of the students entrusted to their care, no matter what their IQ.

Knowledge, as it is so often conceived in our culture, is value-free, universal, contained in statements, often abstract. It is deemed to be religiously neutral. Wisdom, however, is overtly and inextricably linked with questions of value, with everyday problems and personal decision making. As one of the Hebrew sages puts it (Proverbs 24:3–4), knowledge may well provide the furniture, but it is wisdom that builds the house—and builds it, of course, on rock.

The story that has dominated our culture, and most particularly the culture of schooling, is that the supreme values are intellectual, the ultimate excellence is "academic." But values are also ethical, social, economic, aesthetic, and environmental; they concern justice and, above all, faith. In this perspective, "academic excellence" is certainly a legitimate aim of schools, but it must not be the overriding one. (Christian) schools are not to be in the "knowledge business," but in unrelenting pursuit of wisdom, the formation of character.[18] Knowledge does not yield wisdom; information does not guarantee formation.

The Age of Reason, of modernity, far from being surpassed, has come to its peak in the period described as postmodern, in which scientific and technological manipulation of all of life's processes and the rational working of the market's invisible but also iron hand promise heaven on earth. Rational calculation is severed from actual concrete historical events and living, breathing people, who often must be sacrificed to the needs of the system or organization. And rationality is disconnected from a normative framework, so that moral emptiness and a values vacuum substitute for that purity of heart and transparent integrity that are to characterize the servant of God. For where knowledge is impersonal, even transpersonal—the same for all people in all places at all times—wisdom is personal and relational. Truth is not found in "facts," but in Jesus Christ. It is in loving him as Lord and Savior that truth resides.

We hear much in schools about the *disciplines*, but only in Christian schools do we hear about *disciples*. Where the former concern subject matter, the latter requires being subject to the Master. A strength of the Christian school is that it is not neutral with respect to values, that it has a stake in the formation of character, in the forming of its students more and more daily in the image of their Redeemer, who is Wisdom incarnate. It proclaims the values of the gospel, that the goal is a life of service rather than success. The Christian school should seek to embody a different model of excellence from that which is dominant in schooling. "Love, joy, peace, patience, kindness, goodness, faithfulness, gentleness, self-control" (Galatians 5:22)—are there any excellences greater than these?

In one of Geoffrey Robertson's *Hypotheticals,* lateral thinking guru Edward de Bono was asked the question: "You can put genes in for intelligence, but can you genetically improve on wisdom?" He replied, "The difference between intelligence and [wisdom] is like the difference between the horsepower of a car and who drives it. Horsepower doesn't ensure that the car will be driven well." It is, of course, in much more than driver education—let alone sex education—that we want our students to be passionate in the pursuit of wisdom and not just possessors of packets of knowledge.

SECTION IV

Wisdom and Currere

Eisner, in company with many others, counsels that educational improve-ment be incremental. He suggests that what is needed is not the wholesale over-throw of current approaches but a "forceful idea, an attractive conception, an image of [people] and the conditions that foster [their] development. And then we need a small place to begin" (Eisner 1982, 72). In looking for such a place, I first focused on the notion of an integral, problem-posing curriculum (Blomberg 1978, 1980b). In response to the criticism of teachers that the latter tended to promote a negative view of learning, I made more explicit the dimension I came to call "purposeful response." And although the notion of integrality very much emphasized the significance of concrete, everyday experience, the "problem-pos-ing, purposeful response" formulation still seemed to many to foster neglect of this aspect in curriculum planning, which I, in fact, wished to celebrate. Hence, I adopted the term play *in the hope of remedying this inadequacy (Stronks and Blomberg 1993).*

Much has changed since I began my quest, not the least the emergence of a postmodern perspective on curriculum, explored in earlier chapters. I noted at the outset the resonances between that perspective and the one that I am developing in response to a biblical orientation to wisdom. This section seeks to foreground that orientation against a postmodern backdrop; the latter helps to set the stage, but it does not determine what will take place there. One significant postmodern contribution is reflected already in the heading: my emphasis is consciously on currere, *the "running of the course," rather than* curriculum, *the "course to be run." It has always been thus, I suspect, without having been fully articulated. It is implied in my view of curriculum as an organically developing* relationship *between teachers, learners, and subject matter, of curriculum as subject-manner.*

10

Currere: **Running to Learn**

As first proposed by Pinar and Grumet (1976, 51), *currere* is the "self-conscious conceptualization" of the self, the self's exploration of its experiences/experiencing. By an act of recording/reflecting/distancing, one changes one's view of experience; it is "seen differently" because "the problem is different" (53). As Doll points out, there are inherent "Deweyan overtones" in this basically phenomenological perspective. For Dewey, experience has a dual character (as doing/reflecting): "[o]nly when experience is *reflected* upon does it truly become *an experience* . . . only through this secondary, reflective act does meaning get made, do understanding and transformation occur" (Doll 2002, 44).

According to Grumet, *currere* implies "that we first ask the student, 'What does this mean to you?' . . . Here, in this probing, personal questioning . . . lie the beginnings of a dialogic or transformative curriculum. This simple questioning—which Heidegger . . . has called 'the piety of thought' . . .—(re)frames the whole of educational experience; it moves this experience from that [of] being molded or controlled by others to that of dialoguing with others" (Doll 2002, 44).

Though differing in significant respects from the perspective just described—in seeing meaning as given in creation, and thus *responded to* rather than *made*, for instance, and in recognizing a more structurally diverse range of ways in which experience may be transformed—I share with it a sense of the duality of experience, an emphasis on the significance of questioning and dialogue "between ourselves and the text, between ourselves and the students, and among all three" (Doll 2002, 45), and the conviction that education must be about the transformation of experience.

In this and the final chapter, I seek to elucidate further the connections among the three moments I identify in the rhythm of learning and to contextualize this view of (curriculum as) *currere* more explicitly within a wisdom perspective.

167

Learning from Experience: Is It Possible?

The central question about curriculum, unsurprisingly, was given its classical formulation by Plato. "How is it possible ever to learn anything? How is it that a learner is able to understand something new?" This is the question of the *Meno*. It is a question for teachers and learners alike and how they should relate to one another; Socrates' interrogation of the slave boy is a paradigmatic case of the relationship we describe as "curriculum."

Simply put, the conundrum is this: learning must involve an encounter with something new in experience, for I cannot *learn* what I already know. But I cannot come to know something totally new, either, for it would be utterly incomprehensible; it would be as though I had arrived in a foreign country with absolutely no knowledge of the language being spoken. Everything I heard would sound like gibberish.

But the fact is that we do learn that of which we appear originally to be in complete ignorance. Plato thought to resolve the impasse by the notion of past lives and present reminiscences, to which the teacher was but midwife. But the impasse arose in the first place because experience had been dismissed as a possible source of understanding; it suffered this ignominy because Plato could not conceive of *knowledge* arising from the realm of evident impermanence, of "appearance." Reality could only be "seen" by rational processing that unearthed the truths that were buried in the unconscious, if this anachronistic analogy to psychoanalysis may be allowed.

Plato's archetypal protagonist in this respect in the "corridors of philosophy" was John Locke. Contrary to Plato, Locke's empiricist account of experience suggested that *only* through appearance was learning possible. And I use the word *appearance* advisedly, because it was the sensory dimensions of experience alone that concerned Locke and that he thought impressed themselves on the mind in much the way that a stylus might mark cuneiform characters on a clay tablet.

Thus, both Plato's and Locke's accounts were "impressionist," a term in some respects similar to what it came to mean in an artistic context. In the latter, the reference (originally disparaging) was to the attempt to record the impression made by a passing moment, the changing light and color presenting itself in a fleeting fraction of time. Though we are apt to notice the subjective or interpretative nature of this response to experience, the relevant point is the extent to which the Impressionists regarded themselves as faithfully recording what they had actually seen. It is as though they were media only for capturing on canvas the actuality of the moment.

For Plato, it was the heavenly reality seen between one life and the next—in the process of transmigration—that impressed itself on the mind;

for Locke, it was an earthly reality that made its mark, but by pressure just the same. In other words, both perspectives on learning viewed it as predominantly passive. What is missing is an understanding of the extent to which the learner actively engages in experiencing. Both accounts emphasize the objective to the detriment of the subjective side of experience, thus obscuring its integral subject-object relation.

But a further distortion in these accounts of experience lies in their diminution of it to one of its aspects. Although Plato is typically held to be disparaging of experience, it is more accurate to say that he favors the logical-rational dimension of it over all others; it is by rational processing that knowledge emerges from the chaos of sensory experience. Locke is Plato's symbolic rival precisely because he focuses on just this latter dimension, with Berkeley and then Hume following through on some of the implications of his empiricism.

I have described this question as the central one of curriculum, and not just of learning, because if teachers could discover the mystery of learning, they would be well placed to be its servant. For if learning is a matter of conversion (as I have noted that Plato suggests), of turning to face the truth, "this business of turning the mind round might be made a subject of professional skill, which would effect the conversion as easily and effectively as possible," Plato (1955, 283) pointed out in *The Republic*. And this professional skill becomes embodied in the curriculum, as the relationship between teacher and learner.

According to Plato, the learner remains relatively passive in this process, though so also, it must be acknowledged, does the teacher, in Plato's *account* at least, if not in his interrogatory practice. If we leapfrog from the fourth century BC over the seventeenth to the twentieth, we see that passivist views of learning continued their dominance in the latter, in the form of positivist philosophical and behaviorist psychological perspectives. Common to all of these accounts is the notion that "the facts of the matter" impose themselves on the human organism.

> "Now, what I want is, Facts. Teach these boys and girls nothing but Facts. Facts alone are wanted in life. Plant nothing else, and root out every thing else. You can only form the minds of reasoning animals upon Facts: nothing else will ever be of any service to them. This is the principle on which I bring up my own children, and this is the principle on which I bring up these children. Stick to Facts, sir!" (Dickens, *Hard Times*, Chapter I)

Dickens was writing in the nineteenth century, of course, but his parody and his critique remained relevant into the twentieth. As that century progressed, however, the move was toward the recognition of the inextricable linking of "facts" and "values" and of the interactive connections between subject and object in experience. The former is evident in the Kuhnian and Quinean critiques of empiricism, and the latter in Deweyan and Vygotskian theories of learning, for example. This move is characteristic of the period we describe as postmodern.

Humans are valuing creatures, who reach out to their environments and select amongst it from the earliest age. They *notice* things and pay them differential attention. But never do they do this in isolation. One of the limitations of Piaget's investigation of learning—as "genetic epistemology"—was that it focused on individual cognitive attainments, on developing intellectual structures within this or that child, though seemingly common across children. Vygotsky recognized that thought is much more like an internalized conversation than a (mollusk-like) organic growth following its own internal laws. Children are immersed from the beginning in a culture, in social interactions, and it is this that provides the conditions that are necessary for learning. Never mind learning a foreign language, children would not even learn their own language if they were deprived of linguistic interaction in their early years.

The child reaches out to its environment, exploring it, engaging with it, making contact. It touches and it sucks, and it values its mother's breast for giving it the feedback it seeks (if the pun may be pardoned). Humans as image-bearers are not passive organisms upon which the world impresses itself, but active searchers after meaning, makers of connections: learners.

It is this requirement of the learning environment that Vygotsky sought to describe in his notion of the "zone of proximal development," i.e., the gap between present and new experience must be, like Goldilocks' porridge, "just right." Opportunities for growth must be at hand, in reach.

Wisdom and Experience

Curriculum has to do not only with the "how," of course; it also concerns the "what." Herbert Spencer is credited with the classical formulation here: "What knowledge is of most worth?" —or as I would say, "value." I have been exploring the likely shape of a curriculum directed toward wisdom, as the *realization of value*. And I have been arguing that wisdom is not a body of knowledge to be attained: it is a way of being. One may have gathered a comprehensive collection of wise sayings, but being wise is always situation-specific, and such situations exceed by far in their complexity whatever can be encapsulated in propositions or even aphorisms.

If curriculum is the merging of the how and the what, the former should, for greatest effectiveness, be isomorphic with the latter. As learning a way of living, it requires mentoring by a series of mistresses and masters who embody their subject matter. "Do as I say," must be supported by "Do as I do." With a recognition similar to Vygotsky's of the significance of the social environment, social learning theorists emphasize the importance of modeling in learning.

It is a commonplace that we learn from experience (and equally, that we do not always do so). But what is "experience"? For a more comprehensive perspective than that provided by Plato or Locke, and looking in the direction to which Vygotsky and Bandura point, we turn once again to the Wisdom Literature. A recent study of this tradition draws together many of the themes we have just been exploring:

> The starting point for education and learning, for living well, is experience. Simply put, we learn how to live well by living. Therefore, everyday life is where we begin and where we end. . . . Beginning then, with our own experience and that of others . . . the task of education is to use our reason as we address questions about good and right living. . . . This kind of questioning and self-conscious, even introspective, reflection on the world we live in and on our behavior patterns and values always takes seriously the social matrix in which we find ourselves. (Morgan 2002, 122)

As I noted previously, one of the major theoretical issues with which I have wrestled over many years is how to honor both the learning that comes through immersion in experience (in play) and that which comes in moments of withdrawal (via problem-posing). These seem like contrary, if not contradictory, moments. Morgan's (2002, 169) comments resonate here also: "Wisdom leads us along a precarious but exciting path, and to negotiate it well we must be open to the new even as we rely on old ways of understanding that have worked successfully in the past." In many respects, wisdom is concerned with this relationship between the old (what we know) and the new (what we need to learn), and is thus a reformulation of the dilemma of the *Meno*.

> . . . wisdom is, and always has been, to be found in the dialogue between the order established in creation and the ever new ways in which that order and life are given to us. To understand this, to live well in such a world, requires that we hear the old and the new, with as many sage opinions as possible. (Morgan 2002, 170)

The wisdom perspective takes seriously creational order, and the mediate social structures (the family, cultus, government, and so on) and traditions framed within this order. This is because it was in wisdom that God created the world and thus wisdom is itself "built into the created order" (Morgan 2002, 37).

Hence, the biblical wisdom perspective points us toward both the continuity of experience in an ordered creation and the need for openness to ever-new experience as God continues to be actively engaged with his world. This parallels the proper conditions for learning, which occurs at the intersection of stability and flexibility. As has been well said, what is required for learning is neither a brick (which is enduring) nor a beach (which changes with every tide), but a brain. I noted previously that for Piaget, assimilation and accommodation must function interactively for learning—indeed, life—to occur. Too much stability, and nothing is learned; one is content with what one already knows. Too much change, however, and nothing remains from one experience to the next. Conservation is a basic requirement of healthy human functioning: too much change too quickly leads to breakdown, but at the same time it is necessary to rehearse/practice behaviors if they are to remain within one's repertoire. The experience on which we take our stand is what we presume to *know*; problems posed are occasions for growth in this knowledge, and so, too, is extended "unproblematic" experience. Maturana and Varela (1987) describe this ordered openness to change as the "structural plasticity" of a system, and it is this that makes it a *learning* system.

Because wisdom is part of the created order, seeking after it is also built into who we are; as image-bearers of the one who is Wisdom, our hearts are restless until they find their rest in God. The object of the search "is to find the one who gives us life and to be in relationship with that one" (Morgan 2002, 169).

A Psychological Perspective

With this orientation to transcendence and ultimacy, wisdom may be characterized as a "superlative" concept. If we turn now from the Wisdom Literature to contemporary psychological studies, we find the suggestion that it may "be regarded as the ultimate possible achievement of a normal person's growth. It is the category that describes the moment . . . when the psychological system becomes fully co-ordinated across experiential contexts and across alternative forms/modes of processing" (Pascual-Leone 1990, 245). As such, wisdom deserves to be privileged as a primary goal of education; and schooling, as a subset of the latter, can legitimately take this as its aim, though cognizant always of its elusiveness.

From another standpoint, education and wisdom alike can be seen to be concerned with the "optimization of experience," what Dewey meant by continual growth. In this context, though not explicitly using the term, Csikszentmihalyi provides the following characterization of wisdom, which echoes the preceding (with one caveat):

> To create harmony in whatever one does is the last task . . . present[ed] to those who wish to attain optimal experience; it is a task that involves transforming the entirety of life into a single flow activity, with unified goals that provide constant purpose. (Csikszentmihalyi 1991, 213)

A life of wisdom is a life of integrity, of character. The caveat—implicit in the notion of integrity—is that optimal experience does not ensure that the ends in view are normative. A thief may be "fully engaged in cracking a safe" without being adjudged to be doing "good work" (Gardner, Csikszentmihalyi, and Damon 2001, 5). Wisdom requires pursuit of normative goals, not merely self-chosen ones.

The extensive psychological studies of Csikszentmihalyi and his colleagues have identified the following characteristics of optimal experience (which they describe in terms of "flow"): "a sense that one's skills are adequate to cope with the challenges at hand, in a goal-directed, rule-bound action system that provides clear clues as to how well one is performing" (Csikszentmihalyi 1991, 71). Because there will be an appropriate distance between the level of the challenge and the skills possessed (reminiscent of Vygotsky's "zone of proximal development"), it will provide "a sense of discovery . . . transform[ing] the self by making it more complex" (74). A self "in flow" is one who has "self-contained goals" (209), inbuilt criteria of what he or she is seeking to achieve and criteria by which to judge achievement; such a person is designated "autotelic." Simply, the autotelic person sets goals for her- or himself, becomes immersed in the activity, pays attention to what is happening, and learns to enjoy immediate experience (208–13).

In seeking to define wisdom, Labouvie-Vief (1990, 52–53) suggests that it consists in a "relatively balanced dialogue between two modes" of knowing. "In that dialogue, one mode provides experiential richness and fluidity, the other logical cohesion and stability." She cites Piaget in support, for whom one of these modes (assimilation) "is best exemplified by play. Here, a ludic orientation prevails in which the individual is not concerned with the demands of outer reality." Freud, Werner, Mead, Macmurray, Rorty, Olson, and Bruner ("narrative" and "paradigmatic" modes) are also called to testify to this duality (54–55), which Labouvie-Vief herself prefers to characterize in terms of *mythos* and *logos*. In the same volume, Pascual-Leone (1990, 264) distinguishes two aspects of experience: thinking as thanking (impression) and willing as the operative expression of the person on reality. Though I will differ from each of these thinkers in my explication of this duality (as play and problem-posing), the pervasiveness of this distinction is persuasive, and I locate it in the first sense of *realization*. The second sense has to do with judgment issuing in normative action. Thus, learning (to be wise) has three dimensions.

Howard Gardner (1993) has sought to broaden the notion of intelligence in the direction of wisdom, I believe—from a purely cognitive/intellectual ability to one that includes various kinds of ability to find and solve problems and to create products that are of value/valued in a particular culture. Of course, as the reference to the autotelic thief above suggests, what is valued (by an individual or even a culture) is not necessarily what is valuable, of true value. We need normative structural principles (which the Scriptures identify with the order of creation) to sort between competing (or merely differing) value claims.

This pursuit of the truly valuable is itself a fraught undertaking. But here, too, there is wise counsel. The Western pursuit of knowledge has been predominantly a quest for certainty, a fundamentalist drive that extends, of course, to faiths of many colors (Christianity not excluded). Whether in respect to science or religion, however, wisdom recognizes the necessity of living with uncertainty and ambiguity—but having nonetheless to *act*. For Descartes, "radical doubt" was not a destination, but a starting point en route to indubitable knowledge; for wisdom, living with ill-structured, "wicked" problems is a condition of life's journey. Not hypothetical syllogisms but sensitive judgments are the motor of progression.

Wisdom has been characterized from Socrates on as "knowing that one does not know"; it requires a recognition of the limits to knowledge, a dialectical balance between knowing and doubting (cf. Meacham 1990, 190–91). As Descartes understood, one cannot live in doubt, but it is a *practical* rather than an intellectual resolution that is required: "judgments are necessary to complete the situation" (Kitchener and Brenner 1990, 221). Such judgments depend not on theoretical certainty, but on "firm values and ideals to guide behavior" (Kohut 1977; cit. Orwoll and Perlmutter 1990, 161). Thus, for Dewey, wisdom is not

> systematic and proved knowledge of fact and truth, but a conviction about moral values, a sense for the better kind of life to be led. Wisdom is a moral term, and like every moral term refers . . . to a choice about something to be done, a preference for living this sort of life rather than that. It refers not to accomplished reality but to a desired future which our desires, when translated into articulate conviction, may help bring into existence. (Dewey 1982, 44)

I quote these sources because they provide both *post hoc* support and a helpful further introduction to the model I am presenting in this final part of the book. In these terms, play may be referenced to "knowledge," that which is (taken to be) given. But the given is never certain nor is it complete; rather, it is dynamic and open-ended, suffused with gaps, traces, metaphors, embedded questions: it is evocative of doubt, if one has ears to hear—and wisdom hears, for it is perhaps "more a matter of interrogatives than of declaratives," it is "the art of problem finding" (Arlin 1990, 231). Problem-posing is thus not the antithesis of play, but its complement. And finally, wisdom does not come to fruition without "purposeful response," the "ability to act effectively," for we may err either by acting impulsively and foolhardily on the one hand, or with too great a reticence and caution on the other (Birren and Fisher 1990, 320)—an evaluation obviously reminiscent once more of Aristotle in the *Nicomachean Ethics.*

Employing traditional psychological categories, Birren and Fisher suggest that wisdom may be construed as

> the integration of affective, conative and cognitive aspects of human abilities in respect to life's tasks and problems. Wisdom is a balance between the opposing valences of intense emotion and detachment, action and inaction, and knowledge and doubts. (Birren and Fisher 1990, 326–27)

If one accepts for the sake of Birren and Fisher's argument the psychologist's traditional locating of values in the affective domain (to which credence is added by the work of Damasio [1995], for example), then their summary of the research papers contained in the edited volume they are concluding—*Wisdom: Its Nature, Origins and Development* (Sternberg 1990)—and which I have been instancing in this section, provides a tidy overview of a holistic personality, which we also describe by recourse to the notion of *integrity.* It adds further weight to my argument that schooling in wisdom, which is also education for the formation of character, is a worthwhile goal. Though I have the suspicion that their summary is indeed *too* tidy, and while I would not wish to maintain a one-to-one correspondence between each of these three categories and each of mine, I do draw encouragement from this further indicator of the integrality of a wisdom perspective. And its rehabilitation of conation would be applauded by at least two prominent Christian educationalists, Thomas Groome and Nicholas Wolterstorff (Groome 1991; Wolterstorff 1980), most specifically in respect to the importance of acts of the will.

The View from TQM

The Total Quality Management (TQM) movement has been very much concerned with the processing (verb) involved in production, and not merely the quality of the product (noun). In the last decade or so, many educators have sought to apply the insights of TQM to the practice of schooling (e.g., Bonstingl 1992); others have been stimulated by it to explore more deeply and broadly the meaning of "quality" and its possible applications to education (e.g., Carr 1989; Cumming 2002; Glatthorn 1994; Stones 1994). It will be instructive to consider how these concerns with quality might bear on our evaluation of schools committed to an education for wisdom.[19] After all, the "realization of value" is an attempt to "capture" quality.

Aspin and Chapman (1994, 139) are in accord with me that matters of value are logically (and I would say, ontologically) quite different from "mere matters of taste and individual preference." Values and value judgments function as "the rules, conventions or principles implicit in certain manners of proceeding" that then "act as a standard of discrimination (a criterion) against which other procedures, etc. can be measured and assessed. . . . Their interpersonal significance we regard as commendatory, action guiding and generally prescriptive." They further support my claim that there are "a number of different kinds of value: moral, religious, aesthetic, social, political, educational, technical, economic, and so on," noting, however, that the question of their distinctive differences is still an open one (cf. Aspin 2002).

Aspin and Chapman (1994, 41–42, 123) have argued, on the basis of their empirical research, that schools committed to quality educational provision need to embrace:

- problem-posing,
- the principle of inclusivity, and
- "the four themes of quality schooling—efficiency, equity, choice and variety" (Caldwell 1990)

in order "to enable [students] to acquire the abilities . . . to participate in [society] . . . in appropriate social, political and moral ways." These are all themes that pervade my discussion, and I will briefly suggest how I believe that my proposals would address their concerns.

The normative social participation that Aspin and Chapman describe is a primary objective of a wisdom paradigm for schooling; it is important to underscore that the social, jural, and ethical modes are not the province of those particularly gifted in these ways, but are the calling of all students, while at the same time some will take specific leadership roles. The goal must be education of the "whole person," in accord with what Mant (1997) describes as the need for "broad-band" intelligence. As an education in the realization of value(s), schooling for wisdom sees "values education" not as an *add-on,* but as a pervasive commitment to *adding value,* guiding the enriching and complexification of students' responses to ever more sophisticated levels. In this respect, it may be seen as taking up Brian Hill's (2001, 10) challenge to provide "a robust mandate" for education, which "itself is a value project . . . ."

A wisdom curriculum, allowing for the recognition of multiple modes of meaning, rather than the bipolar options of theory and practice, would enable us to transcend the duality of liberal (or "general") and vocational education. We would recognize that much that goes under the name of liberal education is, in fact, vocational preparation for the professions, and that what is labeled *vocational* can bring a broadening for every student that would make education truly general.[20] The emphasis in the last decade on competencies speaks to the growing recognition that knowledge and skills, though they may be distinguishable, are not separable in actual life situations. Though the focus has been on "vocational education and training" (VET), the wisdom paradigm counsels that it needs to be extended to education in general—so long as we remember that it is our life orientation rather than specific skills or competencies that is the ultimate determinant of how we act (cf. van Manen 1991).

Indeed, "academic achievers" will benefit just as much from programs that put them in touch with other ways of being in the world—vegetable gardening as well as botany, sculpting chess pieces as well as playing chess—and with existential, real-life issues, rather than only abstract analytical manipulations, that acknowledge that wisdom is in the heart and the hands, and not just in the head. I have already suggested (in Chapter 2) the similar import of the Karpin Report's "enterprise skills": accepting responsibility, being flexible, evaluating, initiating, deciding, negotiating, organizing and managing resources, taking risks, and thinking creatively (Meredith, Speedy, and Wood 2001, 29–36); each of these qualities is a feature of wise action.

From such a perspective, there would be scope for the recognition of truly alternative learning pathways, not "more rigorous" and "softer" options ("better" vs. "VET-ter"?) but a horizontal differentiation acknowledging a range of significant human abilities. The curriculum would be truly inclusive, serving the needs of all within a school's walls—and indeed, recognizing that much significant learning might need to occur outside these confines, with the school functioning as "learning headquarters" rather than "teaching fortress" (Schools Council 1994, 76). Partnerships with business and industry can allow these sites and their resources to be used for educational purposes, without schools having to duplicate either the specialized equipment or the expertise that is available there.

An *inclusive* curriculum—one that seeks to address the educational needs and to maximize the educational attainment of all students, rather than sorting them into successes and failures—would be more *efficient*, in allowing students to pursue studies in line with their gifts. (Though there may appear to be a tension here, given the usual connotations of "efficiency," my point is that a curriculum that matches "courses to horses," will enable students more readily to attain their goals. Neither, however, is this to be understood as an argument for mediocrity.) In providing a more *varied* offering, it would thereby allow greater *choice*, which, by not treating students as though they were cast in a uniform mold, would be more just and *equitable*.

Schools should evidence that education is ultimately not about information, but transformation, about discipling rather than disciplines, because "learning may usefully be considered as the development of a capacity for judgment" (Hager and Halliday 2001, 17). They will be schools of rainbowed *quality*, not merely of *academic* excellence. Aspin and Chapman, in suggesting a range of problems that might form the basis of the curriculum, argue that schools need to attend:

> above all, perhaps, [to] the problem of how to assist human beings to acquire and retain their values of humanity, sensitivity, sympathy and compassion, at a time when the emphasis upon what Habermas (1972) called "technocratic rationality", upon technicization and the dominance of particular kinds of economic interest, threaten us with the loss of a sense of individual worth and commitment to a set of values that will help define and enrich the quality of human relationships between ourselves and others—what we might call the problem of the need for the *humanization* of the present-day curriculum. (Astin and Chapman 1994, 123–24)

Where some might balk at "humanizing" the curriculum, I empathize with the intentions expressed in this paragraph; for to be authentically Christian is to be on the way to fulfilling the potential of normal humanness.

It remains for me to draw the threads together in a concrete proposal for curricular practice, which I will endeavor to do in the following, final chapter.

11

Play, Problem-Posing, Purposeful Response

Where conventional education deals with abstract and impersonal facts and theories, an education shaped by Christian spirituality . . . means being drawn into personal responsiveness and accountability to each other and the world of which we are a part.

Parker Palmer (1983, 14–15)

The Play/Problem-Posing/Purposeful Response model is intended not as an algorithm but as an evocative/provocative concrete metaphor for the rhythm of learning. As a perspective on learning, it seeks to move away from those theories that "offer little more than an accretion mechanism" (Meacham 1990, 183), to a view of learning as *transformation*. It is a small place to begin for teachers who are wanting to "do school differently" and to "do it" more faithfully to a biblical view of the person and the world. It would be worse than foolhardy to imagine that it provides a comprehensive formal system that resolves all of the issues of learning, epistemology, pedagogy, and so on that are of interest to educators. Simply, it attempts to depict *moments of experience viewed as learning*.

It has been my claim that wisdom is the proper goal of learning. I have described wisdom as the "realization of value," in the two senses of realization, and suggested in the previous chapter that we need to distinguish two orientations in the first sense of "realization." Thus, in the characterization of the curriculum as a rhythm of play, problem-posing, and purposeful response:

- *Play* points to that primal encounter and engagement with creation that is the basis of all learning. The play of creation on us draws us outward and onward as we interact playfully with it. By connotation, it is intended to remind us that our privilege as God's image-bearers is to *enjoy* him and all that he has made (1 Timothy 4) and that the appropriate response to this gift is, in the first place, love and thanksgiving (Romans 1). Learning starts at birth (if not before), with a *broadening* experience of rich, multidimensional contexts; schools

179

should continue this orientation rather than substituting extensively theorized, abstracted, and artificial "lessons." Play opens up possibilities, gathers "grist for the mill" of learning. It requires initiation into new areas, gives insight into existing realities: it is *realization 1a*, **making connections**.

- *Problem-posing* suggests that our experience of creation is *deepened* in a complementary manner to that which occurs through play, by addressing questions to/that arise from this primordial and ongoing encounter. Play also opens up problems: what ought I do, and how am I to accomplish it? How do I move in a normative direction? These "values-in-view" create a "problem-space" (which is bounded also by the constraints of the present situation, including knowledge): this is *realization 1b*, **breaking and remaking connections**.

- These problems invite responses-in-action, the instantiation of value. *Purposeful response* underscores that most important in this responsive encounter is not a detached contemplation of propositional truths, but *normative action,* developing over time into a disposition to act normatively. Because creation is complex and problems are many-sided, wisdom is pluriform: there is a range of ways of wisdom, according to the variety of norms that invite realization. This is *realization 2*, **staking oneself on the connections**.

Bigge speaks in similar vein of this ternary process as *simultaneous mutual interaction,*

> a cognitive experiential process within which a person . . . reaches out to his [/her] psychological environment, encounters some aspects of it, brings those aspects into relationship with himself [/herself], makes something of those aspects, acts in relation to *what he (she)* [sic] *makes of* them, and realizes the consequences of the entire process. (Bigge 1982, 340)

Though the distinctions do not map precisely onto one another, they are (un)remarkably close: *realization 1a* corresponds to the reaching out and encountering phase, *realization-1b* "makes something" of the encounter, and *realization 2* is consequential action, in which one "realizes the consequences."

In this view, teaching and learning are the playfully shared exploration of a normed (value-laden) problem-space. This space is defined by a single question, though it takes multiple forms: "Where is wisdom to be found?" In other terms: "How is value to be added? What would make the situation as I now experience it more valuable? What is a normative response?"

You will see why I find the quotation of Parker Palmer with which I open this chapter so congenial, emphasizing as it does the importance of students "being drawn into personal responsiveness and accountability to each other and the world of which we are a part." Although Palmer's terminology also does not parallel mine exactly, the moments of *being drawn into*, *responding*, and *accountability* echo the three moments I have identified. In similar vein, Oppewal (1985) suggests a triad of *consider*, *choose*, and *commit*, and Whitehead (1967) a rhythm of *romance*, *precision*, and *generalization*.

The following account by a teacher captures these three dimensions of learning succinctly, though illustrating how intertwined with one another they also are (they are moments, not compartments):

> In terms of what I teach, which resources will I use? How connected to the present reality of students is the material we are dealing with? I'll never forget the reaction I got when I sent a Grade 8 student into a store in Quebec City. We were spending a week there, and for many of our students it was their first experience away from home. To build confidence, I gave one of them the task of going into a store to ask a rather simple question in French: "What time is it?" Two minutes later he bounded out of the store, face aglow, yelling, "It works!" I was astounded. For the first time I, as a teacher, realized that for many students the learning of French was so far removed from their lives, that for all they knew it was a secret code I had made up. We, as French teachers, need to search for ways to make French present and authentic by using people and resources that open their eyes to a different world that actually does exist. (Vanderkooy 2002, 4)

In this final chapter, I turn to a more detailed elaboration of these three moments. A focus on a single aspect of the rhythm of learning invites the likelihood of reification, the freezing of a moment in time as though it were the flow of life, thus presenting a distorted picture. This is the ever-present danger in analysis, of assuming that when two features of experience are distinguishable, they are also separable. But although I can indeed think the color *brown*, and I can think the notion *house*, I can never experience a colorless house or a nonsituated brown. In the same way, play, problem-posing, and purposeful response permeate one another in our experience. They are three ways of looking at the one "object," three sides of the one coin—the obverse, reverse, and rim, if you will. There will thus be a certain "fuzzy logic" (i.e., not strictly bivalent) in what follows. This is inevitable if one is seeking to realize a range of norms simultaneously.

Play: An Engaging Encounter

When God said, "Let there be—" to the very underpinnings of the earth,
[I was right there!]
Yes, I was God's very own protégé.
And I was enjoying myself day after day, playing around
    all the time in front of God's face,
playing through the hemispheres of God's earth,
having fun with all of humankind. . . .

(Proverbs 8:29–31, based on Seerveld 1980, 43)

Wisdom was there at the beginning, but wisdom is here in the present, continuing to play through creation, as wisdom will do at creation's consummation. For Wisdom is personified—no, incarnated—in Christ, by whom and for whom all things were created, and in whom all things hold together (Colossians 1:16–17). All creation is redeemed at root, all creation is of value, its "very good-ness" reaffirmed.

Thus, the wisdom and grace of God extend to each and every inch of his world, including to me individually, and this twice over. For not only my life but my new life in Christ—my life returned to me when I had given it away—is dependent on his grace. God's gifts of creation and new life call us to lives of thankfulness, "thick" rather than "thin" lives, in which we revel in the abundance of what God has made, experiencing as many different sides of creation as we can each day. This is not experience for experience's sake, a greedy consumption of the world for pleasure above all; it is because in experience, the unfolding of history, we meet God and his purposes. This is the positive side to the Teacher's message: eat your bread with enjoyment, drink your wine with gladness, enjoy life with the ones you love, work hard at whatever you are called to do, accept with thankfulness what God has given you under the sun. Celebrate life! Everything is a gift from God, not the product of our own striving, whether this be for good or—once again, thank God—for evil.[21] It is this positive view of experience in its richness that informs our commitment to the development of the whole person, made wholly in the image of God, not just of the intellect or of the capacity for economic productivity.

Joyful Responsiveness

A rich encounter with God's world involves a joyful responsiveness to what God has made, rather than an overriding concern with control.[22] Because God is in control, we are able to give ourselves up to him and his world without fear. We can play in his world and thus allow it to play on us. God's grace calls me to joy in the abundance and richness of life, without pretending (as the Teacher did not) that its pain and suffering are an illusion: with C. S. Lewis, I am surprised by joy. Because all life is learning, because we have been created to *grow* in understanding, appreciation, and Christlikeness, and not to repeat routines *mechanically*, learning, too, is meant to be a joyful activity. Because of the gospel, all of life is touched with a song. In this encounter, this mutuality, comes our first (ontologically, not merely chronologically) moment of realization—*realization 1a*. It is our primary mode of responsiveness, paying attention, dialoguing, and conversing with the world.

An enjoyable conversation is one in which there is a relaxed playfulness. A conversation with friends has no agenda, no outcome to be achieved. It does not rule out serious matters by any means, nor will it rule out disagreements or even arguments; but there is a trust in the relationship that undergirds and pervades these moments as well. It has been said that "quality time is wasted time," and it is in the free flow of openness to one another, of respecting and valuing someone enough to be ready just to "waste time" with them, that one comes to learn and love more.

Creation is Revelation

So it should be with our growing understanding of the world in general. We ought not to set out in the first place to master, to conquer, but instead to submit ourselves to what the world has to teach us. And teach us it will, for creation is revelation. We learn as we rest in the coherence of the world that is our home, as we are sensitively open to what will come upon us not as a prize that we have struggled to win but as a gift bestowed. Our attitude then is not one of coercion or subversion, but of respecting the integrity of the Other as subject, allowing it to respond, as it invites us to respond—to subject ourselves—to it. We must first of all let the world play on us, even play us as its instruments, for we are called to serve it. As I have mentioned, Straus (1966) has used the term *pathic* to describe this invitational character of the world: the ocean waves invite us to plunge in, the glass of water invites us to drink, and the structure of government invites us to do justice (cf. van Manen 1990). Umberto Eco puts this in characteristically more whimsical fashion:

> We produce signs because there is something that demands to be said. To use an expression that is efficacious albeit not very philosophical, the Dynamical Object is Something-that-sets-to-kicking-us and says "Talk!" to us—or "Talk about me!" or again, "Take me into consideration!" (Eco 1999, 14)

The wisdom writers have reminded us that when the world speaks to us in this way, it speaks also with the voice of God. As Martin Buber says,

> God's speech . . . penetrates what happens in the life of each one of us, and all that happens in the world around us, biographical and historical, and makes it for you and me into instruction, message, demand. Happening upon happening, situation upon situation, are enabled and empowered by the personal speech of God to demand of the human person that he take his stand and make his decision. (Buber 1958, 136–37)

The world is revelation, if only we have ears to hear, if only we will *realize*. And this revelational world is not merely "natural," it is "biographical and historical," social and cultural. It is *Little Dorrit* and lemonade, Saddam Hussein and Sydney Harbour, Beethoven's Fifth and Beresford's films: "events" of all kinds can be occasions of epiphany.

Thus, and not infrequently, our encounters are of the nature of an "annunciation":

> . . . the source of a profound response of recognition, joy and wonder is not the responding person, myself, but the presence to which I am responding. What we call the object of our response is really the subject and activator. . . . the line we like to draw between subject and object, between that which calls and that which answers, grows faint and finally disappears. As soon as "being" becomes "presence" it has already become a part of that to which it is present. (Taylor 1972, 13)

The world reveals itself to us, unbidden. What is valuable is suddenly crystal clear. As Henry Adams (1999, 283) puts it, in reflecting on his own "education," "he knew no quicker mode of learning a lesson than that of being struck on the head by it. . . ." But it helps if we put ourselves in the way of the possibility:

> Sam went to Bermuda for a Christmas holiday with his father when he was fifteen. At the time, he had no idea of what he wanted to do with his life . . . no clearly differentiated goals; he wanted exactly what other boys his age are supposed to want. . . . Sam's father took him on an excursion to a coral barrier, and they dove underwater to explore the reef. Sam couldn't believe his eyes. He found the mysterious, beautifully dangerous environment so enchanting that he decided to become more familiar with it. He ended up taking a number of biology courses in high school, and is now in the process of becoming a marine scientist.
>
> In Sam's case, an accidental event imposed itself on his consciousness. . . . He had not planned to have this experience; it was not the result of his self or his goals having directed attention to it. But once he became aware of what went on undersea, Sam *liked* it. . . . He felt the experience was

something good, something worth seeking out again. (Csikszentmihalyi 1991, 34–35)

Teachers can well be those who put their pupils in the paths of possibilities.

Playing with the World

Play is necessary if children—and not only they!—are to encounter the world in its many-sidedness and make those connections between the various aspects of their experience that are so important to effective learning. To bring together seemingly unconnected things in playful ways—as in humor or scientific theory-building, the "ha-ha" and "ah-hah" of creativity in Koestler's (1975) terms—is a productive rather than a wasteful activity, conducive to deep rather than surface learning.

It is play that nurtures our imagination and creativity, playing around that enables us to put together ideas that haven't been put together before. Messing around in the world, getting our hands dirty, allows us to experience creation in its many-sided concreteness, its historical-situatedness. It enables us to make connections and see relationships that we otherwise would not have encountered. It gives us the space to see things from different angles, freeing us from the tunnel vision of logical processing, and thus freeing us *for* different ways of knowing. (At the same time, it provides the raw materials for logical deduction, for a conclusion can only state what is entailed by the premises; concepts without intuitions are empty.)

Playfulness encourages students to cross boundaries and to connect their school learning with their everyday experience. The many children in (especially, high) school who would rather be somewhere else—*anywhere else*—feel this way because they see no connection with anything they find meaningful or relevant to their own lives. Where they are restless because of enforced physical inactivity, inattentive to the requirements of the teacher's lesson plan, their "failure" ought to be considered (at least in part) an artifact of the system. And that part is what we as teachers and administrators have the possibility and thus the responsibility of addressing.

Things in Relation

For many students, school is an alienating theoretical interruption to their daily lives, a disconnect. Theory abstracts from concrete individual things and the relationships between them, converging on the generalities, as it were; skills broken down into their components, fragments to be repeated by rote, evince this same disconnection. Wisdom, on the other hand, intensifies our perception of the individual, invites us to know this or that creature, including the social relationships that God has created for us to live within, as it is in its uniqueness, without isolating it from its various relations.

Thus, while wisdom thinks in terms of concrete things, it at the same time invites us to compare thing to thing, the one to the other, encouraging us to go to the ant for an example of diligence and to lovers as an example of how we are to serve one another. It invites us to live in metaphor: "A stone is heavy, and sand is weighty, but a fool's provocation is heavier than both" (Proverbs 27:3). And metaphor is divergent in character, turning outward in reference to other meanings at the same time as it turns in. Metaphor is reflexive and reflective, construing identity in the individual's mirroring of the other. It is allusive, nuanceful, referring beyond itself to its connectedness with the rest of the plush tapestry of creation.

Trust

Not only as an English teacher, but in my daily life, I find excitement in the exploration of etymologies and word families, of connections across languages. Words always point beyond themselves, and my students and I have played many times with these linkages. Language is not a logical construction, it is a response to lingual (and other) norms. A language with such a complex history and composition as English can only be understood—and yes, enjoyed—if this richness is reveled in. Unfortunately, many adults have learned to fear rather than to trust language.

We cannot truly play if we do not trust, if there is not *shalom* and security. Children in the family home play carefree in the yard; they may not these days, however, be allowed to venture to the park. Fear takes our freedom from us, but free of fear we can take risks, imagine new possibilities, dare, laugh, and fantasize. Some of the things we try will fail, but this does not defeat us: we have room to move at play. We owe our students this freedom to make mistakes, otherwise creativity and the confidence it requires are crushed.

Language in this context is itself but a metaphor for the connection of all things to everything else.

> One way to teach children the potential of words is by starting to expose them to wordplay quite early. Puns and double meanings may be the lowest form of humor for sophisticated adults, but they provide children with a good training ground in the control of language. . . .
>
> The major creative use of language . . . is poetry. Because verse enables the mind to preserve experiences in condensed and transformed form, it is ideal for giving shape to consciousness. Reading from a book of poems each night is to the mind as working out on a Nautilus is to

the body—a way for staying in shape. (Csikszentmihalyi 1991, 130)

Wonder

In form and content, Gerard Manley Hopkins' poem "Pied Beauty" evokes the sense of play I am exploring here: utter and almost unutterable joyfulness in the fecundity of creation, natural and cultural, and its proper outcome, praise of the Creator (Romans 1:21).

> Glory be to God for dappled things —
> For skies of couple-colour as a brinded cow;
> For rose-moles all in stipple upon trout that swim;
> Fresh-firecoal chestnut-falls; finches' wings;
> Landscape plotted and pieced — fold, fallow, and plough;
> And áll trádes, their gear and tackle trim.
>
> All things counter, original, spare, strange;
> Whatever is fickle, freckled (who knows how?)
> With swift, slow; sweet, sour; adazzle, dim;
> He fathers-forth whose beauty is past change:
> Praise him.
>
> (Hopkins 1953)

In the study of animals and literature, technology and economics, if our curricula could evince—induce—the merest shadow of the wonder that Hopkins captures here, we would already have done much of our job as teachers. Indwelling a book, reading it just to enjoy it (before one engages in critical analysis), stepping into a painting so that it becomes a world in itself, encountering mathematical questions in planning or executing a building project, interpreting statistics in an epidemiological context: all of these are examples of that engaging, active encounter that is the well-spring of learning, which itself is responsiveness to creation.

The Discipline of Play

Hopkins' poem is but a structured form of play, hard work though it might be for poet and reader alike. Much play is by no means an undisciplined affair; nor is it devoid of problems to be addressed. Huizinga observes in his classic study of play that

> we must not think of seriousness degenerating into play or of play rising to the level of seriousness. It is rather that civilization gradually brings about a certain division between two modes of mental life which we distinguish as play and seriousness respectively, but which originally formed a continuous mental medium wherein that civilization arose. (Huizinga 1949, 133)

Playing the piano is a rigorous activity, requiring much diligence even as one is "playing." I remember hearing Claudio Arrau perform at the Sydney Opera House: our enjoyment was almost spoiled by the labor of his breathing, so intense was his effort. And music in itself suggests something further about the nature of play: it has an order and a structure, but it is the unpredictability of the particular notes—the fact that each note is utterly and inexorably contingent and apparently spontaneous—that gives to music both its ethereality and its concreteness.

Most forms of structured play require alertness and attentiveness, ability to focus on the task, precisely because one cannot predict what is going to happen next. (Interestingly enough, in light of the previous paragraph, Begbie [2000] makes a similar observation concerning the incompleteness and openness of music.) It is the skilled player's ability not only to initiate but also to respond to the unexpected and serendipitous (the "problematic") that gives a game much of its interest. It is what brings the crowd to its feet in an outburst of exuberance. And we remember that it is not only knowing how, but knowing *when* to respond aright, that the Hebrews meant by wisdom.

A Critical Edge

Thus, although there is a native naivety to wisdom, it also has a critical edge. It seeks the right response to the order of creation, to the way in which God would have us go, by sensitively seeking out the contours of the other we encounter: the clay one molds, the concert one attends, one's spouse with whom one converses and couples. A term such as *play* can, perhaps paradoxically, sharpen our awareness of this critical component to wisdom, as it suggests a counter to the technical, bureaucratic rationality characteristic of our culture: the connotations of play are at odds with the mechanistic worldview that such thinking entails, the "Taylorist, Tylerist" take on teaching. It alludes to the primacy of being over doing, that our worth resides first and foremost in who we are as images of God. Just "to be" is enough, is glory in itself.

Wisdom cautions sensitivity to each situation, rather than a detachment that would have us categorize an event as one instance of a general class. Similarly, authentic play revels in the spontaneity of the here and now, seeking no end beyond itself. It embodies responsiveness, just as the *play* in a rope or the *play* of light through the leaves connotes a freedom of response.

Deep Learning

I can sympathize with a probable skepticism about the "Romantic" and "progressive" overtones of this conception. It is thus important to emphasize that playfulness promotes not only concrete learning but academic learning as well. What characterizes the difference between "deep" and "surface" learners is the quality and quantity of the connections that are made, especially in the extent to which details are related to larger contexts (Biggs and Telfer 1987). "Deep" learners will take the facts of genetics, for example, and relate them to history, literature, ethics, economics, and their broad personal experience. They move outside of the established channels: there is playfulness rather than rigidity in their learning. Not only will they have a richer understanding of genetic concepts, they will also retain this understanding more lastingly and be able to apply it in a wider range of contexts than "surface" learners. The latter tend to see pieces of information in isolation from each other, as discrete facts to be learned and applied in specific circumstances (not unusually, an examination); their understanding is brittle and tense, keeping everything on a tight rein.

And further with respect to academic expectations, I trust that it is evident from my earlier comments that "playing around" with texts, periods of history, languages, and so on—immersing students in the rich traditions of their culture—is also what I intend by the moment of play in curriculum. It is not that I wish to exclude the vital role in education of introducing students to, even *initiating* them into, their cultural heritage; rather, that I wish to stress the importance of the concrete encounter with "the things themselves," with the plays of Shakespeare and the quandaries of Galileo, with the Aboriginals of Central Australia and the homeless on the city streets, firsthand rather than at one remove. My own introduction to Handel was at the hands of older friends who insisted that I be seated and immerse myself in *The Messiah*; out of this being placed in the presence of possibility, this annunciation, I learned not merely to tolerate, but to love, classical music (while not renouncing The Beatles or The Bee Gees).

If we want our students to be deep learners, we must allow them the freedom to play. I clipped the following comment from a college newspaper some years ago:

> There seems to be a discontinuity of the approaches used between grade school and grad school. In grade school one learns by playing. In grad school one uses research (an adult designation for the word playing). Alternatively, in high school and college one seems to think that one is too old to learn by playing and too young to learn by doing research. We continue to use inadequate techniques, the spoon-fed approach. (Vander Kreek 1992)

189

Playing at Knowing

Learning is playing at knowing. We reach out in exploratory fashion, not yet having what we seek within our grasp, but trusting that if we continue seeking, we will find. The material with which we work, whether it is timber and tin on a building site or periods and paragraphs on a page, will only yield its meaning as we try out various solutions to its puzzle (and here, the "problematic" emerges again). We can do many things with our eyes closed, our minds asleep, we can habituate ourselves in certain reactions (and this in itself is by no means always negative), but if we are not responsive, we are not *learning*. The more we are fully present as persons, engaging the various dimensions of our humanness and wholeheartedly accepting a challenge, the more we learn. The more we enter empathically into the other, responding to it (as "Thou") and allowing it to respond to us, the more we will come to know it. If we *play* the role of the other, whether an historical personage, a character in a novel, or even atoms bonding in a molecule, regarding it not just as object to be mastered but as subject to be listened to, the deeper will be our understanding. In playing a part, we learn to play our part.

A teacher describes a project in which her accounting students created their own businesses (on paper); she reports the following about one child whose learning style she was monitoring:

> From the beginning of the project Ezra was the business, no longer was he trying to muddle his way through the interpretation of another's actions. These were his own, he was flying across Canada to build a skate park in Vancouver. The accounting became a natural process, an extension of his ideas. He could see the supplies he was using and he knew the company he had bought them from (and still owed money to). No longer hindered by the requirements to read and interpret words on a page Ezra was able to translate the images in his head into financial records. (Dibbits 2002, 4)

The "structure" of the World Wide Web is a powerful metaphor for learning: connections are not prescribed, there is no one sequence set. It is like one of those books where you choose the plot as you go; if you would like Sue to procrastinate in the face of a moral dilemma, go to page 59, if you would prefer she plunge immediately into action, go to page 64. Positively, it puts control into the hands of learners themselves, to determine their own running—*currere*. Is not all learning really re-search—and thus a form of play?

Similarly, the best way to learn to use new software is to play around, to experiment with it in a disciplined context. Complete a few of the tutorial sessions, certainly, and then get on with the work one would normally be doing—a meaningful task, not a rote activity—and refer to the online help facility or the manual when problems arise. (In more "primitive" times, this is the way I learnt to touch-type.) Learning as play is situated and shared with the tools one is using; understanding is in the hands as well as in the head: this is as true for the surgeon as for the motor mechanic. Even as I write, the words speak back to me and ask me questions, and the words I ponder pull me in different directions—which one will I follow?

Vulnerability vs. Performativity

What does it mean to be *alive* if not to be open, responsive—and yes, vulnerable—to the world? Vulnerability: this is the proper condition of play. Opening oneself to the other without fear. Opening oneself to the moment. As Papert (cit. Whitaker 1995, 12) has noted, "Education has little to do with explanation and everything to do with engagement—or falling in love with the material." (And I wonder whether Papert recognized the allusion to the pledging of troth in that word *engagement;* probably he did, but *I* did not see it the first time around.)

How different is the post-/high-modernist preoccupation with performativity, which threatens to shut down learning rather than to open it up? As Alfie Kohn says:

> "Although it's important for students to think about how well they're doing, students also need substantial time freed from pressure to improve, to be deeply engaged with ideas they're *playing* with". . . . Students need time to be tentative, when they can stop worrying how good they are. "Fixing students' attention on their performance may come at the expense of their *playing* with ideas, words, and numbers," he cautions. (Association for Supervision and Curriculum Development, 1996, 5 [emphases mine])

Becoming deeply involved with other people and with everyday activities is a condition of "finding flow," which Csikszentmihalyi (1997) refers to as "mundane immersion." It is a phrase that reminds me first of the claim that the Wisdom Literature is concerned with the demands of *secular* life here and now, and second of my own use of the term *immersion*. Be that as it may, what is important throughout this discussion of learning, and what teachers ought to do to promote it, is active engagement with the creation.

Problem-Posing: The Transformation of Experience

The picture of learning as play that I painted in the preceding section might seem somewhat Edenic. And this is purposely so, for, contrary to some Christian traditions, I affirm the continuing goodness of all that God has made and God's faithfulness in sustaining the world by the power of the Word, maintaining it as a habitable home for us and all creatures. But there is more to be said. If the purpose of the previous section was to illustrate how we *do* learn from experience, the purpose of this one is in many respects to account for why it is that we do not *always* learn from experience, that we do not always learn what we should, and that we sometimes learn better than at other times.

And where better to start than with myself as teacher? My own teaching style has been described by more than one observer as "Socratic," which suggests that I rely a great deal on questioning students, prodding them to formulate answers. I might speculate that this is also because I trust that there is an order to the world that people can come to understand if they are open to it, not because of past lives, but because of God's presence. (With Augustine, I, too, believe that God is ultimately the teacher.) Others (generally adults) have stressed that I am "enigmatic." The two descriptions are related, of course, and they do reflect my view of what teaching should be like. It is not that I believe that the teacher should not give information and answer questions. It is rather that leading the growth and self-formation of students in lives of service has a greater priority than the transmission of knowledge, and the former is not well served by an overwhelming reliance on the latter. Teaching is about helping students see what is of most value in their experience and guiding them to value that which is truly valuable.

Change and Order

Learning occurs when what we do brings about a relatively permanent change in our way of being in the world. It is interesting to observe that this definition depends on there being an orderliness in the environment. As Stones (1966, 52) observes in one of the more interesting (if dated) of the ubiquitous texts entitled *Educational Psychology*, "[i]f the environment were completely chaotic . . . organisms would be unable to build up . . . relatively permanent patterns of responses. . . . [I]t would be virtually impossible for an organism to adapt."

The biblical account of creation obviously expresses the conviction that we live in an orderly environment, one that owes its order to its Creator. I spent many hours of student debate speculating on what conditions were like pre-Fall. The serious intention underlying these otherwise fruitless discussions—whether there were mosquitoes in the Garden, and if so, whether they would bite you, and if they did, whether it would itch, and more importantly, would they transmit disease (the answer to the latter was obvious, that to the second and third questions, not so)—was an attempt to determine the nature of creational givens. What was the order of creation, and what was postlapsarian?

Creation is Dynamic

The Wisdom Literature is oriented to creation, in its human and social dimensions as well as its "natural" aspects. Creation has been entrusted into the hands of humankind to shape it according to God's purposes—the so-called Cultural or Creation Mandate (Genesis 1:28). Creation is dynamic—it is living and growing from its genesis to its consummation. This condition of dynamic harmony is described by the biblical authors as *shalom,* which we usually translate as "peace." Peace in this sense is thus not a mere absence of conflict but the connectedness and fittingness of all things one to another, which the New Testament tells us has its origin, focus, and purpose in Christ (Colossians 1:15–20). Creation is dynamically structured, organically integrated, and, as God's image-bearers, we are to help direct its unfolding in positive rather than negative ways—by adding (realizing) value, one might say, rather than devaluing what God has made. There is in this respect a "distance" between what is and what *could* be, and this constitutes the space in which we are called to be culturally formative. Adam and Eve were placed in the Garden as stewards, to till it and keep it, indeed, to serve it, and this evidently required them to plant and tend crops, to prune and harvest fruit trees, to breed and feed animals. (I don't think that my speculations are taking me too far afield here.) They were part and parcel of the creational dynamic that would enable it (along with them) to be fruitful and multiply.

But (whatever our position on mosquitoes) creation also bears pervasively the marks of the Fall, and this implies a tension between what is and what *ought* to be that, while not primeval, is pervasive in our present experience. I have referred to this feature as "directional" (Wolters 1985), in the sense that it is ultimately a matter of what prime value, what vision of "the good, the true, and the beautiful" (God or a substitute) we will serve, what direction our lives will take. There is thus a *directional* as well as a *structural* dimension to the distance we experience, and these two features—our fallibility and our formativity—are inseparable in our experience of the world. Together, these features underlie the problematic, challenging character of the human calling and require a humble wisdom if we are to realize value.

Our Formative Task

Our intrinsic task is to assist our fellow creatures (human or not) in their calling to express the will of God. Strange as it may seem, Roget (1966) suggests *normative* as a synonym for *formative,* perhaps because giving form to something has a positive connotation ("the world was without form, and void"). The word *normative* derives from *norma,* Latin for a carpenter's square. If a building is to be properly formed, it needs to be square (though many exceptions will test this rule). It must be properly framed or else it will fall.

Formativity in a fallen world requires wise framing. Schön has alerted us to the importance of this framing of problems in professional practice, but the significance of this extends far beyond that realm to include all practice. And these frames are necessarily evaluative in kind. It is values that frame problems in practice and establish a problem-space.

In exploring wisdom as an alternative to the theory-into-practice paradigm in the practice of schooling, my concern is with learning that actively engages students unto good, that empowers them to carry out their formative task. When Freire (1972) popularized the notion of "problem-posing," he, too, was very much concerned with empowering the oppressed with whom he worked by giving them the ability to name properly the reality they encountered. His "cultural circles" commenced with the identification of emotively and evaluatively charged terms, which then became the occasion not only for literacy education but for political and "cultural action for freedom" (Freire 1975). Properly framing problems, validly assigning value, was the starting point for increasing *shalom.*

The terms that peasants identified arose, of course, from experience as it played out in the *favela.* Problem-posing was a matter of focusing differently on this experience, and the teacher helped them in this process. Without the cultural circle and the teacher-student, they would have remained victims of rather than becoming victors in that experience. For while it is true that we learn *only* from (and in) experience, we do not *always* learn from experience; and when experience is nasty, brutish, and short, what we learn will in many respects not be beneficent.

Choice of Direction

Thus, though I have highlighted the contribution of immersion in experience as a structural component of learning, I have no desire to romanticize it. The wisdom writers remind us forcefully enough that the daily life in which we play in the fields of the Lord presents us with messy, ill-structured problems, none more emotionally and physically demanding that those that befell Job and his family, none more psychologically enervating than those that oppressed the Teacher. And Proverbs leaves us in no doubt that experience might just as readily seduce us into evil company as persuade us to sojourn with Wisdom. There are choices of direction at stake—the broad or the narrow path, the boulevard of the fool or the walkway of the wise.

Choice is always and everywhere at work in experience. For experience, I have emphasized, is interactive; the world does not merely impress itself upon us, we select, organize, and prioritize within it. The ability of humans to envisage goals—to pursue the realization of values—that transcend the immediate and the present, is one of the marks of personhood. Though important elements of both are in operation, we are neither exclusively instinctively driven nor environmentally determined. At the heart of what it means to be human is the freedom to choose rather than merely to be impelled, to go beyond the limitations of the present moment in shaping the next. At the same time, our freedom is located within a lawful order that needs to be respected if truth is to be done. Our active experiencing of the world thus involves taking distance from it, as a complement to our active immersion in it. In this way, we intentionally constitute the situation as problem: we problematize our experience, we *problem-pose*.

Problems Posed to Us

As well as problems we set ourselves, however, if we are alive to the world we continually encounter events evoking curiosity and wonderment, the recognition that there is something addressing us that we cannot encompass, something that calls us beyond the settled contours of our experience to a relationship we do not presently enjoy. These events—challenges, opportunities—are also "problems." (As Huizinga [1949, 138] points out, *probléma* means literally "what is thrown before you.") We confront "arrests" (Oakeshott 1966) or disruptions in our experience, situations in which our accustomed responses are inappropriate. Judgment and decision are then required: we are challenged to respond in a normative way, perhaps in deciding on a course of action in concert with others, perhaps in realizing new color combinations when decorating a room, or perhaps in determining how resources may be most equitably distributed. These are examples of sociopolitical, aesthetic, and economic problems respectively; each is indicative of the fact that problems (in this case, as arrests that generate goals) are framed by normative or value stances. Thus, problems are *posed to us* by/in our experience; we are thrown out of kilter and challenged to find an appropriate response.

Such evocative events put a question, and as an echo of what someone has said, inside every question is a workshop. This is why "problems are our friends" (cf. Fullan 1993, 25–28). If we may indeed use the language of friendship in this respect, recognizing it as a form of love, we may conceive of problem-posing as not the opposite but the obverse of play, neither its contradiction nor its contrary, but its companion. There is not an antithetical relation between the two, but a mutual embeddedness. They are complementary modes of realizing value.

In the notion of learning as play, I focused on the recognition that much learning/knowing is unproblematic, tacit, embedded (in experience). Mostly, I do not have to focus on how to walk, for example, I just do it, and because I can just do it, I am even able to chew gum at the same time. But when I was learning to walk, this was fraught with challenges, and if now as an adult I am hiking in the mountains (or I am transplanted to Toronto, where the "footpaths" are "sidewalks" and, more significantly than this change in signifiers, bear the treacheries of ice and snow), I need often to focus my attention on where to place my feet. In these contexts, I learn step by step how to walk with greater facility, how to relate properly to the earth as I move across it. But it is only because I have largely resolved the problem of how to walk that I can turn my attention to other things—"Smell the roses!"—and learn further from the world through which I move. If I were not able to "forget," to (sub)merge in my bodily (un)consciousness, what I know, if all that I know were ever-present to mind, I could not know anything for the cacophony that would result. To call to mind, I have also to be able to put out of mind. The purpose of learning is that, having learned, I can go on and learn new things.

Learning as Transformation

If learning means undergoing a relatively permanent change in behavior, this can occur by broadening, enriching, and consolidating experience (in play) or by deepening it (through problem-posing): a person is somehow different as a result. How this change occurs will affect the status of what is learned in the sense of how it is interrelated with previously existing understanding and ability. The more coherent the connections, the more seamless the fabric, the more whole-bodiedly integrated this learning is, the more effective it has been. Such integration will frequently require a reinterpretation of experience.

Reinterpretation of previous learning is necessary if new (and better) understandings are in conflict with existing ones. An inadequate learning style favors accretion, not transformation. It allows learners to add new information "as a veneer of knowledge that they do not appreciate conflicts with their old beliefs." This reinterpretation can only occur if the adequacy of existing beliefs is somehow called into question: "The learner must be dissatisfied with his or her existing conceptions, and must find the new conception intelligible, plausible and fruitful" (Gunstone, White, Fensham 1988, 522). A problem with current understanding, if it exists, must be recognized if it is to be corrected.

It is in confronting and acknowledging uncertainty, one's own fallibility, and the ongoing mystery of existence that much valuable learning occurs. It is for this reason that Dewey (1966, 154) may claim that "the most significant question which can be asked . . . about any situation or experience proposed to induce learning is what quality of problem it involves." Like myself, Dewey has a very broad sense of the latter term, suggesting in another context that it refers to "whatever—no matter how slight and commonplace in character—perplexes and challenges the mind so that it makes belief at all uncertain" (Dewey 1933, 12–13; cit. Foshay 1998). Uncertainty is not to be our permanent condition, but it is important to know when to be uncertain as well as that there is a time to be sure.

Humble Sensitivity

A wise person is an integrated character, in which the values that govern life's decisions are complementary and capable of simultaneous realization. But the wise person knows also that in a less than perfect world, if something is worth doing, it is worth doing badly (as Chesterton remarked). There is no theoretical blueprint, no guarantee of sound judgment, no infallible prediction of all consequences. Wisdom revels in creation's fecundity, as it simultaneously accepts the challenge of bringing healing where there is brokenness. While the theory-into-practice paradigm promises us certainty about what is true at all times and in all places, wisdom counsels a humble sensitivity to the moment-by-moment demands of particular situations. It accepts that ambiguity and uncertainty are intrinsic to our present condition. A timed creation calls us to timely response, in the midst of experience, not in abstraction from it. "There is a time for everything, according to its purpose"; wisdom entails knowing when.

The major justification for schools is that we should not leave learning to chance, nor should we trust the vagaries of experience. Because not only may experience affect us negatively, our responses in it may be mistaken, we may misinterpret, fail to distinguish clearly, to phrase properly, to react sufficiently quickly—in other words, we may fail to value rightly. The order of creation does not merely impress itself on us: it invites us to respond normatively to it.

A Program of Problem-Posing

On the view of learning that I have been outlining, schooling ought to be conceived in part as the endeavor to encourage the student to explore a problem-space by taking into account the various norms that are to govern action in this concrete situation. For example, while it is in most cases true that novels are written in the first place to be enjoyed, to immerse their readers in plots, characters, and themes, they also raise questions and issues that must be addressed. How would I have acted if I had been in Paul Morel's place? Is that decision one with which I would choose to identify? Is that choice of words and imagery appropriate to convey the mood the author intends? The task of the teacher charged with leading students in the study of a novel is to lead them to question where they would otherwise take for granted, so that they come to see depths that would else have eluded them, allusions that would have simply not have been recognized. The kind of meticulous study of a novel that is characteristic of English classes may indeed detract from the flow of simple enjoyment, but the purpose is to deepen students' perceptiveness of the many other texts they will read in life, and not only of texts, but of life contexts. The teacher must often unsettle the convictions and prejudices that students bring with them to the task, so that they will develop a more sophisticated evaluative competence, a more nuanced sensitivity to the world.

When I take a Grade 10 Biology class on an excursion to Westernport Bay, and they classify the organisms dredged from the bottom, the purpose is both to broaden their experience and to deepen their responses to it. The questions that I pose are questions they may not themselves have asked, but which I hope will contribute not only to a store of information about mollusks, crustaceans, and sea grasses, but to the development of an inquiring mind that will see more deeply and engage more extensively with the biological world, that will value more meaningfully the fragile forms of life. Perhaps none of them will follow Sam into a career in marine biology, but I hope that all will be disposed to relate to the sea more sensitively.

A group of Grade 7 students who are invited to select a scrap piece of timber and to shape it and sand it to bring out the natural grain, and even to savor the smell, to feel the resistance, and to be respectful of the properties of the piece, are learning to value what they might otherwise have regarded as rubbish. In our teaching, we are inviting students to pay attention to differences in species, character, significance of historical events, to the unique qualities of a painting or a piano concerto, to finding a solution to an algebraic equation and balancing chemical formulae—and asking them to *value* and *evaluate* all these things (in the context of the Most Valuable).

These problem-posing encounters are not primarily reflective moments, though they will involve these. The language of reflection, like that of "reasoning about," is too passive and intellectualistic to capture the quality of responsiveness in its various evaluative modes that I am arguing is at the heart of good learning/teaching. As I have reiterated, there are as many primary modes of responsiveness as there are primary modes of value/normativity; these include the theoretical-analytical, but also the lingual, techno-cultural, social, economic, aesthetic, jural, ethical, and confessional.

Discerning Student Needs

When advocating a problem-posing pedagogy above, I added the qualification "in part"; a significant caveat is in order: no one should be left in a continuing state of cognitive dissonance. Teachers will need to be sensitively discerning of the needs and characteristics of their students, as individuals and as a group; they should in particular be aware of the developmental level of students. Though the teacher I quote once more is well aware of the significance of dissonance for learning, she is equally aware that she must introduce this in an appropriate manner, under conditions that she has carefully considered.

> I purposely end the unit on Quebec with a French poem called *Speak White*, even though each year again, I have reservations about teaching it. I hesitate because it calls up such negative feelings on the part of students. It is a poem written in 1967, the year Canada celebrated its centennial. It was recited for the first time in Montreal at the height of the quiet revolution, the beginning of Quebec's movement towards independence. After situating the poem in its historical context, I play the video, one in which the author, Michele Lalonde, reads the poem. It is a powerfully bitter and angry poem which ends on a note of resignation. After watching the video, the class is eerily silent, uncomfortable, crestfallen. "What do you think?" I ask. Well, they hate it! They feel shame, guilt and anger. Responses are immediate and defensive. The students tend to personalize this poem, seeing it as an attack on themselves. And the forcefulness of their response makes me wonder yet again whether I have undone what I have worked hard at doing—building an understanding and appreciation for Quebec and its people.
>
> I would never teach this poem to a group of students I do not know nor would I place this poem at the beginning of the unit. Being familiar with my students, having worked with them in our communication unit on building a classroom environment which is hospitable to learning, allowing students to express what they think without feel-

ing threatened, all allow this to be a valuable learning experience. It is important when implementing curriculum, to have a clear sense of purpose, to understand the why of what we are including so that we cannot be too easily derailed by student reaction. That is not to say that we are unwilling to adjust the curriculum as students give us feedback, but our decisions should not be based **solely** on the reactions of students to the material. The temptation might be to cushion our students from situations which make them uncomfortable or stretch their understanding, yet, with forethought and careful debriefing, these are the learning opportunities which stay with them the longest. (Vanderkooy 2002, 5–6)

Problems are Our Friends

Our pedagogy should enable us to honor the challenge continually present in experience to be more responsive to God and his world, and the privilege we have as image-bearers to be purposefully and personally responsible in all our actions, including the act of learning. For learning involves acting, choosing, deciding—not just receiving. And though I have been focusing more on learning than on teaching, this is supported by the conviction that the processes of learning and teaching map onto one another, are "coextensive" (Ikuenobe 2001, 326) and ought in practice to complement each other as a hand fits a glove.

Problems are our friends; tasks come with gifts in their hands. If the role of fairy tales is "to prepare children for later traumatic experiences," as Peter, Paul & Mary suggested, then schooling must also have this inoculatory or preparatory role. Children who do not live in cocoons will be exposed to many events in their lives that will cause them pain, and they will bring this pain with them to school. But even when the pain is real, neither to be denied nor downplayed, the promise is of patience to be learned, endurance to be nurtured, character to be built. As the German pedagogical tradition reminds us, being educated is *Bildung:* self-formation and transformation (cf. Bauer 2003).

Purposeful Response: The Formation of Character(s)

In this concluding section, I wish to focus on the role of purposeful response, first in the formation of *character* and second, in the formation of *a character.* "Purposeful response" is my shorthand for freely chosen action directed by and toward normative ends; it is wisdom as *realization 2.* I doubt that anyone (whatever their personal religious convictions) would argue with me that what we seek above all is not people who (merely) know what the truth is, but people who do the truth, people who are truthful, trothful. In this sense, we hope to build in ourselves and others—to en*cour-age*—virtue, integrity, character.

And I would go one step further: we seek to do this not merely by inducing a doctrinaire conformity (indoctrinating) but by respecting the freedom of choice given to people as differing *characters*. Wisdom requires "freedom in the presence of knowledge" (Whitehead 1967, 30). If the "wizardry" of the *Harry Potter* series indeed incorporates some "wisdom," then it might lie in the words of his Hogwarts headmaster, Albus Dumbledore: "It is our choices, Harry, that show what we truly are, far more than our abilities" (cit. Grossman 2003, 54).

This last quotation presents a timely occasion to comment on the first moment of learning, *realization 1a*. For I came upon it in the normal course of my daily life, that "broadening of my experience" that is part and parcel of being open to the world, of "living." (Which is why Adams [1999], who reminded us that learning often occurs by being "struck on the head," entitled his autobiography, *The Education of Henry Adams*.) It was unproblematic, so to speak; that it addressed a need I had was serendipitous. I had to respond purposefully to it, *notice* it and *value* it, but it did not evoke any dissonance. In the context of the formal planning of a school program, it is analogous to teachers taking children "out to play," in the fields of literature, history, science, basketball, or ballet. It is curriculum as *extension* of experience.

I wish to orient the ensuing discussion around the *intension* of experience, however, because an important and probably more difficult part of teaching and learning has to do with pruning and weeding the garden rather than with planting and watering. In other words, I will focus on purposeful responses to problems posed (in the play of experience).

Goals and Constraints

I suggested in the previous section that problems, whether posed by or to us, are characterized by the values that are prominent in a situation, indicating a discrepancy between what is and what one considers (could and) ought to be. They present a challenge that needs to be addressed (see Robinson 1993, 25).

As well as setting a goal to be attained, a problem-space is bounded by a set of constraints; together, these define the task to be achieved (Doyle 1983; Nickles 1981). These constraints may be determinative or normative. The former are factors that set the boundaries of what is possible and that may stand as (in)surmountable obstacles on the path to reaching the goal; these are the regularities and events the natural sciences seek to describe, but which are experienced as physical, physiological, or psychological barriers and opportunities in everyday life. We meet the latter as imperatives that may be honored or repudiated—ethical, economic, ecological and political demands, for example.

Determinative constraints may be formulated in rules and customs, in theory, etiquette, organizational policy, moral codes, legislation, or even "common sense"; normative demands must necessarily be given some such form. Examples of the first include Newton's Laws, driving on the "right" (which might be the left) side of the road, "stay away from hot objects or the edge of a cliff or . . ."; of the second, the Law of Thirds, do not/do burp after a meal (am I in France or Fiji?), honor your father and mother, treat persons not as means but as ends. Such rules can and often do themselves function as goals for behavior and establish a problem-space.

Realizing a goal—*realization 2*—involves meeting and overcoming the constraints of that problem-space in purposive action. A referee may achieve 100 percent in a test on the rules of the game, but still hesitate—not *know when*—to blow the whistle in the face of an infringement; he or she may be stymied from responding purposefully. Players may know well enough that the goal is to score goals, within the physical constraints of the field of play, the shape of the ball and the size and position of the target, and the normative constraints of the laws of the game, but lack the skill, ingenuity, or timeliness to do so. It is not enough then to simply "follow the rules," for they are but a framework within which action occurs.

A purposeful response is neither a conditioned or automatic reaction to a situation (a "stimulus-response" link in a chain of such responses, which I consider *reactions* rather than *responses*) nor an arbitrary even if totally voluntary rejoinder. A response is purposeful if it seeks the resolution of a problem by attaining a valued (i.e., value-laden) goal. We accomplish tasks by interpreting the problem-space and organizing resources in ways that enable us to address it adequately. The notion of "problem resolution" is used advisedly: it is not necessary, or even possible, to *solve* every problem we meet, in order to grow in understanding or improve in practice. Such tidiness is rare. All that we seek is an enhancement of our ability to resolve other problems that we experience (cf. Walker 1987).

Normative Growth

This may seem an overly pragmatic criterion, not far removed, if at all, from Dewey's central conception of growth. But Dewey was as concerned as I am in stressing the need for purposeful, normative response, to distinguish between educative and miseducative experience. The latter is one "that has the effect of arresting or distorting the growth of further experience. An experience may be such as to engender callousness; it may produce lack of sensitivity and responsiveness. Then the possibilities of having richer experience in the future are restricted" (Dewey 1965, 25). For Dewey (68–69), an emphasis on *activity* is inadequate, for this mistakes the immediate gratification of desires for true freedom; where he would say the latter issues only from the goal of *intelligent* activity, I would broaden the goal to include normative activity of diverse kinds (which has a similar effect to Gardner's pluralizing of intelligence). Just the same, one needs criteria by which to make the distinction, and with Dewey, I think that this lies in large part in encouraging students' responsiveness, for responsivity is of the essence of abundant life.

A formative emphasis on growth (rather than, say, performance indicators or learning outcomes, as summative attainments) comports well with a Christian eschatological perspective, with its recognition of the "now but not yet" character of life. Perfection is not a state that may be attained here and now. Yet a movement toward maturity is expected, and, because it is expected, it is possible; "sanctification" is one way of describing the process. Problems—the ultimate ones of injustice, suffering, and death—cannot be obliterated. It is not the solution or avoidance of problems that is promised, but the strength and courage to deal with them with faith, hope, and, above all, love (1 Corinthians 13:13). It is worth not only citing, but quoting, the Apostle Paul at this point:

> Therefore, since we are justified by faith, we have peace with God through our Lord Jesus Christ. Through him we have obtained access to this grace in which we stand, and we rejoice in our sufferings, knowing that suffering produces endurance, and endurance produces character, and character produces hope, and hope does not disappoint us, because God's love has been poured into our hearts through the Holy Spirit which has been given to us. (Romans 5:1–5, RSV)

The life of "character" is one of hope, which looks beyond the present in the expectation of the future. Brown (1996) suggests that the *formation*, *deformation*, and *reformation* of character is a key to understanding the Wisdom Literature, which demonstrates that the life of character is not one of "rule-following," because it requires an openness and vulnerability to life's slings and arrows, an ability to endure. As I have suggested, rules may establish constraints, but they cannot dictate action—normative activity—that is truly sensitive to the moment. A person of character is a person of integrity, who responds faithfully to the norms for human living. Such a person knows the right thing to do and is disposed to do it. And such is a wise person.

Suffering rivals ecstasy as an experience of life at its most intense. Thankfully, for most of us most of the time, ordinary life is just that—ordinary; even ecstasy cannot be typical. And in ordinary life, which transpires outside of strictly theoretical parameters, learning, which is also enduring toward the deformation or reformation of character, is not a matter of following rules. Grammar, for example, is useful largely for critiquing sentences already constructed (Bereiter 1991; Evers 1993). Forming a sentence may be regarded as a paradigm case of learning: in response to a situation in which we are immersed, we address a particular communicative goal, not by regurgitating a sentence we have previously prepared and stored in a necessarily finite repertoire, but by drawing on our vast experience with language to form an expression that is apt and, to all intents and purposes, unique. Thus, we can tap the infinite. And there is always something mysterious about an utterance or an inscription, for we only rarely know the conclusion when we commence. Even sentence formulation is impelled by hopefulness!

Education is a normative undertaking. Though arguments will rage about the extent to which the individual or society ought to be targeted as the primary beneficiaries, the ethical creed of the doctor applies to the care of students in schools as much as it does in medicine: "Do no harm." As with the Ten Commandments, this *proscription* is not the impediment that it might appear, for it opens up a large space within which the requirement is to "Do good" without *prescribing* exactly how this is to be done. It is a guarantee of freedom, not its prohibition. At the same time as it does not prescribe, however, it counsels attention to the normative dimensions that will promote a life of human flourishing.

Schools and teachers will thus seek to encourage and nurture some kinds of purposeful response on the part of students, and they will seek to discourage others. The criteria that are applied to sort better from worse responses will derive from the larger value or worldview framework endorsed by the sponsoring community. Such frameworks will not, of course, generally be incommensurable between communities: seeking "the truth of the matter," though necessarily being also "a matter of judgment," will be a goal that we may presume will be common to all.[23]

For the Christian community, these criteria will be derived from a judgment concerning how the gospel impinges upon daily life and what it means to be a Christian in contemporary society. The normativity or otherwise of a student's *purposeful response* to *problems posed* in the *play* of experience is to be discerned in the context of a fallen but redeemed-at-root creation: is it in the service of the Prince of Shalom, who has reconciled all things to himself? Thus, the *what* and the *how* are both important in the curriculum, for here matter and method merge in subject-*manner* : will it invite and enable students to lead serviceable lives? Is it structurally and directionally facilitative?

Realizing Value(s) in the Curriculum

If wisdom and character entail a disposition "to do the right thing," while it is true that this "right" is at root unitary, it also comes to expression in diverse, complex, differentiated forms. The example of speaking a sentence requires the resolution of a lingual problem, a purposeful effort to realize lingual norms in a concrete action: we have to choose our words. Similarly, in dealing with aesthetic or ethical problems, such as how to capture the play of light on a rock or in trying to decide whether to confront someone with a perceived disloyalty, different sorts of judgment must be exercised than are encompassed by the "scientific method" or its analogs. The moments of "reflection" in the painting of a picture are not theoretical in character; the painter is not concerned with the articulation of principles but with the production of an object that tacitly embodies aesthetic norms. It is by moving back and forth between the concrete material and an attitude of aesthetic distance that the material is shaped according to these norms. This is praxis, in which it is not practice and theoretical abstraction that are involved, but experience and an aesthetic mode of wisdom (cf. Macmurray 1969, 181).

The successful entrepreneur, the groundbreaking artist, the social prophet, the literary innovator: each displays an ability to perceive possibilities and then to actualize them. This is wisdom as the "realization of value"—hearing the call of God in creation and making it present to others. The biblical perspective on wisdom, with its openness to the richness and diversity of daily experience, gives us a perspective from within which to recognize that there are many ways other than theory that we can come to an understanding of God's world, many other kinds of value besides the theoretical that can define a problem-space and guide a response to it. If life is appropriately characterized not in rationalistic terms but as requiring the realization of a multiplicity of norms, then it is this whole range of norms that ought to map the contours for schooling. The everyday locus of human activity is not theoretical thought but concrete experience.

Different Abilities of Equal Value

If wisdom has pluriform instantiations and schools are to "do no harm," the various ways of wisdom must be honored when designing curriculum, in recognition of the biblical teaching that everyone is of ultimate value in the eyes of God and that everyone has been gifted by him according to his purposes. These purposes, in this specific as well as in the much more general sense, must be respected in discerning between students' purposeful responses. We met Bob Clifford, the boat-building entrepreneur who was a failure at school, in an earlier chapter. Rather than a merely vertical differentiation of human ability, the Bob Cliffords of this world—and we have known many, many of them in our journeys as teachers—challenge us to recognize and encourage a horizontal differentiation of abilities, one that ranks students not in order, from top to bottom, from first to last, but that ranges them in parallel, as possessing abilities that are equal in value.

As children develop, they do not merely string out along the same track, they choose different courses, whether or not the school formally allows for these—by which I mean, that students will often find their own ways of developing their interests and talents, while their in-school time merely acts as an impediment to their education. One will indeed sprint to the tape, but another exits the stadium to return several hours later having explored the surrounding streets, a third prefers the challenge of the hurdles, while a fourth would rather hop, step, and jump. There are yet others who are content for their peers to work themselves into a senseless sweat while they instead wander into the crowd for conversation, contemplate the blades of grass, opt to sit and read a good book, or to cheer on their confreres. And this is still to forget the judges and timekeepers, compilers of statistics, sketchers of competitors, reporters of events, organizers of award ceremonies and the musicians who play in them, and so on.

There are more intelligences than can be thought of in conventional psychology, as Gardner (1993) has most famously explored and learning styles theorists in their own way affirm. The structure of schooling will in many contexts militate against the realization appropriate to this recognition, which is why the notion of the "integral curriculum" seeks to locate this concern at its heart. Gardner believes that the intelligences evolved to help people do things that matter in the real world, and he argues that schools should seek to relate all of their activities to something that is *valued* in the world. He regards this as the core idea of multiple intelligences (Checkley 1997, 12). Along with the rubric to respect individual differences, this is a salutary reminder to schools of their mission: to nurture their students in the *realization of value.*

How would schools be organized differently if they were for the getting of wisdom in its various modes? Every classroom is peopled with unique individuals, each made in the image of God and thus of intrinsic worth, each gifted (and limited) in his or her own way. You know the Michaels and Michelles, the Jessicas and the Julians who greet you each day. Each of them is "a character," each of them in their (self-)formation is developing the characteristics that will further distinguish them from their peers as they mature. Though I have explored the formation of people of character, and there are many qualities that such people have in common, many attributes that are universally valued, it is also clear that they respond to these norms in ways that are not only situation-specific, but also specifically individual. Character takes on the profile of the characters who bear it. This is partly to do with temperament and personality, but these are also linked with and affected by each character's value choices and preferences.

If you had in your classroom an infant Martin Luther or an adolescent Mother Teresa, a Winston Churchill, Rupert Murdoch, Pablo Picasso, Gerard Manley Hopkins, Frank Lloyd Wright, Peter Singer, or even a Bob Clifford, how would you teach them? In an integral curriculum, the luminaries like these, and the multitude who share their kinds of talents if not their renown, could pursue in a unit on ancient Rome, for example, their confessional, ethical, political, aesthetic, and other understandings and contribute to the understanding of the whole class out of the depth of their particular insights. Winston could practice his oratory—"I come to bury Caesar"—as well as investigating the ins and outs of senatorial life; Rupert could publish the class newspaper, *Ancient Times,* recounting the news on the streets; the young Teresa could explore the social support networks at the same time as she worked alongside those with learning difficulties, bearing their burdens; Pablo could paint cityscapes or backdrops for the production of *Julius Caesar*—and Susan could calculate the mathematical intricacies of the Pantheon or the Coliseum, Terry could design and make clothes, Barbara could investigate forms of transport and build models of drays and chariots, Todd could cook traditional delicacies (and foods not so delicate), Louise could explore the sanitary systems, and so on.

Learning in Community

"The ways of wisdom are pleasant ways, and all her paths are peace" (Proverbs 3:17). In this linkage of wisdom with peace, it is important to remember that *shalom* is not to be understood negatively or passively, as the mere *absence* of conflict, but vibrantly and dynamically, as the mutual responsiveness and interdependence of all of God's creatures. It includes the dynamically harmonious interaction between individuals in a learning community, teachers as well as students, that the wisdom paradigm seeks to promote. Such a community is one where "justice and peace embrace"

(Psalm 85:10), where all people are given the space to "be"; wisdom's concern with justice has in large part motivated my quest, and only in a just community can there be real peace.

The foregrounding of wisdom gives scope for a communal rather than an individualistic conception of learning (as Hirst [1993] now also realizes). Theory purports to deliver truths that are the same for all people in all times at all places: if there is that one truth, then the goal of education is that everyone acquires it, if to a greater or lesser extent. If, however, one recognizes that the truth of a complex situation is many-sided, requiring the realization of many values, the contributions of people with different kinds of understanding—wisdom—becomes necessary. Schooling at all levels can become a site for cooperative learning, indeed, should do so, for here is the most effective means of preparing people to live in society in cooperative rather than competitive ways. Part of the "situatedness" of cognition is its communality. It is not each individual "covering" the whole curriculum, but the depth of individual insight contributing to a broad communal understanding, that will ensure equity and quality.

The Teacher's Calling

The calling of the teacher is to create that safe, pleasant, and peaceful space for learning in which, as Parker Palmer (1983) says, obedience to truth may be practiced. Such *obedience* to truth in its varied expressions—not merely the *description* of it—is wisdom. In the end, what I hope to have achieved in this project is a similar "creation of space." To conclude with prescriptions would be to violate the spirit of wisdom; rather, I offer an invitation to explore this space in your own classroom, your own school, indeed, your own life.

ENDNOTES

1. This approach to curriculum is not as outré as it might seem. A report on the "Schools" page of *The Australian* (3 April 2000, 15) describes "A radical blueprint for reform of Queensland's public schools," in which "School renewal will be built on an integrated reform of teaching practice, curriculum and assessment. The emphasis is on flexibility, with schools and teachers left to make key decisions according to their judgment of local needs." Students will engage with areas "by completing a series of intellectually demanding, practically oriented projects known as 'rich tasks.'" These tasks must "be 'problem-based and relevant to new worlds of work and everyday life' and must be seen to be so by parents and the community." They should also be "transdisciplinary, drawing from a range of operational fields."

2. I acknowledge that this description reflects an earlier period in the life of the school; though much has changed in the concrete expression, and in exciting ways, the vision remains essentially the same, as a recent visit to the school has confirmed. The dialogues in later chapters are imaginative accounts in which traces of people and events at Mount Evelyn will however be identifiable by some; I trust these dialogues will be accepted as celebration of the rich communal life and dedicated enthusiasm for the calling of Christian teaching that I have sought to capture in these pages.

3. "Prep" is the colloquial term for "Preparatory Grade," the first year of formal schooling in Victoria, and is equivalent to "Kindergarten" in North American usage. (In Australia, "Kindergarten" refers to pre-schooling.)

4. The use of this term in the present context is owed to Israel Scheffler (1964).

5. There do seem to be echoes of the Old English and German in Shakespeare's use of *wis*, to which Robin Small has pointed me. However, it apparently has the sense of "suspect," falling short of the certainty of knowledge, a more limited notion than the one we find in "wisdom," the tolerance of uncertainty in the latter notwithstanding. See *King Richard III*, I:3; *The Taming of the Shrew*, I:1; *The Merchant of Venice*, II:9.

6. It is perhaps offensive in this context to mention the witticism, "One man's fish is another man's *poisson*," but the levity of this remark may also help us to capture the realization that it is not only in the extremes of horror, the almost *de rigeur* citing of Hitler, Stalin, and Pol Pot, that we see "man's inhumanity to man," but in the daily denial in so many countries of an ethnic and/or religious group's right to live out its own vision of life. The recent treatment of refugees or "boat people" by the

Australian government has been seen by many as an echo of horrors more readily recognized.

7. These two words of French provenance—*conversation* and *intercourse*—were originally interchangeable in English, but even the hymn that speaks of "intercourse at hearth and board" is apt to raise a chuckle these days. However, there is in the intimacy of intercourse in its full-bodied sense—of Eve-*knowing*-Adam-*knowing*-Eve—an even more powerful metaphor for knowledge and wisdom than we find in a purely verbal exchange.

8. Several months after writing this paragraph, I read Toulmin's *Cosmopolis*. It included a section that made similar observations to mine here. Indeed, I was encouraged to find quite a number of other similarities—specific, not merely general—in Toulmin's account (Toulmin 1990).

9. The emphasis is on curriculum as verb, on running the course, rather than on the noun form, the course that is to be run. In other words, the focus is on the learning rather than on what is to be learned, on the becoming rather than on the representation of being. I will explore this further in the next and a later chapter.

10. For example, Isocrates distinguished seven forms of knowledge (Muir 1998, 18). Aristotle identified differing aims of human activity that led to three ways of knowing, namely science, art, and politics (of which the former was the most important); these categories are echoed by Habermas. As Putnam points out, Kant began to develop a differentiated view, but scientific thought again maintained priority:

    > . . . I think we see, especially in the third Critique and in Kant's post-critical writings, a *tendency* towards genuine pluralism. . . . In effect, Kant begins to speak not only of a moral image of the world and a scientific image of the world, but also . . . of a religious image of the world, one which is subservient to the moral image of the world, but beginning to develop some autonomy of its own; and he also begins to speak . . . of what one might call aesthetic images of the world, and also of legal images of the world, and so on. To be sure, Kant, like Quine in our day, continued to insist that only the scientific image of the world contains what can properly be called "knowledge." (Putnam 1995, 30–31)

11. Warnock (1977) discusses these issues more broadly, without making the comparison I have drawn. You may hear perverse echoes of Alfred North Whitehead in these sentences (see Chapter 8).

12. Saul's choice of metaphor is unfortunate, to the extent that it plays on the unearned stigmatization of the child born out of wedlock, where, in fact, he is wishing to emphasize the active corruption of Voltaire's heritage by *usurpers* of the latter's good name. Bastardization is a more or less conscious debasement of something, and the perpetrators of such acts, unlike the labelled and libelled children from whom the term

derives, are deserving of moral condemnation. I thank Allyson Dziedzic for drawing this to my attention.

13. Even when these ideas are transmogrified into "sense data," a concept—like *idea* itself—that is the product of a sophisticated theoretical system.

14. Our inescapable bodiliness—the fact that moment by moment, breath by breath, we exchange matter/energy with our environment; that we ingest, digest, and eliminate; that we each share some of the molecules that once invested the body of Paul, and indeed, the body of Jesus, for Jesus, too, ate real food, before but also after his resurrection—constitutes an unabashedly physicalist basis for the notion of immersion, if this is what one requires.

15. Christian personalist, John Macmurray (1969, 54–57, 73), argues for the priority of the "I do" over the "I think":

    Action is primary and concrete, thought is secondary, abstract and derivative.... [T]he distinction between "right" and "wrong" is constitutive for action, is the primary standard of validity; while the distinction between "true" and "false"' is secondary. (Macmurray 1969, 89)

16. Interviewed by Paul Collins in *God's Earth* (ABC Television, 15 March 1998). Straus (1966) uses the term *pathic* to describe the invitational character of the world. This captures an aspect of the more tendentious side of the co-responsive relationship that I am describing here. In biblical terms, it is a reference to the revelational character of creation.

17. It is just that Plato thought the True—and the Good and the Beautiful—were abstract entities to be approached through abstract thought. But value—nor truth, for that matter—is not a quality attaching solely to propositions.

18. Though I have not explored the Aristotelian perspective on *phronesis* or practical wisdom herein, it is worth noting Dunne's (1997, 290) observation in respect to this that "it is not the case that one is first of good character, and *then* can have phronesis. Rather, being phronetic is itself part of what it means to be of good character." As Noel (1999, 286) comments, "we cannot separate *phronesis* from the moral character of the person who exhibits it, the *phronimos*."

19. It is also worth keeping in mind Davis's (1997, 4) warning about the dangers of preferring "best practices" to "wise practices" and remembering that the latter are "idiosyncratic, contextual, textured, and probably inconsistent."

20. Aspin and Chapman (1994, 112) comment: "We should . . . still want every student to be given the chance to develop as far as their interests and ambitions take them. But this means the provision of opportunities and appropriate teaching and learning styles to allow all students to

advance and grow in domains other than the merely cognitive."

21. There is evident ambiguity in this sentence, but the emphasis is on thanking God for saving us from the full consequences of our individual and collective *striving* after evil, not on thanking God for evil. Just as we cannot guarantee positive outcomes by our own efforts alone, but receive goods ultimately as gifts from God, neither can we pursue evil to its ultimate, God's gift to us in this case being the restraints placed on us.

22. Doll (2002) explores the embeddedness of control and method in the very conception of curriculum, as it was introduced into educational discourse by Peter Ramus in 1576 and adopted, interestingly enough, by the Calvinist-influenced universities of Leiden and Glasgow. He suggests connections to Calvin's frequent references to life as a "race" or a "racecourse" and the use of the phrases *vitae curriculum* and *vitae curriculo* in the final, 1559 edition of the *Institutes*.

23. Australian readers will notice here an allusion to the constitutional crisis of 1975, when the Whitlam government was dismissed by Governor-General Kerr. The two phrases in quotation marks were titles of their respective accounts of the events of the period.

BIBLIOGRAPHY

Adams, H. *The Education of Henry Adams*, Oxford World's Classics ed. New York: Oxford University Press, 1999.

"A radical blueprint for reform of Queensland's public schools," *The Australian* (3 April 2000), 15.

Aristotle. *The Ethics of Aristotle*. Translated by J. A. K. Thomson. New York: Penguin, 1953.

Arlin, P. K. "Wisdom: The Art of Problem Finding." In *Wisdom: Its Nature, Origins, and Development,* edited by R. J. Sternberg, 230–43. Cambridge: Cambridge University Press, 1990.

Aspin, D. N. "An Ontology of Values and the Humanisation of Education." In *Values in Education,* edited by S. Pascoe, 12–24. Deakin West, ACT: Australian College of Educators, 2002.

Aspin, D. N., J. D. Chapman, with V. Wilkinson. *Quality Schooling: A Pragmatic Approach to Some Current Problems, Topics and Issues.* London: Cassell, 1994.

Association for Supervision and Curriculum Development. *ASCD Education Update* 5 (June 1996).

Association of Parents for Christian Education Mount Evelyn. *Senior Secondary Education: A Proposal.* Melbourne, 1976.

Bantick, C. "Leave a Boy in School but You Won't Make Him Think: Success Should not be Equated with University Admission Scores." *The Australian*, 17 July 2001, 15.

Bates, R. "Educational Research and the Economy of Happiness and Love." *The Australian Educational Researcher* 22, no. 1 (1995), 1–16.

Bawden, R. "Problem-based Learning: An Australian Perspective." In *Problem-based Learning in Education for the Professions,* edited by D. Boud, 43–57. Sydney: Higher Education Research and Development Society of Australasia, 1985.

Begbie, J. *Theology, Music and Time.* Cambridge: Cambridge University Press, 2000.

Bell, D. *Cultural Contradictions of Capitalism.* New York: Basic Books, 1976.

Bereiter, C. "Implications of Connectionism for Thinking about Rules." *Educational Researcher* 20, no. 3 (1991), 10–16.

Bigge, M. L. *Learning Theories for Teachers,* 4th ed. New York: Harper & Row, 1982.

Biggs, J. B., and R. Telfer. *The Process of Learning,* 2nd ed. Sydney, NSW: Prentice-Hall of Australia, 1987.

Birren, J. E., and L. M. Fisher. "The Elements of Wisdom: Overview and Integration." In *Wisdom: Its Nature, Origins, and Development,* edited by R. J. Sternberg, 317–32. Cambridge: Cambridge University Press, 1990.

Blake, N., P. Smeyers, R. Smith, and P. Standish. *Thinking Again: Education after Postmodernism.* Westport, CT: Bergin & Garvey, 1998.

Blomberg, D. G. *The Development of Curriculum with Relation to the Philosophy of the Cosmonomic Idea.* Unpublished Ph.D. Dissertation. Sydney: University of Sydney, 1978.

———. "Toward a Christian Theory of Knowledge." In *No Icing on the Cake: Christian Foundations for Education in Australasia,* edited by J. Mechielsen, 41–60. Melbourne: Brookes-Hall Publishing Foundation, 1980a.

———. "Curriculum Guidelines for the Christian School." In *No Icing on the Cake: Christian Foundations for Education in Australasia,* edited by J. Mechielsen, 111–22. Melbourne: Brookes-Hall, 1980b.

———."Developing a Christian Curriculum, Part II." *Nurture* 20, no. 3 (1986), 9–10.

———. "The Teacher as Evaluator." *Curriculum Perspectives* 11, no. 4 (1991), 32–41.

———. "Teacher as Researcher, Curriculum as Hypothesis: Implications for the Education of Educators." In *Educating Christian Teachers for Responsive Discipleship,* edited by P. DeBoer, 63–84. Lanham: University Press of America, 1993.

———. *Ways of Knowing and the Task of Teaching, with Implications for Teacher Education.* Unpublished Master of Educational Studies Thesis. Melbourne: Monash University, 1994.

———. "Teachers as Articulate Artisans." In *Nurturing Reflective Christians to Teach,* edited by D. C. Elliott, 99–118. Lanham: University Press of America. 1995.

———. "Maintaining the Boundaries: Secular Versus Sacred." In *Humans Being: Essays Dedicated to Stuart Fowler,* edited by D. Blomberg, 15–38. Sydney: National Institute for Christian Education, 1996.

———. "Wisdom at Play: In the World but Not of It." In *The Crumbling Walls of Certainty: Towards a Christian Critique of Postmodernity and Education,* edited by I. Lambert and S. Mitchell, 120–35. Sydney: Centre for the Study of Australian Christianity, 1997.

———. *Living with Ambiguity.* Unpublished manuscript. Toronto: Institute for Christian Studies, 1998a.

———. "The Practice of Wisdom: Knowing When." *Journal of Education & Christian Belief* 2, no. 1 (1998b), 7–26.

———. "An 'Epistemology' of Teaching." *Philosophia Reformata* 64 (1999), 1–14.

———. "Ways of Wisdom: Multiple Modes of Meaning in Pedagogy and

Andragogy." In *Ways of Knowing, In Concert*, edited by J. H. Kok, 123–146. Sioux Center: Dordt College Press, 2005.

Bonsting, J. J. *Schools of Quality*. Alexandria, VA: Association for Supervision and Curriculum Development, 1992.

Bowles, S., and H. Gintis. *Schooling in Capitalist America: Educational Reform and the Contradictions of Economic Life*. London and Henley: Routledge & Kegan Paul, 1976.

Bringuier, J.-C. *Conversations with Jean Piaget*. Translated by B. F. Gulatis. Chicago: University of Chicago Press, 1980.

Brown, J. S., A. Collins, and P. Duguid. "Situated Cognition and the Culture of Learning." *Educational Researcher* 18, no. 1 (1989), 32–42.

Brown, W. *Character in Crisis: A Fresh Approach to the Wisdom Literature of the Old Testament*. Grand Rapids and Cambridge: Eerdmans, 1996.

Brueggemann, W. *The Creative Word: Canon as a Model for Biblical Education*. Philadelphia: Fortress, 1982.

Bruner, J. S. *Acts of Meaning*. Cambridge: Harvard University Press, 1990.

―――. *Actual Minds, Possible Worlds*. Cambridge: Harvard University Press, 1986.

―――. "Frames for Thinking: Ways of Making Meaning." In *Modes of Thought: Explorations in Culture and Cognition,* edited by N. Torrance and J. P. Torrance, 93–105. Cambridge: Cambridge University Press, 1996.

Buber, M. *I and Thou*. Translated by R. G. Smith. Edinburgh: T. & T. Clark, 1958.

Caine, R. N., and G. Caine. *Making Connections: Teaching and the Human Brain*. Alexandria, VA: Association for Supervision and Curriculum Development, 1991.

Caldwell, B. "School-based Decision-making and Management: International Perspectives." In *School-based Decision-making and Management*, edited by J. Chapman. London: Falmer, 1990.

Carr, W., ed. *Quality in Teaching: A Sample of Cases*. London: Falmer, 1989.

Chalmers, A. F. *What Is This Thing Called Science?* 2nd ed. St. Lucia, Qld.: University of Queensland Press, 1982.

Chomsky, N. Television interview, 30 March 1978. *The Listener,* 6 April 1978.

Clements, R. E. *Wisdom in Theology*. Carlisle/Grand Rapids: Paternoster/ Eerdmans, 1992.

Clouser, R. A. *The Myth of Religious Neutrality: An Essay on the Hidden Role of Religious Belief in Theories*. Notre Dame and London: University of Notre Dame Press, 1991.

Code, L. *What Can She Know? Feminist Theory and the Construction of*

Knowledge. Ithaca and London: Cornell University Press, 1991.

Concise Oxford Dictionary of Current English. Adapted by H. W. Fowler and F. G. Fowler from *The Oxford Dictionary.* 4ᵗʰ ed. Oxford: Clarendon Press, 1952.

Connelly, F. M., and J. Clandinin. "The Promise of Collaborative Research in the Political Context." In *Teacher Research and Educational Reform,* edited by H. Sockett, 86–102. Chicago: University of Chicago Press, 1994.

Crenshaw, J. *Old Testament Wisdom: An Introduction.* Atlanta: John Knox, 1981.

Csikszentmihalyi, M. *Finding Flow: The Psychology of Engagement with Everyday Life.* New York: Basic Books, 1997.

———. *Flow: The Psychology of Optimal Experience.* New York: HarperCollins, 1991.

Cumming, J., et al. *Teacher Standards, Quality and Professionalism: Towards a Common Approach. Report of a National Meeting of Professional Educators.* Canberra: Australian College of Educators, 2002.

Damasio, A. R. *Descartes' Error: Emotion, Reason, and the Human Brain.* New York: Avon, 1995.

Danzig, T. *Number: The Language of Science.* Garden City, NY: Doubleday-Anchor, 1954.

Davies, P. *The Mind of God: Science and the Search for Ultimate Meaning.* Harmondsworth: Penguin, 1993.

Davis, O. L. "Editorial: Beyond 'Best Practices' Toward 'Wise Practices.'" *Journal of Curriculum and Supervision* 13, no 1 (1997), 92–113.

de Graaff, A. H., and J. Olthuis, eds. *Joy in Learning: An Integrated Curriculum for the Elementary School* (Vol. I). Toronto: Curriculum Development Centre, 1973.

Derrida, J. *Of Grammatology.* Translated by G. C. Spivak. Baltimore: Johns Hopkins University Press, 1976.

Dewey, J. *Democracy and Education.* New York: Free Press, 1966.

———. *How We Think: A Restatement of the Relation of Reflective Thinking to the Educative Process,* new ed. Boston: D. C. Heath, 1933.

———. *Logic: A Theory of Inquiry.* New York: Holt, 1938.

———. *Experience and Education.* New York: Collier, 1965.

———. "Philosophy and Democracy." In *The Middle Works: 1899–1924,* Vol. 11, edited by J. A. Boydston, 41–53. Carbondale: Southern Illinois University Press, 1982.

Dibbits, T. *Taking Action: Helping Students Learn.* Unpublished Master of Worldview Studies Essay. Toronto: Institute for Christian Studies, 2002.

Dickens, C. *Hard Times.* London: Nelson, n.d.

Doll, W. E., Jr. "Ghosts and the Curriculum." In *Curriculum Visions,* edited by W. E. Doll, Jr. and N. Gough, 23-70. New York: Peter Lang, 2002.

———. *A Post-Modern Perspective on Curriculum.* New York and London: Teachers College Press, 1993.

Dooyeweerd, H. *A New Critique of Theoretical Thought,* Vol. I–IV. Philadelphia: Presbyterian and Reformed, 1953.

Dordt College. *The Educational Task of Dordt College.* Sioux Center: Dordt College, 1979/1996. (See *Celebrating the Vision: The Reformed Perspective of Dordt College,* edited by J. H. Kok, 1–16. Sioux Center: Dordt College Press, 2004.)

Doyle, W. "Academic Work." *Review of Educational Research,* 53 (1983), 159–99.

Duckworth, R., ed. *This Is the Word of the Lord. Year A. The Year of Matthew.* Oxford: Oxford University Press, 1980.

Dunne, J. *Back to the Rough Ground: Practical Judgment and the Lure of Technique.* Notre Dame: University of Notre Dame Press, 1997.

Eco, U. *Kant and the Platypus: Essays on Language and Cognition.* Translated by A. McEwan. San Diego: Harcourt, 1999.

Eisner, E. W. *Cognition and Curriculum: A Basis for Deciding What to Teach.* New York and London: Longman, 1982.

———. *The Educational Imagination.* New York: Macmillan, 1979.

Elbow, P. *Embracing Contraries: Explorations in Learning and Teaching.* New York and Oxford: Oxford University Press, 1986.

Eliot, T. S. *The Collected Poems and Plays of T. S. Eliot: 1909–1950.* New York: Harcourt, Brace, and World, 1971.

Elliott, R. K. "Education, Love of One's Subject, and the Love of Truth." *Proceedings of the Philosophy of Education Society of Great Britain* 8, no. 1 (1974), 135–53.

Evers, C., and G. Lakomski. *Knowing Educational Administration.* Oxford: Pergamon, 1991.

Evers, C. W. *Administrative Decision-making as Pattern Processing.* Unpublished paper. Clayton, Vic.: Monash University, 1993.

Foshay, A. W. "Problem Solving and the Arts." *Journal of Curriculum and Supervision* 13, no. 4 (1998), 328–38.

Fowler, J. W. *Stages of Faith.* Blackburn, Vic.: Dove Communications, 1981.

Fowler, Stuart, ed. *Christian Schooling: Education for Freedom.* Potchefstroom, RSA: Potchefstroom University for Christian Higher Education, 1990.

Frankl, V. *Man's Search for Meaning: An Introduction to Logotherapy.* New York: Pocket Books, 1963.

Freire, P. *Cultural Action for Freedom.* Harmondsworth: Penguin, 1975.

————. *Pedagogy of the Oppressed*. Harmondsworth: Penguin, 1972.

Fullan, M. *Change Forces: Probing the Depths of Educational Reform*. London: Falmer, 1993.

Gadamer, H.-G. *Truth and Method*, 2nd rev. ed. Translated by J. Weinsheimer and D. G. Marshall. New York: Continuum, 1989.

Gardner, H. *Multiple Intelligences: The Theory in Practice*. New York: Basic Books, 1993.

Gardner, H., M. Csikszentmihalyi, and W. Damon. *Good Work: When Excellence and Ethics Meet*. New York: Basic Books, 2001.

Gellner, E. *Words and Things*. Harmondsworth: Penguin, 1968.

————. *Words and Things: An Examination of, and an Attack on, Linguistic Philosophy*. London and Boston: Routledge & Kegan Paul, 1979.

Glatthorn, A. A. *Developing a Quality Curriculum*. Alexandria, VA: Association for Supervision and Curriculum Development, 1994.

Goethe, W. *Goethe's World View, Presented in his Reflections and Maxims*. New York: Frederick Ungar, 1963.

Goldman, R. *Religious Thinking from Childhood to Adolescence*. London: Routledge & Kegan Paul, 1968.

Goldsworthy, G. *Gospel and Wisdom: Israel's Wisdom Literature in the Christian Life*. Carlisle: Paternoster, 1995.

Goodlad, J. I. *Teachers for Our Nation's Schools*. San Francisco: Jossey-Bass, 1990.

Goudzwaard, B. *Capitalism and Progress: A Diagnosis of Western Society*. Translated by J. Zylstra. Toronto and Grand Rapids: Wedge/Eerdmans, 1979.

————. *Idols of Our Time*. Translated by M. Vander Vennen. Downers Grove: InterVarsity Press, 1984.

Groome, T. H. *Sharing Faith*. San Francisco: Harper, 1991.

Grossman, L. "The Story so Far, Book by Book." *TIME Canadian Edition* 161 (23 June 2003), 54–55.

Gunstone, R. R., R. T. White, and P. J. Fensham. "Developments in Style and Purpose of Research on the Learning of Science." *Research in Science Teaching* 25, no. 7 (1988), 513–29.

Hadot, P. *Philosophy as a Way of Life: Spiritual Exercises from Socrates to Foucault*. Translated by M. Chase. Oxford and New York: Blackwell, 1995.

Hager, P., and J. Halliday. *The Importance of Context and Judgment in Learning*. Paper presented at the Thirtieth Conference of the Philosophy of Education Society of Australasia, Claremont Teachers College, WA, 2001.

Hart, L. A. *Human Brain and Human Learning*. New York: Longman, 1983.

Hawking, S. W. *A Brief History of Time: From the Big Bang to Black Holes.* London: Bantam, 1988.

Hayles, N. K. *Chaos Bound.* Ithaca: Cornell University Press, 1990.

Hill, B. V. *Was the Piggy Who Went to Market Satisfied? Educational Aims in a Consumer Society Adrift.* Paper presented at the Thirtieth Conference of the Philosophy of Education Society of Australasia, Claremont Teachers College, WA, 2001.

Hirst, P. H. *Knowledge and the Curriculum: A Collection of Philosophical Papers.* London and Boston: Routledge & Kegan Paul, 1974.

Hirst, P. H., and R. S. Peters. *The Logic of Education.* London: Routledge & Kegan Paul, 1970.

Holy Bible, New International Version. Grand Rapids: Zondervan, 1973, 1978, 1984.

Holy Bible, Revised Standard Version. London: The British and Foreign Bible Society, 1952.

Hopkins, Gerard Manley. *Gerard Manley Hopkins: Poems and Prose,* edited by W. H. Gardner. Harmondsworth: Penguin, 1953.

Hough, M., and J. Paine. *Creating Quality Learning Communities.* South Melbourne, Vic: Macmillan, 1997.

Houston, W. R., and R. T. Clift. "The Potential for Research Contributions to Reflective Practice." In *Encouraging Reflective Practice in Education: An Analysis of Issues and Programs,* edited by M. C. Pugach, 208–22. New York and London: Teachers College Press, 1990.

Huizinga, J. *Homo Ludens: A Study of the Play Element in Culture.* London: Paladin, 1949.

Ikuenobe, P. "Questioning as an Epistemic Process of Critical Thinking." *Educational Philosophy and Theory* 33, no. 3 & 4 (2001), 325–41.

Ilter, T. "The Unassimilable Otherness of the 'Post' of Postmodernism and the Radicality of Radical Sociology." *Critical Sociology* 20, no. 2 (1994), 51–80.

James, W. *The Writings of William James,* edited by J. J. McDermott. Chicago and London: University of Chicago Press, 1977.

Jencks, C. *What Is Post-Modernism?* 2nd enlarged, rev. ed. New York: St. Martin's, 1987.

Jensen, E. *Teaching with the Brain in Mind.* Alexandria VA: Association for Supervision and Curriculum Development, 1998.

Kelly, A. V. *Knowledge and Curriculum Planning.* London: Harper & Row, 1986.

Kilbourn, B. "Fictional Theses." *Educational Researcher* 28, no. 9 (1999), 27–32.

Kitchener, K. S., and H. G. Brenner. "Wisdom and Reflective Judgment." In *Wisdom: Its Nature, Origins, and Development,* edited by R. J. Sternberg,

212–29. Cambridge: Cambridge University Press, 1990.

Kitchener, R. F. *The World View of Contemporary Physics: Does It Need a New Metaphysics?* Albany: SUNY, 1988.

Knight, G. R. *Philosophy and Education: An Introduction in Christian Perspective,* 2nd ed. Berrien Springs, MI: Andrews University Press, 1980.

Koestler, A. *The Act of Creation.* London: Pan Books, 1975.

Kohlberg, L. *The Psychology of Moral Development: The Nature and Validity of Moral Stages.* San Francisco: Harper & Row, 1984.

Kohut, H. *Restoration of the Self.* New York: Princeton University Press, 1977.

Kreeft, P. *Three Philosophies of Life.* San Francisco: Ignatius, 1989.

Lacayo, R. "Mies is More." *TIME Australia* (23 July 2001), 74–75.

Lather, P. "Troubling Clarity: The Politics of Accessible Language." *Harvard Educational Review* 66, no. 3 (1966), 525–54.

Lewis, C. S. *The Abolition of Man: Reflections on Education with Special Reference to the Teaching of English in the Upper Forms of Schools.* London: Geoffrey Bles, 1967.

Loewen, J. W. *Lies across America: What Our Historic Sites Get Wrong.* New York: New Press, distributed by W. W. Norton, 1999.

———. *Lies My Teacher Told Me: Everything Your American History Textbook Got Wrong,* New York: Simon & Schuster, 1996.

Lynn, J., and A. Jay, eds. *Yes Minister: The Diaries of a Cabinet Minister by the Rt Hon. James Hacker MP* Vol. Two. London: British Broadcasting Corporation, 1982.

Lyotard, J.-F. *The Postmodern Condition: A Report on Knowledge.* Translated by G. B. B. Massumi. Minneapolis: University of Minnesota Press, 1984.

MacIntyre, A. *After Virtue: A Study in Moral Theory,* 2nd ed. Notre Dame: University of Notre Dame Press, 1984.

MacKay, D. M. *The Clockwork Image: A Christian Perspective on Science.* London: InterVarsity Press, 1974.

Macmurray, J. *The Self as Agent.* London: Faber and Faber, 1969.

"Make Schools More Responsive." *The West Australian* (31 May 2002), 18.

Mant, A. *Intelligent Leadership.* St Leonards, NSW: Allen & Unwin, 1997.

Marginson, S. *Education and Public Policy in Australia.* New York: Cambridge University Press, 1993.

Maslow, A. H. "Self-Actualizing People: A Study of Psychological Health." *Personality* 1 (1950), 11–34.

Maturana, H. R., and F. J. Varela. *The Tree of Knowledge.* Boston: Shambhala, 1987.

Maxwell, N. *From Knowledge to Wisdom: A Revolution in the Aims and Methods of Science.* Oxford: Basil Blackwell, 1984.

McDermott, J. J., ed. *The Writings of William James.* Chicago and London: University of Chicago Press, 1977.

McDonald, J. P. *Teaching: Making Sense of an Uncertain Craft.* New York: Teachers College Press, 1992.

McLaren, P., and P. Leonard, eds. *Paulo Freire: A Critical Encounter.* London: Routledge, 1995.

Meacham, J. A. "The Loss of Wisdom." In *Wisdom: Its Nature, Origins, and Development,* edited by R. J. Sternberg, 181–211. Cambridge: Cambridge University Press, 1990.

Melchert, C. *Wise Teaching: Biblical Wisdom and Educational Ministry.* Harrisburg, PA: Trinity Press International, 1998.

Meredith, S., R. Speedy, and B. Wood. *Industry and Enterprise Studies: VCE Units 1 and 2.* Port Melbourne, Vic: Heinemann, 2001.

Merton, T. *A Thomas Merton Reader.* New York: Doubleday, 1989.

Morgan, D. F. *The Making of Sages: Biblical Wisdom and Contemporary Culture.* Harrisburg, PA: Trinity Press International, 2002.

Muir, J. "The History of Educational Ideas and the Credibility of Philosophy of Education." *Educational Philosophy and Theory* 30, no. 1 (1998), 7–26.

Munby, H., and T. Russell. "Educating the Reflective Teacher: An Essay Review of Two Books by Donald Schön." *Journal of Curriculum Studies* 21 (1989), 71–80.

Nehemas, A. *The Art of Living: Socratic Reflections from Plato to Foucault.* Berkeley: University of California Press, 1998.

Nickles, T. "What Is a Problem that We Might Solve It?" *Synthese* 47, no. 1 (1981), 85–118.

Noddings, N. *Caring: A Feminine Approach to Ethics and Moral Education.* Berkeley: University of California Press, 1984.

———. *The Challenge to Care in Schools: An Alternative Approach to Education.* New York: Teachers College Press, 1992.

Noel, J. "On the Varieties of *Phronesis.*" *Educational Philosophy and Theory* 31, no. 3 (1999), 273–89.

Oakeshott, M. *Experience and Its Modes.* Cambridge: Cambridge University Press, 1966.

Oliver, D. W., with K. W. Gershman. *Education, Modernity, and Fractured Meaning: Toward a Process Theory of Teaching and Learning.* Albany: SUNY, 1989.

Oppewal, D. *Biblical Knowing and Teaching.* Grand Rapids: Calvin College, 1985.

Orwoll, L., and M. Perlmutter. "The Study of Wise Persons: Integrating a Personality Perspective." In *Wisdom: Its Nature, Origins, and Development,* edited by R. J. Sternberg, 160–77. Cambridge: Cambridge

University Press, 1990.

Palmer, P. J. *The Courage to Teach*. San Francisco: Jossey-Bass, 1998.

———. *To Know as We Are Known: A Spirituality of Education*. San Francisco: Harper & Row, 1983.

Pascual-Leone, J. "An Essay on Wisdom: Toward Organismic Processes that Make It Possible." In *Wisdom: Its Nature, Origins, and Development*, edited by R. J. Sternberg, 244–78. Cambridge: Cambridge University Press, 1990.

Peck, J., and C. Strohmer. *Uncommon Sense: God's Wisdom for Our Complex and Changing World*. Sevierville, TN: The Wise Press, 2000.

Peters, M. "Book Review: *Philosophy of Educational Research*." *Educational Philosophy and Theory* 34, no. 3 (2002), 357–60.

Peterson, C. *Looking Forward Through the Lifespan: Developmental Psychology*, 3rd ed. Sydney: Prentice Hall Australia, 1996.

Pillow, W. S. "Deciphering Attempts to Decipher Postmodern Educational Research." *Educational Researcher* 29, no. 5 (2000), 21–24.

Pinar, W. F. *Autobiography, Politics and Sexuality: Essays in Curriculum Theory, 1972–1992*. New York: Peter Lang, 1994.

Pinar, W. F., and M. R. Grumet. *Toward a Poor Curriculum*. Dubuque: Kendall/Hunt, 1976.

Pirsig, R. M. *Zen and the Art of Motorcycle Maintenance: An Inquiry into Values*. London: Corgi, 1976.

Plato. *The Republic*. Translated by H. D. P. Lee. Harmondsworth: Penguin, 1955.

Pring, R. "Liberal Education and Vocational Preparation." In *Beyond Liberal Education: Essays in Honour of Paul H. Hirst*, edited by P. White, 49–78. London and New York: Routledge, 1993.

———. *Philosophy of Educational Research*. London: Cassell, 2000.

Purpel, D. E. *The Moral and Spiritual Crisis in Education: A Curriculum for Justice and Compassion in Education*. New York: Bergin and Garvey, 1989.

Pusey, M. *Economic Rationalism in Canberra: A Nation Building State Changes its Mind*. Cambridge: Cambridge University Press, 1991.

Putnam, H. *Pragmatism: An Open Question*. Oxford, UK, and Cambridge, MA: Blackwell, 1995.

Robinson, V. *Problem-based Methodology: Research for the Improvement of Practice*. Oxford: Pergamon Press, 1993.

Roget, P. M. *Roget's Thesaurus of English Words and Phrases*, revised ed. Harmondsworth: Penguin, 1966.

Rose, E. "Told she couldn't achieve, woman proudly helps others." *Toronto Star* (17 October 1999), F5, 1.

Roques, M. *Curriculum Unmasked: Toward a Christian Understanding of*

Education. Eastbourne, UK: Monarch Publications, 1989.

Rorty, R. *Philosophy and the Mirror of Nature.* Princeton: Princeton University Press, 1979.

Rotenstreich, N. *Theory and Practice: An Essay in Human Intentionalities.* The Hague: Martinus Nijhoff, 1977.

Saul, J. R. *Voltaire's Bastards: The Dictatorship of Reason in the West.* Toronto: Penguin, 1993.

Scheffler, I. *The Anatomy of Inquiry: Philosophical Studies in the Theory of Science.* London: Routledge & Kegan Paul, 1964.

Schickel, R. "A Cheer for Old Glory: *The Patriot* Comes out Strongly on the Winning Side." *TIME Australia* (17 July, 2000), 78.

Schmidt, J., and T. E. Wartenberg. "Foucault's Enlightenment: Critique, Revolution, and the Fashioning of the Self." In *Critique & Power: Recasting the Foucault/Habermas Debate,* edited by M. Kelly, 283–314. Cambridge: MIT, 1994.

Schön, D. A. *The Reflective Practitioner: How Professionals Think in Action.* New York: Basic Books, 1983.

Schools Council. *The Role of Schools in the Vocational Preparation of Australia's Senior Secondary Students.* Canberra: Australian Government Publishing Service, 1994.

Schubert, W. H. *Curriculum: Perspective, Paradigm, Possibility.* New York: Macmillan, 1986.

Schwehn, M. R. *Exiles from Eden: Religion and the Academic Vocation in America.* New York and Oxford: Oxford University Press, 1993.

———. "Knowledge, Character, and Community." In *Schooling Christians: "Holy" Experiments in American Education,* edited by J. H. Westerhoff, 29–53. Grand Rapids: Eerdmans, 1992.

Seerveld, C. *Rainbows for the Fallen World: Aesthetic Life and Artistic Task,* 1st ed. Toronto: Tuppence, 1980.

———. "The gospel of creation." In *In the Fields of the Lord: A Seerveld Reader,* edited by C. Bartholomew, 46-48. Toronto and Carlisle: Tuppence and Piquant, 2000.

Sfard, A. "On Two Metaphors for Learning and the Dangers of Choosing One." *Educational Researcher* 27, no. 2 (1998), 4–13.

Shulman, J. H., ed. *Case Methods in Teacher Education.* New York and London: Teachers College Press, 1992.

Shulman, L. "Knowledge and Teaching: Foundations of the New Reform." *Harvard Educational Review* 57, no. 1 (1987), 1–22.

Skinner, B. F. *Beyond Freedom and Dignity.* Harmondsworth: Penguin, 1973.

Slattery, P. *Curriculum Development in the Postmodern Era.* New York and London: Garland, 1995.

Steensma, G. J. *To Those Who Teach: Keys for Decision-making.* Signal Mountain, TN: Signal, 1971.

Sternberg, R. J., ed. *Wisdom: Its Nature, Origins, and Development.* Cambridge: Cambridge University Press, 1990.

Stones, E. *An Introduction to Educational Psychology.* London: Methuen, 1966.

―――. *Quality Teaching: A Sample of Cases.* London/New York: Routledge, 1994.

Straus, E. W. *Phenomenological Psychology.* New York: Basic Books, 1966.

Stronks, G. G., and D. Blomberg, eds. *A Vision with a Task: Christian Schooling for Responsive Discipleship.* Grand Rapids: Baker, 1993.

Sylwester, R. *A Celebration of Neurons: An Educator's Guide to the Human Brain.* Alexandria, VA: Association for Supervision and Curriculum Development, 1995.

Taylor, C. *Sources of the Self: The Making of the Modern Identity.* Cambridge: Harvard University Press, 1989.

Taylor, J. V. *The Go-between God: The Holy Spirit and the Christian Mission.* London: SCM, 1972.

Tillich, P. *The Shaking of the Foundations.* Harmondsworth: Penguin, 1962.

Tom, A. R. *Teaching as a Moral Craft.* New York: Longman, 1984.

Toulmin, S. *Cosmopolis: The Hidden Agenda of Modernity.* Chicago: University of Chicago Press, 1992.

―――. *Return to Cosmology.* Berkeley: University of California Press, 1982.

Tremmell, R. "Zen and the Art of Reflective Practice in Teacher Education." *Harvard Educational Review* 63, no. 4 (1993), 434–58.

Van Brummelen, H. *Walking with God in the Classroom: Christian Approaches to Teaching and Learning.* Burlington, ON: Welch, 1988.

van der Hoeven, J. "Christian Philosophy at the End of the 20th Century." In *Christian Philosophy at the Close of the Twentieth Century: Assessment and Perspective,* edited by S. Griffioen and B. Balk, 55–66. Kampen: Kok, 1995.

Van Dyk, J. "Bridging the Gaps: Exploring the Relations between Theory, Educational Philosophy, Teacher Reflection, and Classroom Practice." Discussion paper. Sioux Center, IA: Dordt College, 2002.

Van Manen, M. "Reflectivity and the Pedagogical Moment: The Normativity of Pedagogical Thinking and Acting." *Journal of Curriculum Studies* 23, no. 6 (1991), 507–36.

―――. *Researching Lived Experience: Human Science for an Action Sensitive Pedagogy.* London, ON: Althouse, 1990.

―――. *The Tact of Teaching: The Meaning of Pedagogical Thoughtfulness.* London, ON: Althouse, 1991.

Vander Kreek, P. "Observations: On Grading Students, Not Eggs." *Dordt Diamond* (13 February 1992), 9.

Vanderkooy, A. *A Christian Approach to Curriculum Design.* Unpublished Master of Worldview Studies Essay. Toronto: Institute for Christian Studies, 2002.

Von Rad, G. *Wisdom in Israel.* Translated by J. D. Martin. London: SCM, 1972.

Walker, D. F., and J. F. Soltis. *Curriculum and Aims.* New York and London: Teachers College Press, 1986.

Walker, J. C. "Democracy and Pragmatism in Curriculum Development." *Educational Philosophy and Theory* 19, no. 2 (1987), 1–10.

Walsh, B., and R. Middleton. *The Transforming Vision: Shaping a Christian World View.* Downers Grove: InterVarsity, 1984.

Walsh, P. *Education and Meaning: Philosophy in Practice.* London: Cassell Educational, 1993.

Warnock, M. *Schools of Thought.* London: Faber & Faber, 1977.

Wentz, R. E. *Why Do People Do Bad Things in the Name of Religion?* Macon: Mercer University Press, 1987.

Wertheim, M. *Pythagoras' Trousers: God, Physics and the Gender Wars.* New York and London: W. W. Norton, 1997.

Whitaker, P. *Managing to Learn: Aspects of Reflective and Experiential Learning in Schools.* London: Cassell, 1995.

Whitehead, A. N. *The Aims of Education and Other Essays.* New York: Free Press, 1967.

Williams, M. "Touch Me and Believe: Spiritual Resurrection Redefined." *Pro Rege* XXIV no. 3 (1996), 10–23.

Withers, G. *Life, Learning and Values: An Evaluation of the Values for Life Seminar Program as a Co-curricular Experience for Australian Young People.* Melbourne: Care and Communication Concern, 1997.

Wittgenstein, L. *Philosophical Investigations,* 2nd ed. Translated by G. E. M. Anscombe. Oxford: Basil Blackwell, 1972.

Wolters, A. M. *Creation Regained: Biblical Basics for a Reformational Worldview.* Grand Rapids: Eerdmans, 1985. [2nd ed. 2005]

Wolterstorff, N. "Can Belief in God Be Rational If It Has No Foundations?" In *Faith and Rationality: Reason and Belief in God,* edited by A. Plantinga and N. Wolterstorff, 135–86. Notre Dame and London: University of Notre Dame Press, 1983.

———. *Reason Within the Bounds of Religion.* Grand Rapids: Eerdmans, 1976.

———. *Educating for Responsible Action.* Grand Rapids: CSI Publications/Eerdmans, 1980.

Wright, N. T. "How Can the Bible Be Authoritative?" *Vox Evangelica* 21 (1991), 7–32.

Zinn, H. *A People's History of the United States,* New York: Harper & Row, 1980.

INDEX

Index

233

sensory experience, 59, 169

sensitivity, 5, 91, 93, 121, 129, 178, 188, 197–198, 203

servant(s), 1, 29, 39, 48, 107, 162, 169

serviceable insight, 39

sex education, 163

Shakespeare, William, 54, 104, 189, 209

shalom, 33, 186, 193–194, 204, 207

sharing with, 42

Shaw, George Bernard, 66

simultaneous mutual interaction, 180

Sister Moon, 65

situated(ness), 1, 2, 33, 46, 47, 51–52, 66, 80, 81, 83, 87, 91, 126, 129, 141, 136–138, 155–157, 160, 170, 174, 175, 177, 180, 181, 184, 185, 188, 191, 195, 197, 198–202, 204, 207, 208

Skinner, B. F., 40, 135

slaves, 37

slave boy, 168

Smith, John, 125

social, 2, 3, 21, 41, 51, 67–68, 74, 92, 95, 100, 104, 106, 162, 170, 171, 176, 184–185, 193, 205, 207

competence, 47

Social Studies, 126

Socrates, Socratic, 8, 31, 57, 63–84, 154, 168, 174, 192

Solomon, 8, 63–84

Song of Songs, 88–89

Spencer, Herbert, 85, 170

spiritual(ity), 15, 21, 48, 66, 87, 105–106, 109–111, 125, 157, 179

standard, 86–87, 100, 128, 149, 152, 176, 211

stimulus-response, 202

structural

dimension, 20, 54, 193–194

plasticity, 172

plurality, 5

principles, 17

Structure of Scientific Revolutions, The, 99

student-teacher, 4

Students for a Democratic Society, 100

Study Meeting, 112, 134

subject-centered, 20, 23, 38

subject-subject relation, 90, 93

subjects of schooling, 4

subject manner, 121, 124–125, 165, 205

substances, 58, 69, 133, 146

suffering, 2, 60, 78, 82, 151, 183, 203

survival camp, 34

Sydney, 13,

Harbour, 184

Opera House, 188

Taba, Hilda, 142

Taylor, Frederick, 134–135

teacher, office of, 1, 4, 7–8, 23–24, 31, 39, 55, 69, 77, 85, 110, 117–123, 132, 139, 151–152, 168–169, 181, 185–187, 191–192, 194, 198–199, 201, 204, 206–208

teacher-proof, 120

teacher-student, 4, 194

relationship, 122

teaching fortress, 178

Technical and Further Education, 96

technology, technological, 38, 40, 56, 75, 103, 162, 187

Ten Commandments, 204

Teresa, Mother, 207

tetraktys, 18

Teutonic, 54

thankfulness, 182

theology, theological, 18, 23, 32, 36, 57, 63, 67, 72, 76, 103–106, 107, 108–110, 133, 157

theological text, 105, 110, 123

theoretical, 13–14, 16, 20–21, 23, 46, 53, 55, 61, 63, 73, 80, 120, 130–132, 135, 136, 139, 155, 159, 171, 174, 185, 197, 199, 204, 205, 211

theoria , 78, 157

theory, theorizing, 3, 5, 7–8, 20, 46, 55–60, 63, 73, 75–80, 117, 130–132, 135–136, 144, 154, 157, 177, 185, 202, 205

theory-into-practice paradigm, theory-practice story, 2, 3, 8, 55–57, 73, 120, 130, 131, 135, 154, 194, 197

theory-laden, 60, 136

Thessalonians, 48

thing-ified, thingifying, 9, 118

"Thought thinking itself," 57

time, timed, timely, 2, 7, 78–80, 83, 119–120, 93, 98, 119–120, 156–158, 160, 161, 162, 168, 172, 176, 181, 183, 191, 192, 197, 202, 208

TIME Magazine, 103, 126

tools, 155, 191

totalizing, 55, 101, 127

Total Quality Management, 176

traces, 6, 129, 175, 209

tradition, 2, 8, 25, 31, 48, 51, 63, 65–67, 77–80, 82–85, 88, 98, 101–104, 106–107, 109–110, 118, 124, 129, 156, 171, 189, 200

transcendence, 142, 172

transformation, 27, 140, 146, 154, 157, 167, 178–179, 196–197, 200

transmission teaching, 84, 192

"Like a tree firmly planted by streams of water."
Figure in Landscape No.2 1985
Oil on Canvas 600mm x 900mm

The Australian landscape is populated and characterized by its trees. Each painting in the Figure in Landscape series is a complex metaphor for aspects of human life. I choose trees for their sculptural presence and place them forward and central in the canvas, much like a portrait painting.

In a hidden gorge near Canowindra, Australia, an old gum survives because it has its roots firmly planted. It is scarred by the sharp boulders that flash floods send down the gorge. This tree is a metaphor of a mature life lived in Christ. We may be scarred by events, but if our faith is rightly based, we are able to stand. Psalm 1:3 describes this as "wisdom." We now know this living water: "Christ the Power and Wisdom of God" (1 Corinthians 1:24).

Russell McKane, Artist

"The application of the Old Testament Wisdom Literature to school curriculum and the subsequent development of the organising concept of the 'integral curriculum' is an original and significant contribution. The use of imaginative dialogue is a wonderful literary device employed to great effect. I was particularly impressed with the image of schooling and the curriculum that is distilled in the final chapter. In my view, the Wisdom tradition isn't the only path to creating a welcoming and worthwhile curriculum, but that the Wisdom tradition leads to these conclusions is an affirmation of the value of approaching the curriculum from this standpoint."

Prof. Shirley Grundy, Dean, Faculty of Education
Deakin University, Geelong, Australia

"People who are interested in thinking deeply about schooling will truly enjoy this book. When the going gets tough and the subject matter becomes dense, the author helps the reader along through a clever use of dialog. I visited Mount Evelyn Christian School, the school that is featured prominently in Blomberg's writing, and his description of the curriculum at that school is accurate and exciting."

Dr. Gloria Stronks, Prof. of Education emerita
Calvin College, Grand Rapids, Michigan

CPSIA information can be obtained
at www.ICGtesting.com
Printed in the USA
LVHW091741010921
696696LV00002B/326